W9-BSN-809

Bloom's Literary Themes

Alienation
The American Dream
Civil Disobedience
Dark Humor
Death and Dying
Enslavement and Emancipation
Exploration and Colonization
The Grotesque
The Hero's Journey
Human Sexuality
The Labyrinth
Rebirth and Renewal
Sin and Redemption
The Sublime
The Taboo
The Trickster

Bloom's Literary Themes

THE TABOO

Bloom's Literary Themes

THE TABOO

Edited and with an introduction by
Harold Bloom
Sterling Professor of the Humanities
Yale University

Volume Editor
Blake Hobby

BLOOM'S
LITERARY CRITICISM
An imprint of Infobase Publishing

SIENA COLLEGE LIBRARY

Bloom's Literary Themes: The Taboo
Copyright ©2010 by Infobase Publishing
Introduction ©2010 by Harold Bloom

All rights reserved. No part of this book may be reproduced or utilized in any form or by any means, electronic or mechanical, including photocopying, recording, or by any information storage or retrieval systems, without permission in writing from the publisher. For information contact:

Bloom's Literary Criticism
An imprint of Infobase Publishing
132 West 31st Street
New York NY 10001

Library of Congress Cataloging-in-Publication Data
Bloom's literary themes : the taboo / edited and with an introduction by Harold Bloom ; volume editor, Blake Hobby.
    p. cm.
Includes bibliographical references and index.
ISBN 978-1-60413-444-5 (hc : alk. paper)   1. Taboo in literature. I. Bloom, Harold. II. Hobby, Blake. III. Title.
PN56.T23B56 2010
809'.933552—dc22   2009038090

Bloom's Literary Criticism books are available at special discounts when purchased in bulk quantities for businesses, associations, institutions, or sales promotions. Please call our Special Sales Department in New York at (212) 967-8800 or (800) 322-8755.

You can find Bloom's Literary Criticism on the World Wide Web at
http://www.chelseahouse.com

Series design by Kerry Casey
Cover design by Takeshi Takahashi
Composition by IBT Global, Inc.
Cover printed by Yurchak Printing, Landisville, Pa.
Book printed and bound by Yurchak Printing, Landisville, Pa.
Printed in the United States of America

This book is printed on acid-free paper.

SIENA COLLEGE LIBRARY

Contents

Series Introduction by Harold Bloom:
Themes and Metaphors   xi

Volume Introduction by Harold Bloom   xv

Confessions of an English Opium Eater (Thomas De Quincey)   1
    "Les Paradis Artificiels" by Charles Baudelaire, in *Les
        Paradis Artificiels* (1860)

Dracula (Bram Stoker)   23
    "Suddenly Sexual Women in Bram Stoker's *Dracula*" by
        Phyllis A. Roth, in *Literature and Psychology* (1977)

Howl (Allen Ginsberg)   37
    "Transgression, Release, and 'Moloch'" by Jeffrey Gray

Julius Caesar (William Shakespeare)   51
    "Totem, Taboo, and *Julius Caesar*" by Cynthia Marshall,
        in *Literature and Psychology* (1991)

Lady Chatterley's Lover (D.H. Lawrence)   77
    "1925-30" by Frank Kermode, in *D.H. Lawrence* (1973)

Lolita (Vladimir Nabokov)   91
    "'I have only words to play with:' Taboo and Tradition
        in Nabokov's *Lolita*" by Samuel Schuman

Lord of the Flies (William Golding)   99
    "Men of a Smaller Growth: A Psychological Analysis
    of William Golding's *Lord of the Flies*" by Claire
    Rosenfield, in *Literature and Psychology* (1961)

"The Miller's Tale" (Geoffrey Chaucer)   113
    "Social and Religious Taboos in Chaucer's *The Miller's*
    Tale" by Robert C. Evans

"the mother" (Gwendolyn Brooks)   123
    "The Taboo in Gwendolyn Brooks' 'the mother'"
    by Kate Falvey

Mourning Becomes Electra (Eugene O'Neill)   133
    "'I Forgive Myself!': Escaping the Ever-Present Past
    in Eugene O'Neill's *Mourning Becomes Electra*" by
    Scott Walters

Oedipus Tyrannus (Sophocles)   143
    "Chapter Nine" by Friedrich Nietzsche, in *The Birth of*
    Tragedy (1872)

The Picture of Dorian Gray (Oscar Wilde)   147
    "Taboo in *The Picture of Dorian Gray*" by Arundhati
    Sanyal

The Poetry and Prose of Sylvia Plath   157
    "'God's Lioness'—Sylvia Plath, Her Prose and Poetry"
    by Wendy Martin, in *Women's Studies* (1973)

"A Rose for Emily" (William Faulkner)   165
    "Usher, Poquelin, and Miss Emily: the Progress of
    Southern Gothic" by Edward Stone, in *Georgia*
    Review (1960)

Sabbath's Theater (Philip Roth)   177
    "The Taboo in Philip Roth's *Sabbath's Theater*" by Julia
    F. Klimek

The Satanic Verses (Salman Rushdie)   189
  "Breaking Totems and Taboos: Rushdie's *The Satanic
  Verses*" by Rossitsa Artemis

The Poetry of Anne Sexton   199
  "The Poetic Heroism of Anne Sexton" by Diana Hume
  George, in *Literature and Psychology* (1987)

The Prose Works of Jonathan Swift   217
  "Biographical Introduction" by W.E.H. Lecky, in
  Swift's Tale of a Tub *and Other Early Works* (1897)

Tess of the D'Urbervilles (Thomas Hardy)   227
  "*Tess of the D'Urbervilles*: The 'Pure Woman'" by
  Geoffrey Wagner, in *Five for Freedom: A Study of
  Feminist Fiction*

Ulysses (James Joyce)   251
  "Fetishizing the Bread of Everyday Life: The Taboo
  Gaze in 'Nausicaa'" by Blake Hobby and Dustin Ryan

Acknowledgments   259

Index   261

1. TOPOS AND TROPE

What we now call a theme or topic or subject initially was named a *topos*, ancient Greek for "place." Literary *topoi* are commonplaces, but also arguments or assertions. A topos can be regarded as literal when opposed to a trope or turning which is figurative and which can be a metaphor or some related departure from the literal: ironies, synecdoches (part for whole), metonymies (representations by contiguity) or hyperboles (overstatements). Themes and metaphors engender one another in all significant literary compositions.

As a theoretician of the relation between the matter and the rhetoric of high literature, I tend to define metaphor as a figure of desire rather than a figure of knowledge. We welcome literary metaphor because it enables fictions to persuade us of beautiful untrue things, as Oscar Wilde phrased it. Literary *topoi* can be regarded as places where we store information, in order to amplify the themes that interest us.

This series of volumes, *Bloom's Literary Themes*, offers students and general readers helpful essays on such perpetually crucial topics as the Hero's Journey, the Labyrinth, the Sublime, Death and Dying, the Taboo, the Trickster and many more. These subjects are chosen for their prevalence yet also for their centrality. They express the whole concern of human existence now in the twenty-first century of the Common Era. Some of the topics would have seemed odd at another time, another land: the American Dream, Enslavement and Emancipation, Civil Disobedience.

I suspect though that our current preoccupations would have existed always and everywhere, under other names. Tropes change across the centuries: the irony of one age is rarely the irony of another. But the themes of great literature, though immensely varied, undergo transmemberment and show up barely disguised in different contexts. The power of imaginative literature relies upon three constants: aesthetic splendor, cognitive power, wisdom. These are not bound by societal constraints or resentments, and ultimately are universals, and so not culture-bound. Shakespeare, except for the world's scriptures, is the one universal author, whether he is read and played in Bulgaria or Indonesia or wherever. His supremacy at creating human beings breaks through even the barrier of language and puts everyone on his stage. This means that the matter of his work has migrated everywhere, reinforcing the common places we all inhabit in his themes.

2. Contest as both Theme and Trope

Great writing or the Sublime rarely emanates directly from themes since all authors are mediated by forerunners and by contemporary rivals. Nietzsche enhanced our awareness of the agonistic foundations of ancient Greek literature and culture, from Hesiod's contest with Homer on to the Hellenistic critic Longinus in his treatise *On the Sublime*. Even Shakespeare had to begin by overcoming Christopher Marlowe, only a few months his senior. William Faulkner stemmed from the Polish-English novelist Joseph Conrad and our best living author of prose fiction, Philip Roth, is inconceivable without his descent from the major Jewish literary phenomenon of the twentieth century, Franz Kafka of Prague, who wrote the most lucid German since Goethe.

The contest with past achievement is the hidden theme of all major canonical literature in Western tradition. Literary influence is both an overwhelming metaphor for literature itself, and a common topic for all criticism, whether or not the critic knows her immersion in the incessant flood.

Every theme in this series touches upon a contest with anteriority, whether with the presence of death, the hero's quest, the overcoming of taboos, or all of the other concerns, volume by volume. From Monteverdi through Bach to Stravinsky, or from the Italian Renaissance through the agon of Matisse and Picasso, the history of all the arts demonstrates the same patterns as literature's thematic struggle with itself. Our country's great original art, jazz, is illuminated by what the great creators called "cutting contests," from Louis Armstrong and Duke Ellington on to the emergence of Charlie Parker's Bop or revisionist jazz.

A literary theme, however authentic, would come to nothing without rhetorical eloquence or mastery of metaphor. But to experience the study of the common places of invention is an apt training in the apprehension of aesthetic value in poetry and in prose.

Incest, Shelley remarked, is the most poetical of circumstances. Patricide is a close second, and haunts Shakespearean tragedy. Anyone among the educated in Shakespeare's audience would have known that Plutarch reported the gossip in Suetonius that Julius Caesar was the father of Marcus Brutus. Shakespeare loves to be elliptical and leaves out of the text of *Julius Caesar* that dark rumor, yet he implies it between the lines.

Incest and patricide are the founding taboos of Oedipal tragedy. Why is Hamlet blocked from cutting down Claudius? Doubtless revenge tragedy is beneath the sublime consciousness of Hamlet, who disdains worn-out conventions. And yet taboo is also part of the plot, on a deeply repressed level. How far back does the relationship between Gertrude and Claudius go? Hamlet calls it adulterous and incestuous, and Shakespeare does not disclose the answer. Hamlet, in his darkest conjectures, well may wonder if he is not the phallic son of Claudius.

Shakespeare's Brutus and his Julius Caesar are portrayed as having much in common. Father and natural son alike are imperious, scorning common men and mundane aspirations. As dramatic characters, both are rather cold, and this is much the coldest of Shakespeare's tragedies. Its fire belongs to the taboo of patricide, the true action of the play.

Hamlet, the most intelligent figure in all of literature, cannot be explained simply upon the basis of taboo, even that of father-murder. It may be that his transgressions, and his spiritual heroism, are larger. The wretched Claudius hardly is a fit agonist to contend with Hamlet. His spiritual struggles transcend Elsinore and seek to oppose the spirit of injustice in heavenly realms. And yet he is finally responsible for eight deaths, including his own, leaving the stage finally bare of all its speaking parts except for Horatio, Fortinbras and the fop Osric.

Freud's weird study, *Totem and Taboo*, postulates a Primal History Scene in which the Totem Father is slain and devoured by his many sons, who are a horde of enemy brothers. The dead Father then becomes more revered than the living one had been. Transformed into an ancestor god, he becomes a religious icon. Freud repeated this pattern in his *Moses and Monotheism*, which outrageously says that the Hebrews killed Moses and then founded Judaism upon his martyrdom.

Clearly Freud amalgamated the Totem Father, Moses, and Dr. Sigmund Freud, founder of the New Judaism of his own, supposed science. That is a perpetually challenging story of taboo and its discontents.

CONFESSIONS OF AN ENGLISH OPIUM EATER (THOMAS DE QUINCEY)

❧

"Les Paradis Artificiels"
by Charles Baudelaire,
in *Les Paradis Artificiels* (1860)

INTRODUCTION

A champion of the urbane and modernity, Charles Baudelaire often challenged accepted norms and explored such taboos as sex and illicit drug use. He depicted the dark inner landscape of the melancholic mind, and he died an opium addict, so many people view his life as debauched and tragic. Nevertheless, Baudelaire, in his essays and prose poems, and in his renowned poetry collection, *Les Fleurs de mal* (*Flowers of Evil*), demonstrates critical acumen and poetic genius. Interested in the recreational, spiritual, and imaginative use of drugs, Baudelaire translated Thomas De Quincey's *Confessions of An English Opium Eater* and fashioned his own treatise on this subject, *Les Paradis Artificiels*. In doing so, he broke a longstanding taboo, inviting us to see both the visionary benefits and isolating effects of drug use.

❧

Baudelaire, Charles. "Les Paradis Artificiels." 1860. *Les Fleurs du mal, Petits poèmes en prose, Les Paradis artificiels*. trans. Arthur Symons. London: Casanova Society, 1925. 243–88.

Ma Chère Amie,

Common sense tells us that terrestrial things have but a faint existence, and that reality itself is only found in dreams. As we have to digest our natural and our artificial happiness, one requires all one's courage to swallow it, and those who most merit this happiness are exactly those to whom human felicity, such as we mortals conceive it, has always had the effect of an emetic.

To stupid spirits it might seem singular and even impertinent, that a vision of artificial sensations should be dedicated to a woman, who is the most natural source of the most natural sensualities. At the same time it is evident that as the natural world penetrates the spiritual world, serves as pasturage to it, and thus concurs in operating this indefinable mixture that we name our individuality, that woman is the one being made to project the greatest shadow or the greatest light over our dreams. Woman is fatally suggestive; she lives with another life than her proper one; she lives spiritually in the imaginations that she haunts and fertilises.

Besides, it is of little consequence that the reason of this Dedication should be understood. Is it even necessary, for the writer's satisfaction, that any kind of book should be understood, except by him or by her for whom it has been composed? Is it, indeed, indispensable that it should have been written for *anyone*? I have, for my part, so little taste for the living world that, like certain sensible and stay-at-home women, who send, it is said, their letters by post to their imaginary friends, willingly would I write only for the dead.

But it is not to a dead woman that I dedicate this little book; it is to one who, though ill, is always active and living in me, and who now turns her eyes in the direction of the skies, that realm of so many transfigurations. For, just as in the case of a redoubtable drug, a living being enjoys this privilege of being able to draw wonderful and subtle luxuries from sorrow, from calamity and from fatality.

Thou wilt see in this narrative a man who walks in a sombre and solitary fashion, plunged in the moving flood of multitudes, sending his heart and his thoughts to a far-off Electra who so long ago wiped his sweating forehead and *refreshed his lips parched with fever;* and thou wilt divine the gratitude of another Orestes whose nightmares thou didst so often watch over, and of whom thou didst dissipate, with a light and maternal hand, his slumbers abominable.

C. B.

THE POEM OF HASCHISCH.

I.

The Taste of the Infinite.

Those who know how to observe themselves and who keep the memory of their impressions, those who have known, like Hoffmann, how to construct their spiritual barometer, have constantly chosen to note, in the observatory of their thought, strange seasons, luxurious afternoons, delicious minutes. There are days when man awakens with a young and vigorous genius. His eyelids once lightened of the sleep that sealed them, the outer world offers itself to him with a powerful relief, a certainty of contours, a richness of admirable colours. The moral world opens its vast perspectives, full of dawns and sunsets. The man gratified with this sense of exquisite loveliness, unfortunately so rare and so fragile, feels himself on the sudden more than ever artistic, more than ever noble, more than ever just, if one can express so much in so few words. But what is most singular in this exceptional state of the spirit and of the senses, which I can without exaggeration term paradisal, if I can compare it with the heavily weighted existences who endure the hideous horrors of the night, is that it has not been created by any other cause than what is visible and easy to define. Is it really the result of one's health or of one's wisdom? Such are the first explanations the spirit offers to us; but we are obliged to realise that this miracle, this prodigy, produces as it were the effect of a power superior and invisible, exterior to men, after a period when he has abused his physical faculties. Shall I say it is the reward of an assiduous prayer and of spiritual ardours? It is certain that a continual elevation of desire, a tension of spiritual forces, might be in some sense a remedy against evils, or might create what is glorious in morality; but in virtue of what absurd law are there not manifest manifestations of the guilty joys of the imagination, which is to its honest and reasonable state what dislocation is to the strong gymnasts? That is why I prefer to consider this abnormal condition of the spirit as a veritable grace, as a magic mirror where one's face is splendidly reflected, where one sees oneself transformed, becoming what we ought to be, a kind of angelical excitement, a recall to the sense of order under a complimentary form. In the same manner a certain spiritualistic school, which has its representatives in England and in America, considers supernatural phenomena, such as the apparitions of ghosts, of dark demons, as manifestations of the divine will, attentive in awakening in man's spirit the memory of invisible realities.

Besides, this charming and singular state where all the forces are in equilibrium, where the imagination, marvellous as it is, cannot drag after it the moral sense in its most perilous adventures, where an exquisite sensibility is no longer tortured by diseased nerves, these criminal advocates of crime and of despair, this marvellous state, as I have said, has no premonitory symptoms. It is as unexpected as one's ghost might be. It is an hallucination, but an intermittent hallucination, from which—were we wise—we might derive the certainty of a better world and the hope of attaining it by a daily exercise of our will. This activity of one's thought, this excitement of the senses and of the spirit, must have, for all time, appeared to man as perhaps the best of his belongings; that is why, considering only one's immediate sensuality, he has, without attempting to violate the laws of his constitution, sought to find in physical science, in pharmacopoeia, in the grossest liqueurs, in the most subtle perfumes, under all the climates and in all times, the means of escaping, were it only for a few hours, from its dunghill dominion, and, as the writer of *Lazare* said: "D'emporter le paradis d'un seul coup." Alas! Men's vices, horrible as they are supposed to be, contain the proof positive (were this no more than its infinite expansion!) of his taste of the Infinite; only, this is a taste which often goes astray. One can take in a metaphorical sense the vulgar proverb: *Every road leads to Rome*, and apply it to the moral world; all leads either to recompense or to chastisement, two forms of Eternity. Man's mind is the abode of passions; *he has to sell them over again*, if I may use a trivial expression; but this miserable spirit, whose natural degradation is so immense that his sudden aptitude, half paradoxical, in regard to the most ardent virtues and charities, is pregnant in Paradoxes, which permit him to employ for what is evil what is most excessive, in this overwhelming passion. *Il ne croit jamais se vendre en bloc.* He forgets, in his infatuation, that he gambles toward an end finer and more formidable than himself, and that the spirit of Evil, even if one gives him no more than one single hair, has only one desire: that is, to carry away his head. This visible lord of visible nature (I speak of man) desires to create Paradise by pharmacy, by fermented drinks, exactly like a maniac who wants to replace his solid furniture and veritable gardens with decorations painted on canvas and mounted on easels. It is in this deprivation of the Sense of the Infinite that I find the germ, and the reason, of the most guilty excesses, from the solitary and concentrated intoxication of the man of letters, who obliged to seek in opium solace from some physical suffering, and having there discovered a source of morbid enjoyments, little by little makes of this his one hygiene and the sun of his spiritual life up to the point of the most repugnant drunkenness seen on our Parisian pavements, when a man, his head inflamed with flame and with glory, lets himself roll ludicrously in the midst of the filth of the road. Among the drugs most necessary to create what I name *The Artificial Ideal*, leaving aside the liqueurs, which excite us to the point of fury and which destroy our spiritual force, and the perfumes, the excessive use of which, while they make man's imagination more subtle, gradually exhaust his physical forces, the two most energetic of all substances, those whose use is the easiest and the nearest at hand, are Haschisch and Opium. The analysis of the mysterious and morbid excitements which these drugs might excite, the inevitable chastisements which are the result of too continual a use of them, and finally of the immorality implied in their pursuit of a wrong ideal, constitute the subject of this Study.

The praise of Opium has been made, and in a manner so astonishing, so medical, and so poetical, that I dare not add anything to it. I shall content myself, in another study, by giving the analysis of this incomparable book, which has never been entirely translated into French. The writer, Thomas De Quincey, a famous man, whose imagination is exquisite and powerful, who at the present day lives retired in a kind of hermitical silence, has dared—with a tragic sincerity—to confess the enjoyments and the tortures he derived from Opium, and the most dramatic part of his book is where he speaks of the superhuman efforts of will he was obliged to use so as to escape from the damnation to which he had so imprudently devoted himself.

[...]

III.

The Theatre of Seraphim.

What does one experience? What does one see? Things marvellous, things extraordinary? Is this wonderful and terrible and really dangerous? Such are the ordinary questions that the ignorant address, with a curiosity mixed with conceit, to the adepts. One might say a childish impatience of knowledge, such as that of those who have never left the corner of their fires, when they find themselves face to face with a man who returns from distant and unknown lands. They figure to themselves the intoxication of Haschisch as if it were a prodigious prodigality, a vast theatre of prestidigitation and of jugglery, where all is miraculous and unexpected. That is a prejudice, a complete mistake. And, since for the greater part of readers and of questioners, the word Haschisch gives them the idea of a strange and overthrown world, and the desire of prodigious dreams (it might be better to say hallucinations, which are besides less frequent than we suppose), I shall now remark on the important differences which separate the effects of Haschisch from the effects of sleep. In sleep, this adventurous voyage of every night, there is something positively miraculous; it is a miracle whose punctuality has baffled mystery. Men's dreams are divided in two classes. Some, full of his ordinary life, of his preoccupations, of his desires, of his vices, are combined in a fashion more or less bizarre with the objects seen during the day, that are indiscriminately fixed on the vast canvas of his memory. That is the natural dream: it is the man himself. But the other kind of dream! the dream absurd, unexpected, without any relation with his character, with his life, with his passions as a dreamer! This dream, that I shall call hieroglyphical, represents evidently the supernatural side of his life, and it is justly so because it is absure that the ancients believed it to be divine. As it is inexplicable by natural causes, they have attributed to it a cause exterior to the man; and even to-day, without speaking of the Dream Interpreters, there exists a philosophical school which sees in dreams of this kind now a reproach, now an advice; in one word, a pitiless moral and symbolical picture, engendered in the spirit of the man who sleeps. It is a dictionary that he ought to study, a language of which only the Wise can obtain the key.

In the intoxication of Haschisch, nothing of the kind. Our dreams are natural; our intoxication, however long may be its duration, cannot be, is not, really, more than an immense dream, thanks to the intensity of the colours and to the rapidity of conception; but it must always keep the particular tonality of the individual. Man has desired to dream, the dream must govern the man; but this dream will soon be the son of its father. An idle man uses his ingenuity so as to introduce artificially what is supernatural in his life and in his thought; but he is not, after all and despite the accidental energy of his sensations, more than the same man augmented, the same number elevated to an enormous height. He is subjugated; but, for his sins, he is not subjugated except by himself, that is to say by what is dominant in his nature; *il a voulu faire l'ange, il est devenu une bête*, momentarily very powerful, if always he can call power an excessive sensibility, without government for moderating or for exploiting it.

Let men of the world and those who are ignorant, seriously anxious to find the secret of exceptional enjoyments, know to a certainty that they will not find in Haschisch anything miraculous, absolutely nothing but what is naturally excessive. The brain and the organism on which Haschisch operates, give only their ordinary phenomena, individual, augmented, certainly, as to number and energy, but always faithful to their origin. Man cannot escape the fatality of his physical and moral temperament: Haschisch will be, for the man's familiar thoughts and impressions, a deceptive mirror and a pure mirror.

[...]

It is at this period of intoxication that a rare quality manifests itself, a superior acuteness in all the senses. Smell, sight, hearing, touch, participate equally in this progress. The eyes have the vision of Eternity. The ear perceives almost unseizable sounds in the midst of a vast turmoil. It is then that the hallucinations begin. Exterior objects assume, in succession, singular appearances, they become deformed, transformed. Then, arrives what is equivocal, such as scorn and the transpositions of ideas. Sounds assume colours and colours contain music. This, one might say, is quite natural, and that any poetical brain, in its sane and normal state, easily conceives these analogies. But I have already warned the reader that there is nothing purely supernatural in the intoxication of Haschisch; only, these analogies assume an unusual vivacity; they penetrate, they invade, they weigh down the spirit with their despotic character. Musical notes become numbers, and if your spirit is gifted with some musical aptitude, melody, heard melody, while it preserves its voluptuous and sensual character, transforms itself into a vast arithmetical operation, when numbers beget numbers, of which you follow the phases and the generation with an inexplicable rapidity and an agility equal to that of the executant.

It often happens that the personality disappears and that the objectivity, which is the proper domain of Pantheistic Poets, develops itself in you so abnormally, that the contemplation of exterior objects makes you forget your own existence, and makes you confound yours with theirs. Suppose you look on a tree waved by the wind in a few seconds, what was not in the brain of a Poet no more than a natural comparison, becomes in yours a reality. First you attribute to the tree your passions, your desire and your melancholy; its sobs and oscillations become yours, and before long you are the tree. In the same sense, the bird who flies to the height of the skies *represents* first the immortal desire of flying above things human; already you are yourself the bird. I suppose you seated and smoking. Your attention will find rest in the bluish clouds that rise from your pipe. The idea of an evaporation, slow, successive, eternal, seizes your spirit; and you begin to apply this idea to your proper thoughts, to your thinking matter. Through a singular equivocation, by a kind of transposition or by some intellectual *quid pro quo*, you will feel yourself evaporating, and you will attribute to your pipe (in which you feel yourself crouching in one lump on the tobacco) the strange faculty of smoking yourself (*l'étrange faculté de vous fumer*).

Luckily, this interminable imagination only endured for a minute, for an interval of lucidity, with an effort, when you examine the clock. But another stream of ideas carries you away; which might plunge you in an instant into a living whirlwind, and this other minute must be another eternity. For the proportions of time and of being are completely deranged by the multitude and the intensity of sensations, and of ideas. One might say that one lives several lives in the space of an hour. Are you not then like a fantastic novel which ought to be living rather than written? There is no more equation between the other organs and one's enjoyments; and it is especially from this consideration that the disapproval applicable to this dangerous exercise where liberty disappears, surges.

[...]

For at first, when you are certain that a new dawn has risen on the horizon of your existence, you experience something wonderful; you imagine you are in possession of a marvellous spirituality. But no sooner are you out of bed, than all that remains of the intoxication follows and hinders you, like the chain of your recent servitude. You can hardly walk and you fear at every instant that you might break yourself like any fragile thing. An intense lassitude (there are some who pretend it is not without a charm of its own) seizes your mind and extends itself across your faculties, as a mist over a landscape. You find yourself, for some hours, incapable of work, of action, and of energy. This is the punishment of the impious prodigality with which you have spent your nervous fluid. You have disseminated your personality to the four winds of the world, and, now, what intensity of pain do you not experience in concentrating it and in gathering it together!

IV.

The Man-God.

The time has come to leave aside all this jugglery and these absurd marionettes, born of the smoke of childish imaginations. Have we not graver matters to consider: modifications of human sentiments and, in one word, the *moral* of Haschisch?

So far, in my account of the intoxication caused by Haschisch, I have accentuated the principle traits, especially the material traits. But, what is infinitely more important, I believe, for the spiritual man, is to know definitely the action of the poison on what is spiritual in himself, that is to say, the definition and the exaggeration of his habitual sentiments and of his moral preconceptions, which must present, in this case, in an exceptional atmosphere, a veritable phenomenon of refraction.

The man who, having given himself up for years, bound, bandaged hand and foot, to Opium and Haschisch, has found, weakened as he is by the mere habit of his servitude, the necessary energy needed to deliver himself, appears to me like a prisoner who has escaped. He inspires in me more admiration than the prudent man who has never failed, having always taken care to avoid temptation. The English often use, in regard to the Opium-Eaters, terms that cannot but seem excessive to those innocent creatures to whom the horrors of this forfeiture are unknown: *Enchained, fettered, enslaved!* Chains, in effect, after which all the others, chains of duty, chains of illegitimate love, are no more than webs of gauze and spiders' webs! Fearful marriage of man with himself! "I had become a bounden slave in the trammels of opium, and my labours and my plans had taken a colouring from my dreams," says Ligeia's husband; but, in how many marvellous pages has not Edgar Poe, this incomparable Poet, this irrefutable philosopher—who must always be quoted in regard to the mysterious maladies of the mind—described the sombre and solemn splendours of Opium? The lover of the luminous Berenice, Egoeus the meta-physician, speaks of an alteration in his faculties, which constrained him to give an abnormal, monstrous value to the most simple phenomena. "To muse for long unwearied hours, with my attention rivetted to some frivolous device in the margin or in the typography of a book; to become absorbed, for the better part of a summer day, in a quaint shadow falling aslant upon the tapestry or upon the floor; to lose myself, for an entire night, in watching the steady flame of a lamp, or the embers of the fire; to dream away whole days over the perfume of a flower; to repeat, monotonously, some common word, until the sound, by dint of frequent repetitions, ceased to convey any ideas whatever to the mind: such were a few of the most common and least pernicious vagaries induced by a condition of the mental faculties, not, indeed, altogether unparallelled, but certainly bidding defiance to anything like analysis or explanation." And the nervous Augustus Bedloe, who, every morning before he takes his walk, swallows his dose of opium, assures us that the chief benefit he derives from this daily poisoning, is to take in all things, even in the most trivial, an exaggerated interest. "Nevertheless, the opium has produced the usual effect, which is to give an intensity of interest to the exterior world. In the trembling of a leaf, in the colour of a blade of grass, in the form of a trefoil, in the buzz of a bee, in the lustre of a drop of dew, in the wind's sighing, in the vague odours that escape from the forest, are created an outer world of inspirations, of a magnificent and varied procession of disordered and rhapsodical thoughts."

So expresses himself, through the mouth of his characters, the Priest of the Horrible, the Prince of Mystery. These two characteristics of Opium are perfectly applicable to Haschisch; in one and the other case, one's intelligence, before free as the wind, becomes the winds' slave; but the word *rhapsodic*, which defines a series of sensations suggested by the exterior world and the hazard of circumstances, is veritably truer and more terrible than in the case of Haschisch. Here, reason is no more than a stray at the mercy of all the currents, and the train of thoughts is infinitely more accelerated and more rhapsodical. This is to say, I suppose, in a sufficiently clear manner, that Haschisch is, in its present effect, much more vehement than Opium, much more the enemy of one's regular life; in one word, much more troubling. I query if ten years of intoxication by Haschisch brings with it disasters equal with those caused by ten years of Opium-eating; I say that, for the present hour, and for to-morrow, Haschisch has more ghastly effects on the nerves; one is a peaceful sedative, the other a disordered Demon.

I intend, in this last part, to define and analyse the moral ravage caused by this dangerous and delicious gymnastic; ravage so extreme, danger so stupendous, that those who return from the combat only slightly devastated, appear to me like bandits escaped from the cavern of some multiform Proteus, an Orpheus who has vanquished Hell. Take as you choose this form of language, which might be an excessive metaphor; in any case, I shall avow that these exciting poisons seem to me not only one of the most terrible and most certain means disposed by the Power of Darkness to enlist and to enslave deplorable Humanity, but one of his most perfect incorporations.

This time, so as to abridge my task and make my analysis clearer, instead of bringing together scattered anecdotes, I shall accumulate on a fictitious character a mass of observations. For one thing, I must imagine a soul of my own choice. In his *Confessions*, De Quincey says reasonably that Opium, instead of sending a man asleep, excites him, but that it excites him only in a natural manner, and that therefore, were one to choose anyone to judge of the marvels of Opium, it would be absurd to refer the question to a dealer in oxen; he would not dream of anything but oxen and pasture-lands. I certainly have no intention of describing the heavy caprice of a breeder intoxicated with Haschisch; who would ever consent to read them? So as to spiritualise my subject, I must concentrate on it all the rays in one unique circle, I must polarise them; and the tragic circle where I must assemble them must be, as I have said, a Soul of my own choice, something analogous to what the eighteenth century called *l'homme sensible*, to what the Romantic school named *l'homme incompris*, and to what the mass of citizens generally stigmatize under the epithet *d'original*.

A temperament half nervous and half splenetic, seems to me to be the most favourable for the evolutions of this particular intoxication; to this I shall add a cultivated mind, exercised in studies of form and of colour; a tender heart, fatigued by misery, but still anxious for rejuvenation; I shall go so far, if you desire it, as to admit in him ancient faults, and, what must result from a nature easily excitable, if not positive remorse, at least the regrets of past times profaned. The taste for metaphysics, the acquaintance with different hypotheses of philosophy on human destiny, are certainly not useless complimentary qualities, no more than this love, of virtue, of abstract virtue, of Stoic or mystical, which are found in all those books on which modern children feed their modern souls, as the highest summit to which a distinguished spirit might ascend. If I add to all that a great finesse of the senses that I have omitted as a superogatory question, I believe that I shall have gathered together the general elements commonly attributed to those who are most sensible, of what I might call the *banal form of originality*. Let us now take under consideration what shall become of this individuality driven to distraction by Haschisch. Let us follow this procession of the imagination to the utmost point of its last and most splendid resting-place, and beyond this to man's belief in his own Divinity.

If you are one of these souls, your innate love of colour and of form will find first of all an immense pasture-ground in the beginning of your intoxication. Colours suddenly assume an unaccustomed energy as they enter with an intensity of victory your imagination. Delicate, mediocre, or even evil, the paintings on the ceilings shall surge before you with a terrifying force of life; the dullest wall-papers which cover the walls of several shall change into splendid grimaces. Nymphs with shining flesh shall fix on you their immense eyes deeper than the sky and the sea; figures of ambiguity, rigged out in their sacred and military costumes, shall give you the exchange with the simple regard of solemn confidences. The sinuosity of lines is a definitely clear language in which you must decipher the agitation and the desire of souls. All the same this mysterious and temporary state of the spirit unweaves itself magically, where the depths of our existence, beset with multiple problems, reveals itself absolutely in the spectacle, so natural and so trivial as it might seem to be, that one has under one's eyes—where the first seen object becomes a speaking symbol. Fourier and Swedenborg, one with his *analogies*, the other with his *correspondences*, are incarnated in the vegetable and the animal who fall under your regard, and instead of teaching by the voice they instruct you by the form and by the colour. The intelligence of what means to you allegory seizes in you proportions unknown to yourself. I shall note in passing that an allegory of this *spiritual* kind, which awkward painters are apt to despise, but which is really one of the primitive and natural forms of poetry, takes over again its legitimate domination in one's intelligence when it is dazzled by one's intoxication. Haschisch extends itself across our life like a magic mirror; it colours it solemnly and darkens its depth. Vague landscapes, flying horizons, perspectives of white cities whitened by the cadaverous lividity of the Dawn, or illuminated by the concentrated ardours of setting suns—depths of space, allegory of the depth of time—the dance, the gesture or the declamation of the comic actors, if you happen to be in a theatre—the first phrase that starts to your lips, when your eyes fall on a book—in one world, and finally, the universality of Beings surges before you with an unimaginable glory. Grammar, the arid grammar, becomes something like an evoked sorcery; words resuscitated clothe themselves in flesh and bones, the substantive, in its substantial majority, the adjective, a transparent vestment that colours it like the glazing on a painting, and the Verb, angel of movement, that gives the swing to the phrase. Music, another language dear to idle or to deep minds who seek for relaxation in the variety of their creations, speaks to you and relates to you your Life's Poem; it incorporates itself in you, and you melt into it. Music speaks your passions, not in an indefinite and vague manner, as it does in your negligent nights, or on an opera night, but in a circumstantial, positive manner, each cadence of the rhythm marking the malicious cadence of your soul, each note transforming itself into a word, as the entire poem enters your head like a Dictionary gifted with life.

You must not believe that all these circumlocutions of life produce themselves confusedly in the mind, with the shrill accent of reality and the disorder of exterior life. The inward vision transforms all things and gives to everything that exquisite perfection which makes beauty more beautiful. It is to this essentially voluptuous and sensual phase that one must attribute the love of limpid waters, flowing and stagnant, which develop themselves so astonishingly in the cerebral intoxication of certain artists. The mirrors become a pretext for certain dreams that have a curious resemblance with spiritual thirst, joined with that physical thirst that dries the throat, of which I have spoken; then the escape of waters, *les jeux d'eau*, harmonious cascades, the immense cobalt-blue of the sea, sing, sleep with an inexpressible charm. Water extends before one's vision with a veritable enchantment, and, in spite of the fact that I don't put much trust in the furious follies caused by Haschisch, I can't affirm that the contemplation of a limpid gulf might not be without a certain peril for a spirit amorous of space and of crystal, and that the ancient fable of Undine might not become for the enthusiast a tragic reality.

I have sufficiently spoken of the monstrous exercise of time and of space, two ideas always connected, but which the spirit affronts without sadness or fear. It gazes backward with a certain delirious melancholy over the vast abyss of time, and sinks audaciously into unseen seas. I presume that one divines, in what I have said, that this abnormal and tyrannical increase can be applied equally to all the sentiments and to all the ideas; in the same sense in regard to benevolence; of this I have given, if anything, more than enough in the way of example; in the same sense in regard to Love. The idea of beauty should naturally seize fast hold on what is vast in a spiritual temperament such as I have supposed. Harmony, the balancing of lines, rhythm in move-ments, seem to the observer as necessities; as duties not only for all the beings of the Creation, but for himself, the dreamer, who finds himself, at this period of the crisis, gifted with a marvellous aptitude for comprehending the immortal and universal rhythm. And if our fanatic lacks in personal beauty, you must not suppose he suffers from the confession to which he is constrained, nor that he looks on himself as a discordant note in the world of harmony and beauty improvised by his imagination. The sophistications of Haschisch are numerous and innumerable, only they have a way of leading us to optimism, and the most efficacious of all the principles is that which transforms desire into reality. It is the same no doubt in many cases of ordinary life, but here with how much more of candour and of subtlety? Besides, how can a being so gifted in its fashion of understanding harmony, a kind of Priest of the Beautiful, make an exception and a mistake in his proper theory? Moral beauty and its power, Grace and its seduc-tions, eloquence and its prowesses, all these ideas present themselves as correctives of an indiscreet ugliness, then as consolers, finally as the perfect flatterers of an imaginary sceptre.

As for Love, I have heard many people, animated with an absurd curiosity, trying to instruct themselves from the mouths of those to whom Haschisch is familiar. What could be this amorous intoxication so passionate in its natural state, when it is confined in another form of intoxication, as a sun in a sun? Such is the question that arises in a crowd of people that I shall call the jesters of the intellectual world. So as to respond to a dishonest misunderstanding, to this part of the question which dares not make itself manifest, I shall send the reader to Pliny, who has spoken somewhere of the poisoned contents of hemp seed, in a fashion to dissipate many illusions on this subject. I am certain, besides, that weakness is the most ordinary result of the abuse men make of their nerves and of the substances needed to excite them. For as there is no question here of an effective power, but of emotion and susceptibility, I shall simply advise the reader to consider that a nervous man's imagination, intoxicated by Haschisch, is driven onward in a prodigious degree, as little determinable as the possibly extreme force of the wind in a storm, and his senses subtilised to a point almost too difficult to define. It is thus permissible to believe that a woman's caress might have a value a thousand times more terrible than the actual state of the soul and of the senses, and might conduct them very rapidly to a sudden spasm. But what Haschisch reveals in an imagination too much obsessed with love-adventures and bitter memories to which sorrow and misery add a strange illumination, is indubitable. It is not less certain that a strong dose of sensuality mixes itself with the mind's agitations; and, besides, it is worth noticing—what might be enough to settle for ever this point of the immorality of Haschisch— that a sect of the Ismailites (those Ismailites who are descended from the Assassins) diverted its adorations far beyond the impartial *Lingum*; that is to say, to an absolute and exclusive cult of what is half feminine in the symbol. It might be nothing less than natural, every man being the representative of history, to see an obscure heresy, a monstrous religion produce itself in the spirit which is in a cowardly sense given over to the mercy of an infernal drug.

Since we have seen manifested a curious singularity in the intoxication of Haschisch applied to the Unknown, a kind of philanthropy made more of pity than of love (it is here that the first germ of the Satanic Spirit develops itself in an extraordinary fashion) but which goes so far as the fear of afflicting I know not what, one divines what a localised sensation might become, applied to someone who is dear to us, playing or having played an important part in the moral life of sick people. Cult, Adoration, Prayer, dreams of happiness surge out of us with the fierce energy of fireworks; like powder and the colouring materials of fire they shine and scatter themselves in the darkness. There is no sentimental education—such as Flaubert's—to which some simple slave of Haschisch might not lend himself. The taste of protection, a sentiment of ardent and devoted paternity, might mix itself with a guilty sensuality. Haschisch alone can always excuse and absolve. It goes far beyond that. I suppose the faults one has committed having left in the soul bitter memories, a husband or a lover thinking with a kind of sadness (in his normal state) backward to a storm-tossed past; bitterness might perhaps change into sweetness; the need of pardon might make the imagination more suppliant, and remorse itself, in the diabolical Drama that express itself only in a long monologue, might act as excitant. Was I wrong in saying that Haschisch appeared, to an actually philosophical spirit, like a perfectly Satanical instrument? Remorse, so singular an ingredient of pleasure, can easily be drowned in the delicious contemplation of remorse, in a kind of voluptuous analysis; and this analysis is so rapid that man, this natural Devil, does not perceive how involuntary such sins are, and how near, from instant to instant, he approaches diabolical perfection. He *admires* his remorse, he glorifies it, exactly at the sinister hour when he is about to lose his liberty.

My imaginary man—the spirit of my own choice—has arrived at that peculiar state of joy in which he is *constrained* to admire himself. All contradiction is effaced, all problematical questions are solved. He attains the joy of existence. The plenitude of his actual life inspires in him an immeasurable pride. A voice speaks to him (alas! it is his own voice), and says to him: "You have the right to consider yourself as being superior to the hosts of men; no one knows all that you think and all that you feel. You are a King over all the passions, you live in the solitude of your convictions; you possess an immense contempt."

We can certainly suppose that from time to time a biting sensation traverses one's joy. An exterior suggestion might revive a disagreeable past. How many vile and stupid actions does not one's past reveal to one, which are veritably unworthy of this King of thought and which can soil his dignity? You must believe that the man who takes Haschisch is fated to confront reproachful ghosts of memory that surge before his vision, and that he can derive from these hideous shapes rarer elements of pride and of pleasure. Such must be the evolution of his reason: the first sensation of sorrow once over, he must analyse curiously this action or this sentiment whose memory has disturbed its actual glorification, the motives that made him act in this particular fashion, the circumstances with which he is surrounded, and if he does not find reasons enough in these circumstances, if not for the absolution, at least for the attenuation of his sin, do not imagine that he feels himself vanquished! I assist at his reasoning as at the tricks of a mechanism behind a transparent glass: "This ridiculous, cowardly, vile action, whose memory has for an instant agitated one, is in complete contradiction with my veritable nature, with my actual nature, and the energy with which I condemn it, the inquisitional care with which I analyse it and judge it, prove my haughty and divine aptitudes for virtue. How can one find in the world men clever enough to judge themselves, severe enough to condemn themselves?" And not only does he condemn himself, he glorifies himself. His horrible mind absorbed in the contemplation of a real ideal, of an ideal charity, of an ideal genius, he delivers himself triumphantly to his spiritual Debauch. We have seen that counterfeiting in a sacrilegious fashion the sacrament of Penitence, himself the Penitent and the Confessor; he has given himself a futile absolution, or, worse still, he may have derived from his condemnation a new pasturage for his pride. Now, in the contemplation of his dreams and virtuous projects, he concludes in his practical aptitude for virtue; the enormous energy with which he embraces his phantom of virtue seems to him proof positive, peremptory, of the virility necessary for the accomplishment of his desires. He confounds completely dream with action, and his imagination warms itself more and more before the enchanting spectacle of his corrected and idealised nature, substituting this fascinating image of himself to his real individuality; so weak in will, so vain in vanity, he finishes by decreeing his apotheosis in these simple terms which contain for him a world of abominable Lusts: *Je suis le plus vertueux de tous les hommes!*

Does not this remind you of Jean-Jacques Rousseau how, after having shamelessly confessed himself to the Universe, not without a certain sensuality, dared utter the same cry of triumph (or at least the difference doesn't really count) with the same sincerity and the same conviction? The enthusiasm with which he admired virtue, the nervous tenderness which filled his eyes with tears, at the sight of an excellent action or at the thought of the finer actions he might have accomplished, were enough for him to give a superlative sense of his moral value. Jean-Jacques intoxicated himself without Haschisch.

Shall I continue my analysis of this victorious monomania? Shall I explain how, under the empire of the poison, the man I have imagined supposes himself to be the centre of the Universe? Shall I explain how he becomes the living and outrageous expression of the proverb that declares that passion creates passion? He believes in his virtue and in his genius: does he not divine the end? All these environing objects are so many suggestions that agitate a world of thoughts within him, all more coloured, more living, more subtle than ever, more magic than ever. "These magnificent cities," said he, "where the superb houses are arranged in intervals, look like stage-scenery, this fine ship balanced by the waves on the shore in a nostalgic indolence, and which seem to translate our thought: when shall we set sail for the Fortunate Islands?— these museums which contain such wonderful forms and such intoxicating colours, these libraries where are accumulated scientific books and dreams of the Muse, these instruments which placed together seem as it were to speak with one voice, these enchanting women who are more charming still by the science of their costumes and by the magic of their glances; all these things have been created *for me, for me, for me!* For me, has humanity travailed, been martyred, been immolated, to serve for pasture, for *pabulum*, to my implacable thirst after emotion, after knowledge and after Beauty!" *Je saute et j'abrège.* No one ought to be astonished that a final thought, a supreme sensation should surge from the dreamer's brain: *Je suis devenu Dieu!* that an ardent, a savage cry rushes from his breast with so intense an energy, with so immense a power of projection, which if an intoxicated man's belief and will had an efficacious virtue, this cry would hurl down on the wings of lightning the angels disseminated on the heavenly roads: *Je suis un Dieu!* Suddenly this storm of pride is transformed into a wonderful temperature, and the universality of beings present themselves in coloured shapes and as it were illumined by a sulphurous dawn. If by chance a vague memory glides into the soul of this deplorable man, deplorable simply because he is happy: might there not be another God? be certain that he will rise to his whole height before *HIM*, that he will discuss his will and that he will affront him without terror. Who is the French writer who said—with the intention of mocking modern German doctrines: "*Je suis un dieu qui à mal diné?*" This stinging irony could never sting a man intoxicated by Haschisch; he would reply quietly "Il est possible que j'ai mal diné, mais je suis un Dieu."

V.

Moral.

[. . .]

It is certainly superfluous, after all these considerations, to insist on the immoral character of Haschisch. Were I to compare it with suicide, a slow suicide, with an always blood-stained and an always sharpened weapon, no reasonable man could find anything to say against it. Were I to assimilate it with sorcery, with magic, whose qualities, operating on matter, and by occult and efficacious Arcanas, might conquer a domination interdicted to man or permitted solely to those who are judged worthy of it, no philosophic soul could blame this comparison. If the Catholic Church were to condemn magic and sorcery, it would be because these fight against God's intentions, and because they suppress the travail of the times and because they desire to make superfluous the conditions of purity and morality; and because the church, not considering these as being both real and legitimate, would simply set them down to good or bad intentions. I call by the name of a thief the gambler who has found the means of winning almost every game—perhaps by cheating; how shall I name the man who wants to buy, with a little money, genius? It is certainly the inflexibility of the means that constitutes Immorality, as the supposed infallibility of magic inflicts on it its infernal stigmata. Shall I add that Haschisch, like other solitary joys, makes the individual useless to men and makes society superfluous for the individual, driving him forward to a singular kind of self-admiration and, day by day, precipitating him toward the luminous gulf wherein he admires in his own face the face of Narcissus?

If still, at the price of his dignity, of his honesty and of his free-will, a man can derive spiritual benefits from Haschisch, can he make from it a kind of thinking machine—*en faire une espèce de machine à penser?* That's a question I have often heard said before me, and I can answer it. For, as I have explained at length, Haschisch never reveals to the Individual more than the Individual himself. It is true that this individual is, as it were, driven to the utmost extremity, and as it is equally certain that the memory of impressions and of sensations survive debauches, so the hope of these Utilitarians does not appear at first sight unreasonable. But I must ask them to observe that thoughts—which have to all of us such immense importance—are not really as fine as when they appeared under their momentary travesties covered with magic and faded fineries. They have more hold on the earth than on the sky, and owe a great part of their beauty to nervous agitation, to the avidity with which the spirit casts itself on them. It follows on this, that all vain hope is a vicious circle; admit, for an instant, that Haschisch gives, or at least augments, genius; they forget that it is of the nature of Haschisch to diminish will power, and that thus it gives on one side what it withdraws from another, that is to say, imagination without the faculty of profiting by the imagination. Finally, one must think, supposing a man who is adroit and vigorous enough to escape from this alternative, of another danger, fatal, terrible, which is that of all the customs. All these transformations are necessary. One who could take poison *so as to* think would soon be unable to think without taking poison. Can one conceive the awful state of a man whose atrophied imagination would cease to function without the help of Haschisch or Opium?

In Philosophical studies, the human mind, imitating the stars' eternal movements, ought to follow a curve which brings it back to its point of departure. To conclude, is to enclose a circle. At the beginning I have spoken of this miraculous state, when a special grace seems to descend on a man's mind; I have said that aspiring endlessly to warm his flesh and to raise his body towards the Infinite, he will discover in all times and in all climes, a frantic, a frenzied taste for all the substances, even those that are dangerous, which, as they exalt his personality, might offer for an instant to his eyes a certain Paradise—*ce paradis d'occasion*—in which he desires to attain his ultimate desires, and that finally this hazardous spirit hurling itself, without knowing it, into Hell, must bear witness to its original grandeur. But man is not so abandoned, so deprived of honest means for gaining the sky, as to be obliged to invoke pharmacy and Sorcery; he has no need to sell his soul so as to pay for the intoxicating caresses of Eastern Concubines. What is a Paradise if one buys it at the price of his eternal Salvation? I imagine a man (a Brahman, a Poet, a Philosopher) seated on the summit of the ardent Olympus of his spirituality; around him, the Muses of Raphael and of Mantegna, to console him for his fasts and his assiduous prayers, conceiving the most delicious dancing; the divine Apollo, this Master of Quintessence (that of Francavilla, of Albert Dürer, of Goltzius, or of others, what matters it? Is there not an Apollo, for every man who has the merit of admiring him?) caressing with his bow the most vibrating chords of his divine instrument. Below him, at the foot of the mountain, in the mud and the briars, the multitude of multitudes, the crowd of helots, simulates the grimaces of enjoyment and utters howls against those who tear from it the bite of the poison; and the saddened Poet says to himself: "These unfortunate beings, who have never fasted, nor prayed, and who have refused redemption by travail, demand from Black Magic the means of measuring the extent of their supernatural existence. Magic deceives them and lights for them alluring and deceptive glimpses of disillusions; while all the time, we, Poets and Philosophers, have regenerated our souls by successive work and by an ardent contemplation; by the assiduous exercise of will and by the permanent nobility of intention, we have created for ourselves a garden of sublime beauty. Certain of the word which says that faith transports mountains, we have accomplished the only miracle God ever allowed us to achieve!"

DRACULA
(BRAM STOKER)

❧

"Suddenly Sexual Women in
Bram Stoker's *Dracula*"
by Phyllis A. Roth, in
Literature and Psychology (1977)

INTRODUCTION

In her essay on Bram Stoker's *Dracula*, Phyllis A. Roth summarizes the various interpretations of it that have been proposed to date, including those that deal with taboo fantasies such as Oedipal desire and that seek to show how the novel's fantasies are managed in such a way as to convert horror to pleasure. According to Roth, "Central to the structure and unconscious theme of *Dracula* is, then, primarily the desire to destroy the threatening mother, she who threatens by being desirable." For Roth, the hostility towards female sexuality (itself a social taboo) that is displayed throughout the novel provides much of the appeal for Stoker's audience.

∾

Criticism of Bram Stoker's *Dracula*, though not extensive, yet not insubstantial, points primarily in a single direction: the few articles

Roth, Phyllis A. "Suddenly Sexual Women in Bram Stoker's *Dracula*." *Literature and Psychology* 27.3 (1977): 113–21.

published perceive *Dracula* as the consistent success it has been because, in the words of Royce MacGillwray, "Such a myth lives not merely because it has been skillfully marketed by entrepreneurs [primarily the movie industry] but because it expresses something that large numbers of readers feel to be true about their own lives."[1] In other words, *Dracula* successfully manages a fantasy which is congruent with a fundamental fantasy shared by many others. Several of the interpretations of *Dracula* either explicitly or implicitly indicate, that this "core fantasy"[2] derives from the Oedipus complex—indeed, Maurice Richardson calls *Dracula* "a quite blatant demonstration of the Oedipus complex ... a kind of incestuous, necrophilous, oral-anal-sadistic all-in wrestling match"[3] and this reading would seem to be valid.

Nevertheless, the Oedipus complex and the critics' use of it does not go far enough in explaining the novel: in explaining what I see to be the primary focus of the fantasy content and in explaining what allows Stoker and, vicariously, his readers, to act out what are essentially threatening, even horrifying wishes which must engage the most polarized of ambivalences. I propose, in the following, to summarize the interpretations to date, to indicate the pre-Oedipal focus of the fantasies, specifically the child's relation with and hostility toward the mother, and to indicate how the novel's fantasies are managed in such a way as to transform horror into pleasure. Moreover, I would emphasize that for both the Victorians and twentieth century readers, much of the novel's great appeal derives from its hostility toward female sexuality. In "Fictional Convention and Sex in *Dracula*," Carrol Fry observes that the female vampires are equivalent to the fallen women of eighteenth and nineteenth century fiction.[4]

The facile and stereotypical dichotomy between the dark woman and the fair, the fallen and the idealized, is obvious in *Dracula*. Indeed, among the more gratuitous passages in the novel are those in which the "New Woman" who is sexually aggressive is verbally assaulted. Mina Harker remarks that such a woman, whom she holds in contempt, "will do the proposing herself."[5] Additionally, we must compare Van Helsing's hope "that there are good women still left to make life happy" (207) with Mina's assertion that "the world seems full of good men—even if there *are* monsters in it" (250). A remarkable contrast![6]

Perhaps nowhere is the dichotomy of sensual and sexless woman more dramatic than it is in *Dracula* and nowhere is the suddenly sexual woman more violently and self-righteously persecuted than in Stoker's "thriller."

The equation of vampirism with sexuality is well established in the criticism. Richardson refers to Freud's observation that "morbid dread always signifies repressed sexual wishes."[7] We must agree that *Dracula* is permeated by "morbid dread." However, another tone interrupts the dread of impending doom throughout the novel; that note is one of lustful anticipation, certainly anticipation of catching and destroying forever the master vampire, Count Dracula, but additionally, lustful anticipation of a consummation one can only describe as sexual. One thinks, for example, of the candle's "sperm" which "dropped in white patches" on Lucy's coffin as Van Helsing opens it for the first time (220). Together the critics have enumerated the most striking instances of this tone and its attendant imagery, but to recall: first, the scene in which Jonathan Harker searches the Castle Dracula, in a state of fascinated and morbid dread, for proof of his host's nature. Harker meets with three vampire women (whose relation to Dracula is incestuous[8]) whose appeal is described almost pornographically:

> All three had brilliant white teeth that shone like pearls against the ruby of their voluptuous lips. There was something about them that made me uneasy, some longing and at the same time deadly fear. I felt in my heart a wicked, burning desire that they would kiss me with those red lips.

The three debate who has the right to feast on Jonathan first, but they conclude, "He is young and strong; there are kisses for us all" (47). While this discussion takes place, Jonathan is "in an agony of delightful anticipation" (48). At the very end of the novel, Van Helsing falls prey to the same attempted seduction by, and the same ambivalence toward, the three vampires.

Two more scenes of relatively explicit and uninhibited sexuality mark the novel about one-half, then two-thirds, through. First the scene in which Lucy Westenra is laid to her final rest by her fiance, Arthur Holmwood, later Lord Godalming, which is worth quoting from at length:

Arthur placed the point [of the stake] over the heart, and as I looked I could see its dint in the white flesh. Then he struck with all his might.

The thing in the coffin writhed; and a hideous, blood-curdling screech came from the opened red lips. The body shook and quivered and twisted in wild contortions; the sharp white teeth champed together till the lips were cut, and the mouth was smeared with a crimson foam. But Arthur never faltered. He looked like a figure of Thor as his untrembling arm rose and fell, driving deeper and deeper the mercy-bearing stake, whilst the blood from the pierced heart welled and spurted up around it (241).

Such a description needs no comment here, though we will return to it in another context. Finally, the scene which Joseph Bierman has described quite correctly as a "primal scene in oral terms,"[9] the scene in which Dracula slits open his breast and forces Mina Harker to drink his blood:

With his left hand he held both Mrs. Harker's hands, keeping them away with her arms at full tension; his right hand gripped her by the back of the neck, forcing her face down on his bosom. Her white nightdress was smeared with blood, and a thin stream trickled down the man's bare chest which was shown by his torn-open dress. The attitude of the two had a terrible resemblance to a child forcing a kitten's nose into a saucer of milk to compel it to drink (313).

Two major points are to be made here, in addition to marking the clearly erotic nature of the descriptions. These are, in the main, the only sexual scenes and descriptions in the novel; and, not only are the scenes heterosexual,[10] they are incestuous, especially when taken together, as we shall see.

To consider the first point, only relations with vampires are sexualized in this novel; indeed, a deliberate attempt is made to make sexuality seem unthinkable in "normal relations" between the sexes. All the close relationships, including those between Lucy and her three suitors and Mina and her husband, are spiritualized beyond credibility. Only when Lucy becomes a vampire is she allowed to be "voluptuous," yet she must have been so long before, judging from her effect on men and from Mina's descriptions of her. (Mina, herself, never suffers the fate of voluptuousness before or after being bitten, for reasons which will become apparent later.) Clearly, then, vampirism is associated not only with death, immortality and orality; it is equivalent to sexuality.[11]

Moreover, in psychoanalytic terms, the vampirism is a disguise for greatly desired and equally strongly feared fantasies. These fantasies, as stated, have encouraged critics to point to the Oedipus complex at the center of the novel. Dracula, for example, is seen as the "father-figure of huge potency."[12] Royce MacGillwray remarks that:

> Dracula even aspires to be, in a sense, the father of the band that is pursuing him. Because he intends, as he tells them, to turn them all into vampires, he will be their creator and therefore "father."[13]

The major focus of the novel, in this analysis, is the battle of the sons against the father to release the desired woman, the mother, she whom it is felt originally belonged to the son till the father seduced her away. Richardson comments:

> the set-up reminds one rather of the primal horde as pictured somewhat fantastically perhaps by Freud in *Totem and Taboo*, with the brothers banding together against the father who has tried to keep all the females to himself.[14]

The Oedipal rivalry is not, however, merely a matter of the Van Helsing group in which, as Richardson says, "Van Helsing represents the good father figure"[15] pitted against the Big Daddy, Dracula. Rather, from the novel's beginning, a marked rivalry among the men is evident. This rivalry is defended against by the constant, almost obsessive, assertion of the value of friendship and *agape* among members of the Van Helsing group. Specifically, the defense of overcompensation is employed, most often by Van Helsing in his assertions of esteem for Dr. Seward and his friends. The others, too, repeat expressions of mutual affection *ad nauseum*: they clearly protest too much. Perhaps this is most obviously symbolized, and unintentionally exposed, by the blood transfusions from Arthur, Seward, Quincey Morris, and

Van Helsing to Lucy Westenra. The great friendship among rivals for Lucy's hand lacks credibility and is especially strained when Van Helsing makes it clear that the transfusions (merely the reverse of the vampire's bloodletting) are in their nature sexual; others have recognized, too, that Van Helsing's warning to Seward not to tell Arthur that anyone else has given Lucy blood, indicates the sexual nature of the operation.[16] Furthermore, Arthur himself feels that, as a result of having given Lucy his blood, they are in effect married. Thus, the friendships of the novel mask a deep-seated rivalry and hostility.

Dracula does then appear to enact the Oedipal rivalry among sons and between the son and the father for the affections of the mother. The fantasy of parricide and its acting out is obviously satisfying. According to Holland, such a threatening wish-fulfillment can be rewarding when properly defended against or associated with other pleasurable fantasies. Among the other fantasies are those of life after death, the triumph of "good over evil," mere man over superhuman forces, and the rational West over the mysterious East.[17] Most likely not frightening and certainly intellectualized, these simplistic abstractions provide a diversion from more threatening material and assure the fantast that God's in his heaven; all's right with the world. On the surface, this is the moral of the end of the novel: Dracula is safely reduced to ashes, Mina is cleansed, the "boys" are triumphant. Were this all the theme of interest the novel presented, however, it would be neither so popular with Victorians and their successors nor worthy of scholarly concern.

Up to now my discussion has been taken from the point of view of reader identification with those who are doing battle against the evil in this world, against Count Dracula. On the surface of it, this is where one's sympathies lie in reading the novel and it is this level of analysis which has been explored by previous critics. However, what is far more significant in the interrelation of fantasy and defense is the duplication of characters and structure which betrays an identification with Dracula and a fantasy of matricide underlying the more obvious parricidal wishes.

As observed, the split between the sexual vampire family and the asexual Van Helsing group is not at all clear-cut: Jonathan, Van Helsing, Seward and Holmwood are all overwhelmingly attracted to the vampires, to sexuality. Fearing this, they employ two defenses, projection[18] and denial: it is not we who want the vampires, it is they who want us (to eat us, to seduce us, to kill us). Despite the projections, we should recall that almost all the on-stage killing is done by the "good guys": that of Lucy, the vampire women, and Dracula. The projection of the wish to kill onto the vampires wears thinnest perhaps when Dr. Seward, contemplating the condition of Lucy, asserts that "had she then to be killed I could have done it with savage delight" (236). Even earlier, when Dr. Seward is rejected by Lucy, he longs for a cause with which to distract himself from the pain of rejection: "Oh, Lucy, Lucy, I cannot be angry with you. . . . If I only could have as strong a cause as my poor mad friend there [significantly, he refers to Renfield]—a good, unselfish cause to make me work—that would be indeed happiness" (84). Seward's wish is immediately fulfilled by Lucy's vampirism and the subsequent need to destroy her. Obviously, the acting out of such murderous impulses is threatening: in addition to the defenses mentioned above, the use of religion not only to exorcise the evil but to justify the murders is striking. In other words, Christianity is on our side, we *must* be right. In this connection, it is helpful to mention Wasson's observation[19] of the significance of the name "Lord Godalming" (the point is repeated). Additional justification is provided by the murdered themselves: the peace into which they subside is to be read as a thank you note. Correlated with the religious defense is one described by Freud in *Totem and Taboo* in which the violator of the taboo can avert disaster by Lady Macbeth-like compulsive rituals and renunciations.[20] The repeated use of the Host, the complicated ritual of the slaying of the vampires, and the ostensible, though not necessarily conscious, renunciation of sexuality are the penance paid by those in *Dracula* who violate the taboos against incest and the murder of parents.

Since we now see that Dracula acts out the repressed fantasies of the others, since those others wish to do what he can do, we have no difficulty in recognizing an identification with the aggressor on the part of characters and reader alike. It is important, then, to see what it is that Dracula is after.

The novel tells of two major episodes, the seduction of Lucy and of Mina, to which the experience of Harker at Castle Dracula provides a preface, a hero, one whose narrative encloses the others and with whom, therefore, one might readily identify. This, however, is a defense against the central identification of the novel with Dracula and his attacks on the women. It is relevant in this context to observe how spontaneous and ultimately trivial Dracula's interest in Harker is. When Harker arrives at Castle Dracula, his host makes a lunge for him, but only after Harker has cut his finger and is bleeding. Dracula manages to control himself and we hear no more about his interest in Harker's blood until the scene with the vampire women when he says, "This man belongs to me!" (49) and, again a little later, "have patience. Tonight is mine. To-morrow night is yours!" (61). After this we hear no more of Dracula's interest in Jonathan; indeed, when Dracula arrives in England, he never again goes after Jonathan. For his part, Jonathan appears far more concerned about the vampire women than about Dracula—they are more horrible and fascinating to him. Indeed, Harker is relieved to be saved from the women by Dracula. Moreover, the novel focusses on the Lucy and Mina episodes from which, at first, the Jonathan episodes may seem disconnected; actually, they are not, but we can only see why after we understand what is going on in the rest of the novel.

In accepting the notion of identification with the aggressor in *Dracula*, as I believe we must, what we accept is an understanding of the reader's identification with the aggressor's victimization of women. Dracula's desire is for the destruction of Lucy and Mina and what this means is obvious when we recall that his attacks on these two closest of friends seem incredibly coincidental on the narrative level. Only on a deeper level is there no coincidence at all: the level on which one recognizes that Lucy and Mina are essentially the same figure: the mother. *Dracula* is, in fact, the same story told twice with different outcomes. In the former, the mother is more desirable, more sexual, more threatening and must be destroyed. And the physical descriptions of Lucy reflect this greater ambivalence: early in the story, when Lucy is not yet completely vampirized, Dr. Seward describes her hair "in its usual sunny ripples" (180); later, when the men watch her return to her tomb, Lucy is described as "a dark-haired woman" (235). The conventional fair/dark split, symbolic of respective moral casts, seems to be unconscious here, reflecting the ambivalence aroused by the sexualized female. Not only is Lucy the more sexualized figure, she is the more rejecting figure, rejecting two of the three "sons" in the novel. This section of the book ends with her destruction, not by Dracula but by the man whom she was to marry. The novel could not end here, though; the story had to be told again to assuage the anxiety occasioned by matricide. This time, the mother is much less sexually threatening and is ultimately saved. Moreover, Mina is never described physically and is the opposite of rejecting: all the men become her sons, symbolized by the naming of her actual son after them all. What remains constant is the attempt to destroy the mother. What changes is the way the fantasies are managed. To speak of the novel in terms of the child's ambivalence toward the mother is not just to speak psychoanalytically. We need only recall that Lucy, as "bloofer lady," as well as the other vampire women, prey on children. In the case of Lucy, the children are as attracted to her as threatened by her.

I have already described the evidence that the Van Helsing men themselves desire to do away with Lucy. Perhaps the story needed to be retold because the desire was too close to the surface to be satisfying; certainly, the reader would not be satisfied had the novel ended with Arthur's murder of Lucy. What is perhaps not so clear is that the desire to destroy Mina is equally strong. Let us look first at the defenses against this desire. I have already mentioned the great professions of affection for Mina made by most of the male characters. Mina indeed acts and is treated as both the saint and the mother (ironically, this is particularly clear when she comforts Arthur for the loss of Lucy). She is all good, all pure, all true. When, however, she is seduced away from the straight and narrow by Dracula, she is "unclean," tainted and stained with a mark on her forehead immediately occasioned by Van Helsing's touching her forehead with the Host. Van Helsing's hostility toward Mina is further revealed when he cruelly reminds her of her "intercourse" with Dracula: "'Do you forget,' he said, with actually a smile, 'that last night he banqueted heavily and will sleep late?'" (328) This hostility is so obvious that the other men are shocked. Nevertheless, the "sons," moreover, and the reader as well, identify with Dracula's attack on Mina; indeed, the men cause it, as indicated by the events which transpire when all the characters are at Seward's hospital-asylum. The members of the brotherhood go out at night to seek out Dracula's lairs, and they leave Mina undefended at the hospital. They claim that this insures her safety; in fact, it insures the reverse. Furthermore, this is the real purpose in leaving Mina out of the plans and in the hospital. They have clear indications in Renfield's warnings of what is to happen to her and they all, especially her husband, observe that she is not well and seems to be getting weaker. That they could rationalize these signs away while looking for and finding them everywhere else further indicates that they are avoiding seeing what they want to ignore; in other words, they want Dracula to get her. This is not to deny that they also want to save Mina; it is simply to claim that the ambivalence toward the mother is fully realized in the novel.

We can now return to that ambivalence and, I believe, with the understanding of the significance of the mother figure, comprehend the precise perspective of the novel. Several critics have correctly emphasized the regression to both orality and anality[21] in *Dracula*. Certainly, the sexuality is perceived in oral terms. The primal scene already discussed makes abundantly clear that intercourse is perceived in terms of nursing. As C. F. Bentley sees it:

> Stoker is describing a symbolic act of enforced fellatio, where blood is again a substitute for semen, and where a chaste female suffers a violation that is essentially sexual. Of particular interest in the ... passage is the striking image of "a child forcing a kitten's nose into a saucer of milk to compel it to drink," suggesting an element of regressive infantilism in the vampire superstition.[22]

The scene referred to is, in several senses, the climax of the novel; it is the most explicit view of the act of vampirism and is, therefore, all the more significant as an expression of the nature of sexual intercourse as the novel depicts it. In it, the woman is doing the sucking. Bierman comments that "The reader by this point in the novel has become used to Dracula doing the sucking, but not to Dracula being sucked and specifically at the breast."[23] While it is true that the reader may most often think of Dracula as the active partner, the fact is that the scenes of vampire sexuality are described from the male perspective, with the females as the active assailants.[24] Only the acts of phallic aggression, the killings, involve the males in active roles. *Dracula*, then, dramatizes the child's view of intercourse insofar as it is seen as a wounding and a killing. But the primary preoccupation, as attested to by the primal scene, is with the role of the female in the act. Thus, it is not surprising that the central anxiety of the novel is the fear of the devouring woman and, in documenting this, we will find that all the pieces of the novel fall into place, most especially the Jonathan Harker prologue.

As mentioned, Harker's desire and primary anxiety is not with Dracula but with the female vampires. In his initial and aborted seduction by them, he describes his ambivalence. Interestingly, Harker seeks out this episode by violating the Count's (father's) injunction to remain in his room; "let me warn you with all seriousness, that should you leave these rooms you will not by any chance go to sleep in any other part of the castle" (42). This, of course, is what Harker promptly does. When Dracula breaks in and discovers Harker with the vampire women, he acts like both a jealous husband and an irate father: "His eyes were positively blazing. The red light in them was lurid . . . 'How dare you touch him, any of you?'" (48–49). Jonathan's role as child here is reinforced by the fact that, when Dracula takes him away from the women, he gives them a child as substitute. But most interesting is Jonathan's perspective as he awaits, in a state of erotic arousal, the embraces of the vampire women, especially the fair one: "The other was fair as fair can be, with great wavy masses of golden hair and eyes like pale sapphires. I seemed somehow to know her face and to know it in connection with some dreamy fear, but I could not recollect at the moment how or where" (47). As far as we know, Jonathan never recollects, but we should be able to understand that the face is that of the mother (almost archetypally presented), she whom he desires yet fears, the temptress-seductress, Medusa. Moreover, this golden girl reappears in the early description of Lucy.

At the end of the following chapter, Jonathan exclaims, "I am alone in the castle with those awful women. Faugh! Mina is a woman, and there is nought in common." Clearly, however, Mina at the breast of Count Dracula is identical to the vampire women whose desire is to draw out of the male the fluid necessary for life. That this is viewed as an act of castration is clear from Jonathan's conclusion: "At least God's mercy is better than that of these monsters, and the precipice is steep and high. At its foot a man may sleep—as a *man*. Good-bye, all! Mina!" (4; emphasis mine).

The threatening Oedipal fantasy, the regression to a primary oral obsession, the attraction and destruction of the vampires of *Dracula* are, then, interrelated and interdependent. What they spell out is a fusion of the memory of nursing at the mother's breast with a primal scene fantasy which results in the conviction that the sexually desirable woman will annihilate if she is not first destroyed. The fantasy of incest and matricide evokes the mythic image of the *vagina dentata* evident in so many folk tales[25] in which the mouth and the vagina are identified with one another by the primitive mind and pose the threat of castration to all men until the teeth are extracted by the hero. The conclusion of *Dracula*, the "salvation" of Mina, is equivalent to such an "extraction": Mina will not remain the *vagina dentata* to threaten them all.

Central to the structure and unconscious theme of *Dracula* is, then, primarily the desire to destroy the threatening mother, she who threatens by being desirable. Otto Rank best explains why it is Dracula whom the novel seems to portray as the threat when he says, in a study which is pertinent to ours:

> through the displacement of anxiety on to the father, the renunciation of the mother, necessary for the sake of life is assured. For this feared father prevents the return to the mother and thereby the releasing of the much more painful primary anxiety, which is related to the mother's genitals as the place of birth and later transferred to objects taking the place of the genitals [such as the mouth].[26]

Finally, the novel has it both ways: Dracula is destroyed[27] and Van Helsing saved; Lucy is destroyed and Mina saved. The novel ends on a rather ironic note, given our understanding here, as Harker concludes with a quote from the good father, Van Helsing:

> "We want no proofs; we ask none to believe us! This boy will some day know what a brave and gallant woman his mother is. Already he knows her sweetness and loving care; later on he will understand how some men so loved her, that they did dare so much for her sake" (416).

NOTES

1. Royce MacGillwray, "*Dracula*: Bram Stoker's Spoiled Masterpiece," *Queen's Quarterly*, LXXIX, 518.
2. See Norman N. Holland, *The Dynamics of Literary Response* (New York: W. W. Norton & Co., 1975).
3. Maurice Richardson, "The Psychoanalysis of Ghost Stories," *Twentieth Century*, CLXVI (December 1959), 427.
4. *Victorian Newsletter*, XLII.

5. Bram Stoker, *Dracula* (New York: Dell, 1974), 103–104. All subsequent references will be to this edition and will appear parenthetically.

6. While it is not my concern in this paper to deal biographically with *Dracula*, the Harry Ludlam biography (a book which is admittedly anti-psychological in orientation despite its provocative title, *A Biography of Dracula: The Life Story of Bram Stoker*) includes some suggestive comments about Bram Stoker's relationship with his mother. Ludlam remarks an ambivalence toward women on the part of Charlotte Stoker who, on the one hand, decried the situation of poor Irish girls in the workhouse which was "the very hot-bed of vice" and advocated respectability through emigration for the girls and, on the other, "declared often that she 'did not care tuppence' for her daughters." Too, Charlotte told her son Irish folk tales of banshee horrors and a true story of "the horrors she had suffered as a child in Sligo during the great cholera outbreak that claimed many thousands of victims in Ireland alone, and which provoked the most dreadful cruelties" (New York: The Fireside Press, 1962, p. 14). I cannot help but wonder how old Stoker was when his mother discussed these matters with him. Certainly, they made a vivid impression, for later, Charlotte wrote her story down and Bram based his own "The Invisible Giant" on his mother's tale of the cholera epidemic in Sligo.

7. Richardson, p. 419.

8. C. F. Bentley, "The Monster in the Bedroom: Sexual Symbolism in Bram Stoker's *Dracula*," *Literature and Psychology*, XXII, 1 (1972), 29.

9. Joseph S. Bierman, "*Dracula*: Prolonged Childhood Illness and the Oral Triad," *American Imago*, XXIX, 194.

10. Bentley, p. 270.

11. See Tsvetan Todorov, *The Fantastic*, trans, Richard Howard (Cleveland: Case Western Reserve, 1973), pp. 136–39.

12. Richardson, p. 427.

13. MacGillwray, p. 522.

14. Richardson, p. 428. The Oedipal fantasy of the destruction of the father is reinforced by a number of additional, and actually gratuitous, paternal deaths in the novel. See also MacGillwray, p. 523.

15. Richardson, p. 428.

16. See, for instance, Richardson, p. 427.

17. Richard Wasson, "The Politics of *Dracula*," *English Literature in Translation*, IX, pp. 24–27.

18. Freud, *Totem and Taboo*, trans. James Strachey in *The Standard Edition of the Complete Psychological Works of Sigmund Freud*, Vol. XIII (1913–1914) (London: Hogarth press, 1962), 60–63.

19. Wasson, p. 26.

20. Freud, pp. 37ff.

21. Bentley, pp. 29–30; MacGillwray, p. 522.

22. Bentley, p. 30.

23. Bierman, p. 194. Bierman's analysis is concerned to demonstrate that "*Dracula* mirrors Stoker's early childhood . . . ," and is a highly speculative but fascinating study. The emphasis is on Stoker's rivalry with his brothers but it provides, albeit indirectly, further evidence of hostility toward the rejecting mother.

24. Ludlam cites one of the actors in the original stage production of *Dracula* as indicating that the adaptation was so successful that "Disturbances in the circle or stalls as people felt faint and had to be taken out were not uncommon—and they were perfectly genuine, not a publicity stunt. Strangely enough, they were generally men" (Ludlam, I. 165).

25. See, for instance, Wolfgang Lederer, M.D., *The Fear of Women* (New York: Harcourt Brace Jovanovich, Inc., 1968), especially the chapter entitled, "A Snapping of Teeth."

26. Otto Rank, *The Trauma of Birth* (New York: Harper & Row, 1973), p. 73.

27. When discussing this paper with a class, two of my students argued that Dracula is not, in fact, destroyed at the novel's conclusion. They maintained that his last look is one of triumph and that his heart is not staked but pierced by a mere bowie knife. Their suggestion that, at least, the men do not follow the elaborate procedures to insure the destruction of Dracula that they religiously observe with regard to that of the women, is certainly of value here, whether one agrees that Dracula still stalks the land. My thanks to Lucinda Donnelly and Barbara Kotacka for these observations.

HOWL
(ALLEN GINSBERG)

❧ ❧

"Transgression, Release, and 'Moloch'"
by Jeffrey Gray, Seton Hall University

"Unscrew the locks from the doors!
Unscrew the doors themselves from their jambs!"

—Walt Whitman, "Song of Myself"
(and epigraph to Ginsberg's "Howl")

Among the many parallels between Allen Ginsberg and his literary forefather Walt Whitman is the fact that just as the 1881 edition of Whitman's *Leaves of Grass* was banned from the mail (the U.S. Post Office refusing to handle it), so was Ginsberg's *Howl and Other Poems*, and for the same reasons. In 1957, the second printing of *Howl* was seized by customs as it came into San Francisco from England. The ACLU contested the legality of the seizure, with the result that, after hearing the testimony of witnesses for the defense (including Mark Schorer, Walter Van Tilburg Clark, Herbert Blau, and Kenneth Rexroth), Judge Clayton Horn dismissed the charges, finding poet and publisher Lawrence Ferlinghetti not guilty of publishing obscene writings on the grounds that *Howl* was not written with lewd intent and was not without "redeeming social importance." By the time of Ginsberg's death in 1997, *Howl* had sold 800,000 copies, was translated into at least 24 languages, and is today one of the best-known of American poems.

The similarities between Ginsberg and Whitman do not stop there. They include the two poets' references to sexuality and the body; the

37

exuberant tone, long lines, and catalogues; the sheer length of *Song of Myself* and *Howl;* the collapsing of binary oppositions (soul/body, man/woman, high/low, and others); and the celebration of male camaraderie, both in the homoerotic sense and—in Whitman's case—more often in a spiritualized sense as a remedy for the ills of society.[1] (Whitman was prophetic on this point, as the Civil War demonstrated.)

At the time that the San Francisco district attorney attempted to censor *Howl*, there was still a ban in place on D.H. Lawrence's *Lady Chatterley's Lover* as well as *The Tropic of Cancer* by Henry Miller. Thus, words like "cunt," "snatch," "cock," "fuck," and others in *Howl* were likely included to call attention to the poem, and they did. At the trial Jake Erlich, the lead attorney for the ACLU, defended the word "fuck," quoting groundbreaking precedent in the trial of James Joyce's *Ulysses.* He also quoted Christopher Marlow's sixteenth-century poem "Ignato," which ends with the poet stating that he loves the woman to whom the poem is addressed because "zounds I can fuck thee soundly" (trial transcript, qtd. in Morgan 189).

But as the trial transcripts reveal, it was not principally four-letter words that concerned the authorities. *Howl's* transgressions were (and are) many—sexual, social, aesthetic, religious, and political. Ginsberg's declarations of ethnicity, homosexuality, drug use, and Communist sympathies in both "Howl" and "Kaddish" occurred at a time when these identities and practices were virtually unmentionable. At the same time, Ginsberg's humor and self-parody helped to deflate the repressive power against which "Howl" was especially directed.

In the "tranquilized fifties," as poet Robert Lowell described the decade, American society was ensconced in suburban comfort, conformity, and the official ideology of containment. It was the era of anti-communism and Senator Joe McCarthy, and the U.S. government regarded writers in general as dangerous and seditious. As Jonah Raskin writes, "Hollywood directors and writers were jailed. Irish poet Dylan Thomas was investigated by the FBI and begrudgingly issued a visa. Arthur Miller was denied a passport and not allowed to leave the United States for years. Dashiell Hammett, the author of *The Maltese Falcon* and *The Thin Man*, was sent to prison for refusing to knuckle under to investigators and name names" (5). As for the beat generation, Burroughs wrote *Junkie* under a pseudonym, no one would publish Jack Kerouac from 1950–1955, and *Howl*, of course, was tried for obscenity. Although the ideology of fear, oaths of loyalty, black lists, and public denunciations were winding down by 1955, the nation was still deeply conflicted on questions of loyalty, sexual deviance, and race. Segregation had just been pronounced unconstitutional in 1954, but racial tensions were higher than ever, and Emmett Till was murdered the next year.

Preceded by the notoriety gained from the San Francisco trial, *Howl* burst onto this scene like a firebomb. Perhaps the high degree of societal repression demanded the appearance of a book like *Howl*. Whatever one may have thought of it as poetry, *Howl* represented the return of the repressed—aesthetically, sexually, spiritually, and politically. Like all prophetic and mystical texts, *Howl* transgresses sanity and reason in favor of "mad," paranoid, surreal, apocalyptical consciousness. Of course any incantatory, irrational speech or writing is to some degree anti-hegemonic. But in Ginsberg, the content is explicit. Do radios read minds? Was the CIA involved in publishers' rejections of Kerouac's manuscripts? Do scholars support wars? These conspiracy theories, in retrospect, were not outrageous. Frances Stonor Saunders' *The Cultural Cold War: The CIA and the World of Arts and Letters* (1999) makes it clear that the CIA (and its literary-artistic arm "Congress of Cultural Freedom") was involved in cultural interventions that no one, certainly not the unwitting participants (including Jackson Pollock, Stephen Spender, and Robert Lowell), could have imagined.

The taboos Ginsberg violated with such force in *Howl* were those most entrenched in society: 1. the taboo against the unrestrained sociopathic speech of madness and irrationality; 2. the taboo against sexuality outside of marriage and other moral constraints; and, chiefly, 3. the taboo against mocking and destabilizing the traditional partition between the sacred and the profane, against treating all phenomena, high and low, spiritual and physical, as simultaneous and on an equal plane. Every society is structured upon a division between the sacred and the profane. Indeed, that division can be said to *define* a society. In the "Footnote to Howl," one can see the collapse of the sacred and profane in a single line:

> The world is holy! The soul is holy! The skin is holy! The nose
> is holy! The tongue and
> cock and hand and asshole holy! (27)

SIENA COLLEGE LIBRARY

Most people who consider themselves religious—at least in the western world, where the spiritual and physical have been at odds at least since the Greeks—will subscribe, arguably, to the first two statements (certainly to the second), but from the skin and nose on *down*, things become uncomfortable and finally unacceptable. The "asshole" is not to be talked about, much less declared "holy," much less conflated with things of the "spirit."

Regarding the issue of madness, consider that Ginsberg's usable past was made up of figures like William Blake, Christopher Smart, Charles Baudelaire, Guillaume Apollinaire, and "Plotinus Poe St John of the Cross telepathy and bop Kabbalah" (12),[2] as he writes in "Howl." (In the original manuscript, the list also includes Marx, Genet, Artaud, Rimbaud, Wolfe, Celine, Proust, Whitman, and Buddha.) Whether through drugs, meditation, jazz, sex, or travel, Ginsberg wanted to experience and to depict in the poem the derangement of the senses that Arthur Rimbaud had recommended in the nineteenth century—mad, but also shamanistic, prophetic, bardic, and visionary. Vincent Hugh, at the trial of *Howl* argued that the *book* belonged to a tradition in literature that has roots in Ezra Pound's *Cantos*, Dante's *Inferno*, Joyce's *Ulysses*, and all the "ancient mythologies of the world" (Raskin 223).

Ginsberg's antecedents for alternate states of consciousness were not only literary and mythological; they were also familial. Ginsberg's mother, Naomi Ginsberg, was a paranoid schizophrenic who had many breakdowns, starting almost immediately after her wedding to Ginsberg's father. She saw enemies everywhere, as Raskin recounts:

> President Roosevelt conspired against her; Nazi spies stalked her; her mother-in-law planned to assassinate her; or so she insisted. The whole industrial world aimed to destroy her. That story line was essential to Allen Ginsberg's myth about his mother—the myth that infuses *Howl*. His mother—and all the innocent, idealistic young men and women of the world—had 'human individuality and non-mechanical organic charm,' Ginsberg thought. Like them, Naomi stood in opposition to the 'modern, mechanical, scientific robot government' (Raskin 29–30).

The anti-establishment climax of *Howl* occurs in Part II, an incantation of accusations against Moloch, the ancient Middle Eastern deity to which children were sacrificed, seen now as the technological evil

SIENA COLLEGE LIBRARY

of instrumental reason, Blake's Urizen. Moloch had murdered Naomi and would murder others. But Moloch is clearly also the cities and their buildings. Moloch is the military-industrial complex, CIA, FBI, Blake's "satanic mills," and multinational capitalism all rolled into one. (In early drafts, Ginsberg wrote, "Moloch whose name is America . . ." [AGHO 64], a line he later took out.[3]) This apocalyptic section of *Howl* was written under the influence of peyote, after walking through San Francisco with Peter Orlovsky. He at first saw Moloch as memories of gloomy New York City, but when he stared at the façade of the Sir Francis Drake hotel, "suddenly the gothic eyes of the skull tower glaring out" and "dollar sign skull protrusion of lipless jailbarred inhuman longtooth spectral deathhead. . . ." (from Ginsberg's *Journals: Mid-Fifties, 1954–1958*, qtd. in Raskin 131).

Schizophrenics who believe that the radio is talking to them (as did Naomi Ginsberg and, somewhat differently, as does Allen Ginsberg in *Howl* and later books) are not altogether mistaken. Fifteen years after *Howl*, in *The Fall of America*, Ginsberg writes a long poem that he composes as he is being driven across America, listening to the voices on the car radio hypnotize listeners into shopping and supporting a war in Southeast Asia. Ginsberg was prescient in illustrating the forms that modern hegemony takes, not centralized but dispersed, even "implanted" in each person—another "paranoia" of *Howl*.

"Madness" appears in the very first line of *Howl*: "I saw the best minds of my generation destroyed by madness, starving, hysterical, naked . . ." (9).[4] Ginsberg was thinking of his friends, the petty thief and addict Herbert Huncke, Carl Solomon whom he met in a mental hospital, Phil White (a heroin addict who committed suicide in prison), William Cannastra (who was killed in a subway accident), David Kammerer (stabbed to death by Ginsberg's friend Lucien Carr), Joan Burroughs (shot to death by William Burroughs, by accident presumably, in Mexico) and Kerouac, going through his own mental hell, lost, unpublishable, uncertain.[5] In *Howl*, "madness" becomes a floating signifier. Does it refer to the agonizing schizophrenia that killed Ginsberg's mother? Or does it mean what Whitman signifies when, speaking of the atmosphere, he says "I am mad for it to be in contact with me"? In other words, does it signify not pathology but intensity of experience and of opposition to the system? Like *On the Road*, *Howl* celebrates outsiders, living in the moment. The "negro streets" of *Howl*'s second line drew the young Ginsberg in the same way that rap music today pulls white boys out of the stupefying suburbs.[6] Kerouac, in the same vein, writes that "the only people for me are the mad ones, the ones who are mad to live, mad to talk, mad to be saved, desirous of everything at the same time, the ones who never yawn or say a common place thing, but burn, burn, burn like fabulous yellow roman candles exploding like spiders across the stars and in the middle you see the blue centerlight pop and everybody goes 'Awww!'" (5). "Madness," in this sense, was freedom and a sense of wonder, as well as a way of critiquing Bob Dylan's "Mister Jones," who just doesn't know what's happening. Ginsberg said to Kerouac, in 1948, "I really will go mad and that's what I half hope for" (qtd. in Raskin 83). Ginsberg may have glamorized real madness—pathology, suicide, failure—but much of the time "the mad ones" means the wild, the visionary, and the uninhibited.

Explicit sexual description or reference to bodily functions has been the chief grounds for censorship in the twentieth century. This was true in the cases of D.H. Lawrence, James Joyce, Henry Miller, and those of many lesser known authors. The most egregious passage of this kind in *Howl* reads:

> who howled on their knees in the subway and were dragged off
>   the roof waving genitals and manuscripts,
> who let themselves be fucked in the ass by saintly motorcyclists,
>   and screamed with joy,
> who blew and were blown by those human seraphim, the sailors,
>   caresses of Atlantic and Caribbean love,
> who balled in the evenings in rose-gardens and the grass of
> public
>   parks and cemeteries scattering their semen freely to
>   whomever come who may. . . . (13)

The "saintly motorcyclists" of "Howl" are from "The Wild One" with Marlon Brando. Standing perhaps in Brando's place, Ginsberg's friend Neal Cassady was the handsome, charismatic, car-stealing hero of both Kerouac's *On the Road*, published in 1957, and *Howl*. For Ginsberg, Cassady was the living metaphor for energy, nonconformity, and priapic excess. In 1958, in "Many Loves," Ginsberg calls Cassady by name, but in "Howl," Cassady is always "N.C.," the sexual hero whose bisexuality is in fact concealed:

> who went out whoring through Colorado in myriad stolen
> night-cars,
>> N.C., secret hero of these poems, cocksman and Adonis
>> of Denver—
>> joy to the memory of his innumerable lays of girls in
>> empty lots and diner backyards.... (14)

After Cassady's death in 1968, Ginsberg makes their sadomasochistic relationship clear in the poem "Please Master"; it is even clearer in his journals, where he confesses, "I want to be your slave, suck your ass, suck your cock, you fuck me, you master me, you humiliate me ..." (qtd. in Raskin 147). Although the homosexuality is repressed in *Howl*, the poem's redundant homosociality and Whitmanic male camaraderie—as in *On the Road*—has led to well-founded charges of misogyny. Most of the women in *Howl* are shrews, to whom the narrator's friends have "lost their loveboys" (14). The "three old shrews of fate" are whore-like, seductive, greedy, and "one-eyed."

Much of the transgressiveness of *Howl* can be subsumed under the heading of a particular theme, what one might call the trope of nakedness in U.S. literature—the sense of immediacy, that the reader is getting something more "real" for being unadorned and unabashed. For Whitman, stripping bare is a general metaphor for release. This is equally true of Ginsberg, with the additional dimension that Ginsberg actually stripped naked in front of audiences, breaking a taboo that Whitman, though he took considerable risks for the late nineteenth century, surely never contemplated.

Song of Myself is full of tropes of nakedness, often with reference to immediacy, freshness, and originality: When Whitman writes, "Voices long veil'd, and I remove the veil," the "veil" over the voice is that of custom. He is releasing the voice, his own and those of others heretofore silenced. When he writes, "Loose the stop from your throat" (35), alluding to the stop in an organ that opens and closes the valve through which the air rushes to form a tone, he addresses the impediment of shame or fear in oneself that thwarts speech at its source. Consider the context:

> Loafe with me on the grass, loose the stop from your throat,
> Not words, not music or rhyme I want, not custom or lecture,
> not even the best,
> Only the lull I like, the hum of your valved voice. (35)

Ginsberg, invoking Whitman, often talked of the voice and the breath. The titles *Howl* and *Song* both participate in an oral trope, though *Howl* suggests a sound more painful and frightening than a "song," less a celebration than an agony. We see how deeply the oral trope is woven into and performed by *Song of Myself*, with its many performative vocal sounds ("belch'd," "blab," "yawp," "lull," "hum "), most of them onomatopoeic and without etymology. These words—and the desire to hear "not music or rhyme," "not custom or lecture," no matter how good those may be, but rather the pre-semantic "hum of your valved voice"—represent attempts to reach a space prior to language. Whitman is performing or describing the process of an unmediated vocalizing. Finally, when he writes, "What living and buried speech is always vibrating here, what howls restrain'd by decorum . . ." (39), he seems to be both describing his own effort to disinter (a metaphor that substitutes for denuding) this primal vitality and foreshadowing Ginsberg's parallel effort.

Though Whitman's work was the *Song of Myself*, he made it clear that he meant to speak for many, as Ginsberg also purports to do, from the first line of *Howl* and through the many subordinate clauses beginning "who. . . ." In Whitman's poem, the role of the medium for repressed content is most clear:

> Through me many long dumb voices,
> Voices of the interminable generation of prisoners and slaves,
> Voices of the diseas'd and despairing and of thieves and
> dwarfs,
> Through me forbidden voices,
> Voices of sexes and lusts, voices veil'd and I remove the veil,
> Voices indecent by me clarified and transfigur'd. (57)

The appeal to uninhibited, even pre-semantic utterance—belches, howls, yawps, hums, and more—suggests the other taboo that *Howl and Other Poems* conspicuously broke at a time when, far from continuing the modernists' iconoclastic program of "make it new"

(Ezra Pound), mid-century poets were playing it safe. The issue was Ginsberg's poetics. The prizing of spontaneity, which may in part have come out of Whitman ("Spontaneous Me" was one of Whitman's titles), came for Ginsberg more conspicuously out of jazz, out of the automatic writing experiments of the French surrealists, out of Japanese aesthetics such as brush painting, and especially out of the Buddhist idea, often quoted by Ginsberg, "first thought, best thought."[7] This approach can lead, as it certainly did for Whitman, to fatuity, obviousness, and rhetorical excess: this is the risk one takes. In the context of a critical establishment whose leading lights included John Crowe Ransom, Cleanth Brooks, and Robert Penn Warren, *Howl* was initially seen as having no poetic merit at all (it *did* get attention, owing to the court case and to the growing awareness that there was a "beat generation" and that Ginsberg was its poetic voice). It was said to be loose, obscene, adolescent, pretentious, and amateurish. At best these critics saw it (and Ginsberg to some extent encouraged the view) as the "raw" pole of the raw-vs.-cooked binary opposition popular at the time—i.e. the open vs. the closed, the improvisatory vs. the formal. Marjorie Perloff has argued that this is pure mythology, since Ginsberg "was probably a much truer modernist than were mandarin poets like Louis Simpson or Donald Hall" (29–30). *Howl* can hardly be said to have given up formalism either; given "the use of biblical strophes, tied together by lavish anaphora and other patterns of repetition" (Perloff 30) and given the highly artificial nature of Ginsberg's language—its oxymorons and incongruities, its ellipses and syntactic distortions—no one should mistake it for "unformed speech" as critics have charged (Perloff 35). More than 50 years later, there is still no shortage of critics who see *Howl* as, at best, representative of a period in American culture, and therefore of social or cultural more than of literary interest.

In the end, it is the language of the body that is most taboo. The poet Mark Doty describes hearing Ginsberg read at various points in his career, the last time at a Dodge Poetry Festival in New Jersey, on Teachers' Day, in 1996.

> It's maybe six months before his death, but Allen's in fine and sweetly energetic form, reading/ chanting his late, playful chants—"don't smoke, don't smoke, suck cock, suck cock"—and everyone just loves him. (12)

Following the chants, Ginsberg reads his ode to his sphincter muscle, and Doty steals a glance around the room, to discover the audience loves it. How is this? He wonders. Shouldn't they be offended? Doty concludes that Ginsberg managed somehow to sidestep the question of what is polite or obscene or gay or straight. He created "some zone of permission and distinction for himself that seemed to make all things possible" (13). But perhaps with that particular setting and audience, teachers in the presence of a now legendary cultural figure, those who were disgruntled kept quiet and respectful. One can think of many contexts—not merely the U.S. Senate or the PTA—where these poems would be far from welcome, 50 years after the attempted banning of *Howl*.

The division between the sacred and the profane—the structure of which, though the contents vary, is found in every culture—is destabilized in the long poems of both Whitman and Ginsberg. We saw this in "Footnote to Howl." Consider Whitman:

> Divine am I inside and out, and I make holy whatever I touch
> > or am touch'd from,
> The scent of these arm-pits aroma finer than prayer,
> This head more than churches, bibles, and all the creeds. (57)

This passage in *Song of Myself* is followed by a body-centered incantation, in which the parts of the speaker's body are catalogued and celebrated—"I dote on myself, there is that lot of me and all so luscious"—and in which at several points the last opposition, that of inside and outside, of me and not-me, is collapsed, as we have seen earlier in Whitman's eroticized landscape and atmosphere.

What Ginsberg did is to go far beyond the armpits:

> Holy my mother in the insane asylum! Holy the cocks
> > of the grandfathers of Kansas!
> Holy the groaning saxophone! Holy the bop apocalypse!
> > Holy the jazzbands marijuana hipsters peace
> > & junk & drums! (27)

The sacred and profane come together: clothes and God and decorum on one side; nakedness and excrement and howls on the other. Ginsberg, however transcendent and spiritual, will always be seen as the epitome of the freed libido; the raw vs. the cooked; the naked, the unmediated, in both form and content.

Eventually "mainstream" culture and literature made a place for adversarial culture, as has happened so often in U.S. history. Even Lionel Trilling, Ginsberg's professor at Columbia, who hadn't liked Ginsberg's work at all, included two poems ("Supermarket in California" and "To Aunt Rose") in his 1967 textbook *The Experience of Literature.* Today of course there is no mainstream twentieth-century American poetry anthology that omits Ginsberg; the big ones (Norton, for example) usually printing "Howl" in its entirety. In 1986, Harper and Row brought out the original draft facsimile edition of *Howl,* modeled after the facsimile edition of Eliot's *The Waste Land,* in which Ginsberg explained everything one could possibly want to know about the allusions in the poem, the stages of revision, and the author's life during the process of composition. But, with complete absorption into the culture, can *Howl* still be fresh, transgressive, and revolutionary? It would seem that a breakthrough cannot keep being a breakthrough. Once the shattered icons are lying on the floor, you can't keep shattering them. For Sven Birkerts, seeing Ginsberg in the 1970s was a disappointment:

> [I]t hardly helped matters that the poet himself, that fierce icon breaker, had grown into an avuncular pop icon, all finger cymbals and rolling waves of "Ommmm" that I could not take seriously. And as the years passed, his great outburst acquired its crown of thorny footnotes and worked its way into the canon, the Moloch imprecations sidling up to Walt Whitman's "barbaric yawp." (81)

For Birkerts, this was the last straw: it was now possible to read "Howl" in class.

But text is made oppositional by a context. That means that *Howl* may be oppositional again. And so it came to pass: in the 1980s Jerry Falwell's conservative Christian "Moral Majority" began recruiting members by identifying "obscene" or "indecent" literature that they thought should be prohibited. (Since "obscene had been difficult to define in court, they settled on "indecent" as the best term with which to lobby.) The Heritage Foundation and senator Jesse Helms found this a perfect opportunity to inveigh against "smut" and indecency in music and literature. Feeling the pressure, the F.C.C. ruled that "indecent" material could only be broadcast on the radio between midnight and 6 a.m. Broadcasters then had to decide whether material was offensive to the community or not. In January 1988, "Howl" was scheduled to be read on several radio stations as part of a week-long series on censorship. The broadcasters at five Pacifica stations backed off. No one could fight the censorship, since there was no law to challenge. Meanwhile, the F.C.C. fined several other stations around the country for broadcasting movies and other materials that the commission deemed "indecent" (Morgan). For the time being, Ginsberg's opposition triumphed, returning the nation to the idea that had prevailed in the U.S. prior to 1957, i.e. that all art should be suitable for children.

Howl mirrored the changes Ginsberg saw and heard around him in America. It also advanced those changes. In the 1970s, in the hippie counterculture he had helped to create, Ginsberg promised to rewrite Howl to reflect the euphoria of the hippies. The new Howl would be positive and redemptive, he said, and would begin with the line, "I have seen the best minds of my generation turned on by music." But the poem was never written, perhaps for the good reason that it could not have been transformative; it could not have presented the unknown, the unimagined. It would have been part of the furniture of that era, rather than a living howl in the teeth of the world.

NOTES

1. Throughout this article, "Howl" indicates the title of the poem rather than the book *Howl and Other Poems*.
2. All quotations from "Howl," unless otherwise indicated, will be from the 1956 *Howl and Other Poems*.
3. *AGHO* indicates *Howl: Original Draft Facsimile, Transcript and Variant Versions, Fully Annotated by Author, with Contemporary Correspondence, Account of First Public Reading, Legal Skirmishes, Precursor Texts & Bibliography*.
4. In the original, the line read "starving, mystical, naked . . ."
5. Kerouac's *The Town and the City* was published in 1950 but was unsuccessful. *On the Road* would not be published until 1957.
6. The original line was "dragging themselves through the angry streets at dawn looking for a negro fix. . . ." Ginsberg switched

the two adjectives, not wanting to associate drug addiction with black people.

7. In fact we know that Ginsberg revised, against Kerouac's advice, as Ginsberg explains in *AGHO*.

WORKS CITED

Bidart, Frank. *In the Western Night: Collected Poems, 1965–1990.* New York: Farrar, Straus and Giroux, 1990.

Birkerts, Sven. "Not Then, Not Now." *The Poem that Changed America: "Howl" Fifty Years Later.* Ed. Jason Shinder. New York: Farrar, Straus & Giroux, 2006. 73–83.

Doty, Mark. "Human Seraphim: 'Howl,' Sex, and Holiness." *The Poem that Changed America: "Howl" Fifty Years Later.* Ed. Jason Shinder. New York: Farrar, Straus & Giroux, 2006. 11–18.

Ginsberg, Allen. *Howl and Other Poems.* San Francisco: City Lights, 1956.

———. *Howl: Original Draft Facsimile, Transcript and Variant Versions, Fully Annotated by Author, with Contemporary Correspondence, Account of First Public Reading, Legal Skirmishes, Precursor Texts & Bibliography.* Ed. Barry Miles. New York: Harper & Row, 1986. Rpt. New York: HarperPerennial, 1995.

———. *The Fall of America.* San Francisco: City Lights, 1972.

Kerouac, Jack. *On the Road.* New York: Penguin, 1985.

Morgan, Bill and Nancy J. Peters, eds. Howl *on Trial: The Battle for Free Expression.* San Francisco: City Lights, 2006.

Ostriker, Alicia. "*Howl* Revisited: The Poet as Jew." *American Poetry Review* 26.4 (July-August 1997): 28–31.

Perloff, Marjorie. "'A Lost Battalion of Platonic Conversationalists': 'Howl' and the Language of Modernism.'" *The Poem that Changed America: "Howl" Fifty Years Later.* Ed. Jason Shinder. New York: Farrar, Straus & Giroux, 2006. 24–43.

Raskin, Jonah. *American Scream: Allen Ginsberg's Howl and the Making of the Beat Generation.* Berkeley: University of California Press, 2004.

Saunders, Frances Stonor. *The Cultural Cold War: The CIA and the World of Arts and Letters.* London: New Press, 2000.

Whitman, Walt. *The Portable Walt Whitman.* Ed. Mark Van Doren. New York: Penguin, 1973.

JULIUS CAESAR
(WILLIAM SHAKESPEARE)

❧

"Totem, Taboo, and *Julius Caesar*"
by Cynthia Marshall, in
Literature and Psychology (1991)

INTRODUCTION

Although Freud's *Totem and Taboo* contains no explicit reference to Shakespeare's *Julius Caesar*, Cynthia Marshall describes the way "Freud's concept of taboo culture, the primitive banding together of brothers for the purpose of overcoming the father, recreates Shakespeare's picture of Roman society." By focusing on Freud's obsession with the character of Brutus, a role Freud played as a child, and by exploring the two texts for the way they resonate off one another, Marshall connects the taboo in Freud's text, in Freud's life, and in Shakespeare's play. For Marshall, "The story of Julius Caesar–part myth, part history–exists on the cusp of civilization; the father–son conflict is partly actual and partly symbolic. Yet because Brutus is identified in action, he must fail where Freud, heir to his ambivalence, succeeds: repression of the parricidal wish enables Freud to internalize the father, in the form of taboo law or superego."

❧

Marshall, Cynthia. "Totem, Taboo, and *Julius Caesar*." *Literature and Psychology*. 37.1–2 (1991): 11–33.

Freud's "writings are haunted," writes Marjorie Garber, "by the uncanny reappearance of *Julius Caesar*" (53). Freud is a central player in Garber's perceptive account of historical and literary idealizations of "the idea of Rome" (52). Thus she sees Rome itself, the historical "embodiment of fantasy and desire" (53), as inspiring the passage near the beginning of *Civilization and Its Discontents* where Freud considers "the Eternal City" (69) as an image of the human mind. Freud is seeking an analogue for the mind's capacity to preserve its past, to retain "all the earlier phases of development . . . alongside the latest one." But he quickly abandons the attempt, noting how "historical sequence" cannot logically be represented "in spatial terms" (70). "Only in the mind," he writes, is it possible to preserve "all the earlier stages alongside of the final form." In fact, Freud enacts in the text the preservative "phenomenon" under discussion: by retaining the aborted attempt to "represent this phenomenon in pictorial terms" (71), he illustrates his early effort to create a picture of the mind as well as his later abandonment of the task.[1] He creates both a historical record of his mind at work (the narrative sequence) and a spatial representation (the textual artifact).

Freud repeatedly inscribes himself in the text when responding to Rome and to the preeminent Roman story, that of Julius Caesar. *The Interpretation of Dreams* (1900) and *Totem and Taboo* (1912–13), in particular, exhibit a distinct debt to Shakespeare's *Julius Caesar*. In *The Interpretation of Dreams*—the work with which he so self-consciously established his reputation—Freud, notoriously, cites Brutus as an example of ambivalence, then discloses that he once played the part of Brutus himself. The sections of the text immediately following this revelation, which constitute the textual response to *Julius Caesar*, manifest a paternal anxiety that suggests a certain Roman dimension in the role Freud accords to the Oedipus complex in his formulations about culture and society. *Totem and Taboo* contains no explicit reference to *Julius Caesar*, yet Freud's concept of the taboo culture, the primitive banding together of brothers for the purpose of overcoming the father, recreates Shakespeare's picture of Roman society. Considering these three texts in conjunction affords an opportunity to read Freud's articulations of Oedipal theory and of repression in light of his own inscribed experience. Freud's avoidance in *The Interpretation of Dreams* of the biographical significance of his "Caesar," together with the strongly overdetermined Oedipal conclusion of *Totem and Taboo*, suggest how his extension of individual psychology to social theory enacts the sublimation of parricidal anxieties clustered around and within *Julius Caesar*.

I

Julius Caesar, written the year before *Hamlet*, rehearses some of the attitudes familiar from the more notably Oedipal play. Killing the king is structurally the equivalent of killing the father, and Caesar, traditionally identified as Rome's *pater patriae* (Miola 85), carries a special historical importance to his role of victim. Brutus, the dramatic hero cast as symbolic son,[2] understands his part in the assassination as an act of personal betrayal, yet consents nevertheless. The first two acts of the play turn largely upon Brutus' decision to join the conspiracy. At the moment of his death, Caesar binds Brutus' crisis with his own in a causative relation: "*Et tu, Brute?*—Then fall Caesar!" (3.1.77).[3] In terms of the plot, the play's final two acts concern the political aftermath of the assassination, but considered in psychological terms they illustrate "the return of the repressed" (Garber 62). Caesar's influence seems inescapable; as many critics have noted, his power increases with his death. His "spirit walks abroad, and turns [the conspirators'] swords / In [their] own proper entrails" (5.3. 95–96). Brutus and Cassius kill themselves with his name upon their lips. Moreover, Caesar is reincarnated in several forms: politically in the figure of Octavius Caesar, whose pomp and peremptoriness recall the former Caesar; and emotionally in Brutus, whose, evident resemblance to Caesar grows as the play progresses.

Critics have frequently commented on similarities between the two heroes,[4] not only in terms of their "ideals" (MacCallum 241) but with regard to specific behaviors. So James Siemon, for instance, notes how Brutus' rigidity and "aloofness" in the quarrel with Cassius (4.3) betray his likeness to Caesar. "Even the power of hearing seems to begin to abandon Brutus in this exchange," Siemon writes, for Brutus "has gone more than a little way toward being, as Caesar is, deaf to the empirical evidence contradicting his postures and figures" (175). Norman Rabkin sees an inherent and continual similarity between the two, with the parallel construction of 2.1 and 2.2 designed specifically to call attention to a kind of doubling of character. The similarity between the two characters, at whatever point it is perceived, amounts to a kind of family resemblance between them, and adds to the structural equivalence between king and father in enforcing the play's Oedipal theme.

Hamlet is the Shakespearean play most obviously connected with Freud's formulation of Oedipal theory, but two other plays besides *Hamlet*—*Henry IV, pt. 1* and *Julius Caesar*—receive multiple reference in *The Interpretation of Dreams.* Of this trio of Oedipal dramas, *Julius Caesar* carries special weight as the dramatization of a historical event of wide and seemingly unavoidable importance. Moreover, in *Julius Caesar* the problematic relation of the individual to history is formally explored; the play presents the conundrum of two heroes competing for dramatic priority, each precarious in the position of eminence. The divided dramatic form reflects historical consensus: the question of the significance of Caesar's assassination was by no means settled when the play was written in 1599. Ernest Schanzer traces the tradition of contradictory interpretations of the assassination, a tradition he sees Shakespeare as receiving and transmitting (11–23). Rabkin argues that Shakespeare's historical position with regard to the material was particularly problematic, because of the assassination's "inescapable concern to the unstable moment of history in which he composed his plays" (82). Doubtless, the relative stability of one's own historical moment—how perceived, how valued—necessarily influences an interpretation of Caesar's assassination, an event in itself ambiguously barbarous or liberating. Freud's response to the play reveals how biographical concerns impinge on interpretation as well.

The complexity of *Julius Caesar's* historical material perhaps occasioned the new depth of introspection Shakespeare represents in the character of Brutus. As the tragic hero, his character is developed largely through soliloquy, so that however debatable the morality of his intentions may be, he offers at least the appearance of a revealed interior dimension. The contrast with Caesar's illeistic self-references is clear. The contradiction within Caesar's character[5] consists of a gap between his public reputation, fostered largely by Caesar himself, and the infirm, gullible figure presented on stage. It is a contrariety of self-presentation, and not merely in the dramatic sense—a problem of denoting the self to the exterior world. Brutus' ambivalence, however, is seen as more truly experiential, intrinsic to his reflective, self-examining mind. Brutus, "with himself at war" (1.2.45), questions the relative demands of personal loyalty and public good ("I would not, Cassius; yet I love him well" [1.2.81]), questions his own motives ("I know no personal cause to spurn at him/But for the general" [2.1.11–12]). Brutus' mind is thus divided in the act of self-scrutiny; he is, moreover, doubly divided, since he is conscious not only of self, but of his own conflicting impulses—ambivalent, and aware of his ambivalence. What Freud calls repression is the belated discovery of such an internal division. Significantly, when Brutus abandons the habit of soliloquy—the dramatic figuration of self-awareness—after the assassination, he becomes prey to the ghost, an external projection of his guilt. *Julius Caesar* contains, enacts, and inspires ambivalence,[6] and therefore offers a rich mine for Freud.

II

Brutus appears in *The Interpretation of Dreams* in Freud's discussion of one of his own dreams, in which a dead friend (P.) sits, apparently alive, opposite him.[7] Intending to explain this oddity to a second friend (Fleischl) with the phrase *"Non vivit"* ["he is not alive"], Freud instead says *"Non vixit"* ["he did not live"], and then actualizes the death-wish by giving P. "a piercing look," under the strength of which "his form grew indistinct . . . and finally he melted away" (457). Freud attributes his mistake ("*vixit*" for "*vivit*") to "a convergence of a hostile and an affectionate current of feeling towards my friend," and goes on to explain that "As he had deserved well of science I built him a memorial; but as he was guilty of an evil wish . . . I annihilated him." Noticing the "special cadence" of this last sentence, Freud searches for his "model," "a juxtaposition like this of two opposite reactions towards a single person," and discovers it can be found "only in one passage in literature . . . Brutus' speech of self-justification in Shakespeare's *Julius Caesar* [iii, 2], 'As Caesar loved me, I weep for him; as he was fortunate, I rejoice at it; as he was valiant, I honour him; but as he was ambitious, I slew him.'" The verbal parallel leads Freud to the realization that he "had been playing the part of Brutus in the dream" (459).

The admission occasions his reported memory of acting the part of Brutus "in the scene between Brutus and Caesar from Schiller" when he was fourteen, and to an analysis of his troubled relations with his nephew John, who "had come to us on a visit from England" and who played the part of Caesar. John returns as a *"revenant"* from

Freud's early childhood, when the two had been "inseparable." Freud recalls his youthful hostility toward John, who was a year older than he, and remarks that "There must have been times when he treated me very badly and I must have shown courage in the face of my tyrant." The ghost of this "tyrant" exerted "a determining influence on all my subsequent relations with contemporaries" (460), or as Freud later puts it "All my friends have in a certain sense been reincarnations of this first figure . . . they have been *revenants*" (520–21). Or revenants of a revenant, since John's presence was ghostly in the initially cited episode of playing Caesar.

Freud essentially compounds Schiller's play with Shakespeare's: after quoting Brutus' speech in *Julius Caesar*, he identifies "playing the part of Brutus" with the episode in *Die Räuber*.[8] While I will for the most part follow his lead in considering Shakespeare's version of the story, it is interesting to note the pronounced Oedipal antagonism in "the part of Brutus" that Freud actually played.[9] The story of Julius Caesar figures in *Die Räuber* as the inspiration to achieve greatness—and sacrificing the father is the explicit price of such achievement in the play's plot. Boyhood reading of "the adventures of Julius Caesar"[10] (143) is touted as an early indication that Charles von Moor will neglect his duty to his father. Charles recites the lyric between Brutus and Caesar in the hope that "my slumbering genius may wake up again" (244). Although purportedly his father's rescuer from the destructive intentions of his evil brother, Charles himself "kills" his father with the news of what he has become, captain of a robber band. He is, the robbers say at the end, "infected with the great-man-mania" (277)—the result, in the play's terms, of identifying himself with Brutus.

Moreover, while the character of Shakespeare's Caesar enfolds a ghost, who is released after the assassination, in the passage from Schiller Caesar is simply a ghost, an "unblest shade" returned to haunt Brutus. So Freud's nephew John returns "as a revenant" to play a revenant, whose reality is supposedly secondary to that of the more potent Brutus. The brief lyric expresses Brutus' ambivalence toward the dead Caesar: he first scorns the ghost ("Hence to thy Stygian Flood!"), then pleads with him to remain ("Stay, father, stay!"), and resolves the relationship as a purely oppositional one ("Where Brutus lives, must Caesar die!"). Whereas Shakespeare hints at a parricidal theme, Schiller makes it explicit:

> CAESAR: Thou, too, Brutus? that thou shouldst be my foe
> Oh, son! It was thy father! Son! The world
> Was thine by heritage!..................
>   BRUTUS: Stay, father, stay! Within the whole bright round
> Of Sol's diurnal course I knew but one
> Who to compare with Caesar could be found;
> And that one, Caesar, thou didst call thy son!
> 'Twas only Caesar could destroy a Rome;
> Brutus alone that Caesar could withstand—
> Where Brutus lives, must Caesar die! Thy home
> Be far from mine. I'll seek another land.
>   (4.5; pp. 245–46)

Schiller's Brutus praises Caesar in order to have glory rebound upon himself, as son and successor.

Freud, by recounting his memory of presenting this drama, can attribute back to an early source, his "complicated" (461) feelings about John, the element of hostility in his dream about P. He ascribes central importance to the scene in the dream "in which I annihilated P. with a look" (458). It is worth noting, however, that not only P. but the second friend, Fleischl, is discovered to be "no more than an apparition, a '*revenant*.'" The dream narrative concludes with a strange realization: "it seemed to me quite possible that people of that kind only existed as long as one liked and could be got rid of if someone else wished it" (457). The dream grants Freud the capacity to exorcise his demons—a capacity glimpsed in Schiller's Brutus, but lacking in Shakespeare's character, who must kill himself to silence the ghost of Caesar. Focusing on the relationship with P., Freud leaves unremarked in his analysis the discovery of power over others, of a godlike omnipotence. By tracing his ambivalence to a childhood source, Freud historicizes his feelings but refrains from actually interpreting them. Yet the cathexis of John, the tyrant of Freud's childhood, itself stands in need of analysis. Freud relates "how he was my superior, how I early learned to defend myself against him, how we were inseparable friends, and how, according to the testimony of our elders, we sometimes fought with each other and—made complaints to them about each other" (520). He does not explore the significance of the roles he and his nephew played, nor does he comment on the curiosity of his father being "at the same time John's grandfather" (460)—a situation that casts John in a role equivalent to father, intermediary between Freud and his actual father/grandfather.

But the context in which the dream is discussed betrays the paternal ghost; recalling the figure of Brutus seems to evoke the specter of problematic relationships with the father. The dream of annihilating P., coming at the end of the section on "Calculation in Dreams" in Chapter Six, launches discussion of a series of dreams about fathers that extends through the three following sections. The pattern, considered in relation to Freud himself—and after all, it is he who "played Brutus"—suggests that John, the Caesar of his childhood, the elder, superior figure who evokes hostility, is a surrogate for Freud's father, whom he scrupulously protects from the taint of Oedipal accusations. In his essay on "Screen Memories,"[11] Freud acknowledges the unreliability as facts of childhood memories: "It may indeed be questioned whether we have any memories at all *from* our childhood: memories *relating to* our childhood may be all that we possess" (322). Childhood memories signify in different, more symbolic registers than that of pure narrative history. A memory of dramatic play would be particularly resonant, not only because each participant takes on a role additional to his own, but because subsequent encounters with the play-text become impacted to produce one's total current response to the play, which then colors any memory of the original event. The resonance for Freud of *Julius Caesar* (a textual memory evidently embracing the enacted passage from Schiller) is evinced in the way the play serves as a subtext to this portion of *The Interpretation of Dreams*. Noting the formal and thematic correspondences furthers a specific understanding of how Freud connects the phenomenon of ambivalence with the child's (here the son's) relation to the father, a connection that later forms the foundation for *Totem and Taboo*.

Freud's dream of playing "the part of Brutus" is followed by one dreamed by a patient "who had lost his father six years earlier." The dream involves a railway accident in which the father's "head was compressed from side to side" (461) and the dreamer's subsequent vision of his father with a wound above one eyebrow. Freud makes a connection between the dream and the patient's dissatisfaction with a bust of his father newly rendered by an artist. The dreamer's—and Freud's[12]—concern with statuary parallels that of Shakespeare's Romans, who attach crucial importance to life's monumental dimensions, to ancestry, names, and statuary, the "public rendering of name" (Berry 79). *Julius Caesar* opens with a tribunal reprimand delivered to the citizens for decking "the images" with "Caesar's trophies" (1.1.64,69). Still more central to this connection is Calphurnia's dream on the night before Caesar's assassination. The very presence in the play of Freud's subject, dream and dream interpretation, demonstrates its attraction for him and might justify a connection of these two texts. In his wife's dream, as reported by Caesar, he figures as a statue:

> She dreamt to-night she saw my statue,
> Which like a fountain with an hundred spouts
> Did run pure blood; and many lusty Romans
> Came smiling, and did bathe their hands in it.
>   (2.2.76–79)

Calphurnia sees in the dream "warnings and portents/And evils imminent" (80–81), while Decius cunningly offers an interpretation more flattering to Caesar; he says it "Signifies that from you great Rome shall suck / Reviving blood" (2.2.85–6). Calphurnia's dream foreshadows Caesar's fate; after his death, Antony and the conspirators alike emphasize the number of his wounds and the amount of blood that is shed, and Antony's use of Caesar's body as a prop during his funeral oration grants an iconic quality to the corpse. To reiterate further the monumental aspect of the assassination, Antony describes how Caesar died "at the base of Pompey's statue / (Which all the while ran blood)" (3.2.190–91). Statues represent the great figures of the past; in a sense they are the patriarchal past, frozen into concrete form, ancestry reified. So Freud's dreamer, reacting to the "calamity" of a bust he sees as inaccurate, is attempting to accommodate his vision of his father. The dream expresses hostility, but despite the compressed head and the facial wound, the father's eyes are "clear" (462), suggesting that the dreamer's image of his father is intact, that his anxieties are confronted and controlled.

After considering a fairly impersonal dream about constructing and accepting an image of the dead father, Freud turns to a dream of his own, about his father "play[ing] a political part," interpreted as that of a "presiding judge." He reports seeing a portion of the dream

in miniature, as though it were a picture; this distancing of the material into art corresponds to the experience of drama, as the father's part
here corresponds to that of Caesar. The "wish embodied in the dream,"
whose attribution slides in the course of analysis from Freud himself
to a female patient, is stated thus: "To stand before one's children's
eyes, after one's death, great and unsullied" (464). Strangely, it is
formulated as the father's wish, although both Freud and his patient
dream as children. The wish is projected, in other words, onto the
parent from the child. Reattributed to the dreamer, the wish expressed
in the dream is that of "filial piety"—to have one's father stand after
his death, great and unsullied, heroic, statue-like. This dream, like the
previous dream, concerns the formation of a stable image of the dead
father, the memory of whom is conceptualized in terms of art.

Freud next turns specifically to dreams of the dead returning to
life. To illustrate his discussion of absurdity in dreams, he recounts
one in which a dead man returns to call his grandson to account
(465), and another in which a dead man returns to life unaware that
he is really dead (466). These dreams rehearse the motif familiar
from the second half of *Julius Caesar*, in which Caesar's ghost walks
and his influence over the men of Rome continues to be pervasive.
If some such ghost threatens Freud, he quickly wards it off: although
the content of the following dream (Freud's own) does not concern
fathers, its interpretation—encapsulated as, "It is absurd to be proud
of one's ancestors; it is better to be an ancestor oneself" (470)—
expresses the ambivalence of a struggle with the patriarchal bond. Yet,
as Freud writes in *Totem and Taboo*, "The law only forbids men to do
what their instincts incline them to do" (160); so here the repudiation of patriarchy would be unnecessary were it easy or instinctual to
disclaim pride in one's ancestors.

Without acknowledging his own emotional involvement, Freud
recognizes the pattern at work in this series of reported dreams.
Dreams involving a dead father are especially likely to exhibit absurdity, he maintains, because of the degree of censorship necessarily
exerted over feelings about the father.

> The authority wielded by a father provokes criticism from his
> children at an early age, and the severity of the demands he
> makes upon them leads them, for their own relief, to keep their
> eyes open to any weakness of their father's, but the filial piety

called up in our minds by the figure of a father, particularly
after his death, tightens the censorship which prohibits any
such criticism from being consciously expressed. (471)

The comment renders his mystification of the following dream, in
which he exempts himself from the rule of relations with the father,
all the more astonishing. The dream imputes a number of transgressions to Freud's father: unpaid hospital fees, drunkenness requiring
detention, and a suspicion that Freud himself was born early, in the
year following his father's marriage.[13] In the subsequent analysis Freud
discloses anxieties about his own career, his marriage, his mortality—
but steadfastly denies the existence of doubts or hostilities towards
his father. "Whereas normally a dream deals with rebellion against
someone else, behind whom the dreamer's father is concealed, the
opposite was true here" (472). His father is merely the "man of straw"
hiding the figure of "a senior colleague." Freud insists on his father's
perfection: "the dream was allowed to ridicule my father because in
the dream-thoughts he was held up in unqualified admiration as a
model to other people" (473). As Hamlet would put it, "Hyperion to
a satyr."

Issues so effectively censored by "filial piety" would be expected to
return, according to Freud's own insights into the economies of repression. Both of the dreams that explicitly concern his father resurface
for further consideration in the course of the chapter (484, 486). And
as he has promised, Freud returns to the dream that originally evoked
the ghost of Brutus, the dream in which his friends dissolve into
apparitions. Although he never identifies his "tyrannous," "superior"
nephew with his father, a further reference to Shakespeare implies as
much: "Wherever there is rank and promotion the way lies open for
wishes that call for suppression. Shakespeare's Prince Hal could not,
even at his father's sick-bed, resist the temptation of trying on the
crown" (522).[14] One is reminded of a footnote earlier in *The Interpretation of Dreams*: "A Prince is known as the father of his country;
the father is the oldest, first, and for children the only authority, and
from his autocratic power the other social authorities have developed
. . ." (251n).[15] With the reference to Prince Hal, Freud comes close to
an admission of feeling a "temptation" such as that "of trying on the
crown"; he continues, "But, as was to be expected, the dream punished
my friend, and not me, for this callous wish. 'As he was ambitious, I

slew him'" (522). So apparently he had felt a "callous wish" such as might warrant punishment, but had suppressed his wish, his ambition, more effectively than had his friend P., who had given "loud expression to his impatience" (522) to have his superior out of the way. The crime resides not in the actual desire to displace one's father—how could it, if the desire is ubiquitous?—but in the failure to repress it.

Freud ends the section by remarking on his "self-discipline" in reporting and analyzing his own dreams. He exercises this discipline once more in avoiding the matter of his father, reiterating instead the importance of his nephew in determining the shape of subsequent friendships. He expresses "satisfaction" at having "always been able to find successive substitutes for that figure" and concludes that "no one was irreplaceable" (523). The statement is problematized by the fact that from John's first mention he was already a "revenant," himself a substitute for an earlier presence. Mightn't one suppose that John, as Caesar, was not simply a revenant of his former self, but a reincarnation of the original "tyrant" and "superior"—the figure of the father? Such a connection would explain the drive from the dream realization of mastery—"people of that kind only existed as long as one liked"—to the comfort taken in the later statement (which follows the series of discussions of dead fathers) that "no one [is] irreplaceable." These two statements, taken together, offer assurance that one may destroy one's superiors with impunity—as Brutus did, or rather tried to do. For as *Julius Caesar* illustrates, one guise of the irreplaceable is the inescapable.

Like Brutus haunted by Caesar's ghost, Freud meets the reincarnation of his nephew, his Caesar, in all his "subsequent relations with contemporaries." The contrast between the primarily negative terms in which the nephew is first presented ("treated me very badly," "my tyrant") and Freud's later "satisfaction" at finding replacements for "the friend of my childhood" (523) evinces his acknowledged ambivalence. Nevertheless, by concluding on the positive note he reestablishes emotional control. The remnants of "hostility" toward his "early playmate" (460) are buried beneath a grand statement of the emotional life's ongoing adaptation and fluidity. The section of *The Interpretation of Dreams* following Freud's reference to Brutus is a kind of paean to the repression of Oedipal wishes. No wonder it is filled with revenants, returning ghosts of dead fathers; no wonder it shares numerous elements with *Julius Caesar*.

III

Peter Gay notes Freud's "audacious" ambition in writing *Totem and Taboo*, in which he attempts "to dig down to the most remote foundations of culture" (324). Although it exhibits difficulties characteristic of Freud's forays into fields outside psychoanalytic theory—its anthropology heavily derivative, its history speculative—*Totem and Taboo* contains some of Freud's most brilliant, and certainly his most controversial, formulations regarding collective behavior. Freud himself told Strachey "that he regarded it as his best-written work," although he reportedly experienced "doubts and hesitations about publishing it" (13:xi). *Totem and Taboo*'s problematic status as invented myth was identified early, when in 1920 R.R. Marett labelled it a "just-so story" (Gay 327).

As Freud summarizes his myth in *Civilization and Its Discontents*, "the human sense of guilt," and hence the conscience, derive from an original murder, "the killing of the primal father" (132). The deed is not posited as metaphoric, like the relationship that the mythic and dramatic story of Oedipus supposedly bears to modern parent–child relationships, but rather as an actual originary act, setting in motion the guilt of subsequent generations. Freud qualifies the historical reality of the deed at several points. In a footnote to *Totem and Taboo*, he apologizes for "the indefiniteness, the disregard of time interval, and the crowding of the material" (184n) in the account of how "one day the expelled brothers joined forces ..." (183). And in *Moses and Monotheism* he maintains that these events "occurred to all primitive men—that is, to all our ancestors. The story is told in an enormously condensed form, as though it had happened on a single occasion, while in fact it covered thousands of years and was repeated countless times during that long period" (81). While these qualifications might make it more accurate to speak of multiple originary acts, the essential point is an eventual transformation from historical deed to symbolic fact. Whether occurring once for the species as a whole, or repeatedly within numerous tribes, a first, supposedly real, parricide produces remorse in the murdering sons, who subsequently establish the superego, investing it with the power of the father, and thus creating the law, the "restrictions ... intended to prevent a repetition of the deed." A domino effect of rebellion and guilt is set in motion, with the members of each generation passing through their roles as aggressive sons before assuming positions as repressive fathers. But ultimately the relationship with the parent enters Freud's claimed domain of the symbolic: "Whether one has killed one's father or has abstained from doing so is not really the decisive thing. One is bound to feel guilty in either case, for the sense of guilt is an expression of the conflict due to ambivalence" (132). Freud's attribution of guilt to preexisting ambivalence may produce a circular argument,[16] but at least it accords with his concept of the dichotomous mind. Internal warfare ("with himself at war") is bound to produce repercussions, the dominant side punishing the weaker. The central movement in the establishment of this myth, from the nascent consciousness of a primal ancestor to a shaping historical event, cannot be (and has not been) accounted for so easily.

Freud's general task in *Totem and Taboo*—extending his analysis of the individual psyche to society and culture—bears a decided similarity to the attempted analogy between the human mind and Rome at the start of *Civilization and Its Discontents*. For although he aims explicitly to compare the psyche with the physical structure of Rome—the Palatine, the Temple of Jupiter Capitolinus, the Coliseum, the Pantheon—these sites have meaning, have history, only as the record of human group activity; they signify not as isolated architectural examples, but as imposing remains of a past society. The necessity of establishing the cultural validity of his work outside its analytic utility for individuals was a central challenge facing Freud. What then determines the self-acknowledged success of his "audacious" attempt to connect the individual with the group in *Totem and Taboo*, but his proclaimed failure with the related analogy in *Civilization and Its Discontents*?[17] *Totem and Taboo* exhibits a curious slippage from the claim of general correspondence between savage and modern behaviors to establishing the neurotic as the point of contact. Thus, at the beginning, "we can recognize in [savages'] psychic life a well-preserved, early stage of our own development" (3).[18] By late in the second chapter, however, implicating primitive man as more ambivalent than "civilised human beings," Freud requires a principle of differentiation, and finds it in the stigma of neurosis. It is "neurotics who are compelled to reproduce this conflict" of ambivalence; they retain an "atavistic remnant . . . of an archaic constitution" (88).[19] "Neuroses," moreover, unlike savage behaviors, are asocial formations; they seek to accomplish by private means what arose in society through collective labour" (96). Once he determines the strength of the savage experience of ambivalence—which ultimately means (for him) ambivalence toward the father—Freud moves to limit the stated correspondence with civilised human beings. He distances his authorial self from primitive hostility by objectifying and stigmatizing the "atavistic" neurotic. *Civilization and Its Discontents*, valorizing both the Eternal City and the mind's preservative powers, does not offer this escape. Its formulations of the behavior of men in civilised society tacitly include Freud himself, bringing him uncomfortably close to the experience of Rome, which he enacted as a child playing Brutus.

For *Julius Caesar* too is generally about the experience of the group, most obviously in the sense that the play dramatizes a foundational story for Western culture, a political epic anticipating and shaping later notions of tyranny and the costs of rebellion. Brutus' struggle, in one view an individual Oedipal struggle, can also be construed as the necessary accommodation of personal desires to group requirements. Indeed, Brutus himself sees his conflict in precisely these latter terms: "for my part, / I know no personal cause to spurn at him, / But for the general" (2.1.10–12). Only acting in concert can the conspirators amass the strength to overcome Caesar. Or as Freud, borrowing the Darwinian notion of the primal horde, would put it in *Totem and Taboo*, "together they dared and accomplished what would have remained impossible for them singly" (183). Freud traced the beginning of social organization to the banding together of a tribe of brothers in order to kill and devour sacrificially the primal father. The appearance of this same plot in *Julius Caesar*—an ancient, but not "primal" story—historicizes Freud's originary account, taking it out of the realm of myth by suggesting its recurrence in civilized experience. Moreover, his sense of youthful involvement with the Caesar story brings the plot directly into his own experience. David Willbern calls Freud's youthful translation of *Oedipus Tyrannus* the beginning of his "interpenetrat[ion of] the text of the myth" (107). So here with *Julius Caesar*, another version of the Oedipal myth but with more social emphases, text and history interpenetrate: history consists of an enacted text, while the "invented" text of *Totem and Taboo* reenacts dimensions of Freud's own history.

"Only in one passage in literature" (*Dreams* 459) does Freud find the perfect statement of ambivalence. *Julius Caesar* functions as a conduit between his early experience and his later theory about the foundation of society. The taboo, and hence the founding of totemic culture, is rooted in primitive man's ambivalence: "they hated the father who stood so powerfully in the way of their sexual demands and their desire for power, but they also loved and admired him" (*Taboo* 184). "I would not, Cassius; yet I love him well" (1.2.81). "As Caesar loved me, I weep for him; as he was fortunate, I rejoice at it; as he was valiant, I honour him; but, as he was ambitious, I slew him" (3.2.25–27). Not surprisingly, more than a resemblance between the Roman conspiracy and the primitive band of brothers connects *Julius Caesar* with *Totem and Taboo*. Shakespeare's picture of Roman society demonstrates numerous elements of the taboo culture. It seems, in fact, a historicized, literary, and also biographical illustration of much of Freud's created myth about prehistoric society.[20]

The phenomenology of *Julius Caesar* suggests conditions leading to the related taboos against demons and against naming the dead. Brutus, appealing to the conspirators to "be sacrificers, but not butchers," cries out:

> We all stand up against the spirit of Caesar,
> And in the spirit of men there is no blood.
> O, that we then could come by Caesar's spirit,
> And not dismember Caesar! But alas,
> Caesar must bleed for it.
>
> (2.1.164–71)

Brutus sees the two entities of body and spirit as fundamentally different, separate though lamentably not separable in a living person. Attending to the differentiated fates of Caesar's body, which is an evocative prop in Antony's funeral oration, though a mere "bleeding piece of earth" (3.1.254), and of his spirit, which, "ranging for revenge" (3.1.270) as Antony predicted, defeats the conspirators, the play precisely illustrates the sort of dualism from which demonology develops. The appearance of Caesar's ghost indicates that spirit may be detached from the physical essence. The peculiar potency of Caesar's name is a related phenomenon. When Caesar claims invincibility by intoning, "For always I am Caesar" (1.2.209), or when the Plebian supports Brutus with the nomination "Let him be Caesar" (3.2.52), the name has been decontextualized and granted a kind of magical effect suggestive of the savage notion that one's name is "an essential part and an important possession of his personality" (75).

The fundamental taboo in Freud's scheme involves the vengeful spirit of the slain father, wandering like Caesar's ghost. Freud maintains that taboos develop within animistic cultures and he traces animism itself to primitive observations of the dead and to the experience of dreaming. People for whom immortality is "self-evident" (100) understand dreams to be adventures of the unencumbered soul, prefigurations of the larger adventure of death. Believing human beings to "have souls which can leave their habitation," which are "bearers of spiritual activities and are, to a certain extent, independent of the 'bodies'" (99), animists extrapolate that animals, plants, and objects also have souls, and that some souls may become free, in which case they are called spirits. Animists "do not conceal the fact that they fear the presence and the return of the spirit of a dead person" (77). After the murder of the primal father, taboos develop in the attempt to exculpate the wrath of the father's spirit. Yet this is only a partial explanation, for taboo outlives the belief in spirits in the form of the "sense of guilt of the son" (185). The spirit of the father is eventually internalized as taboo or totem law, although according to Freud it was not always so.

In order to account for a historical difference, Freud must posit a fundamental change in human consciousness. Accordingly, he supposes primitive experience to be directed outward, with "inner perceptions" projected "to the outside" by a "primitive mechanism" (85), "perhaps genetically connected" with the creature's original attention to the world outside the self. Hostile impulses were automatically projected onto others, for the concurrent absence of language and of abstract thought made introspection impossible.

> Only within the development of the language of abstract thought through the association of sensory remnants of word representations with inner processes, did the latter gradually become capable of perception. Before this took place primitive man had developed a picture of the outer world through the outward projection of inner perceptions, which we, with our reinforced conscious perception, must now translate back into psychology. (85–86)

In searching the mythic equivalent of Oedipal guilt, Freud is engaged
in the opposite act of translation, working backward from psychology
and its "language of abstract thought" to the "outward projection of
inner perceptions," the demonized spirit of the father. The salient
model was *Julius Caesar*, resonant from Freud's own past.

Freud, no animist himself, accounts for the invincible power of the
taboo, and tacitly for the power of Caesar's ghost, not by supposing that
spirits of the dead are *a priori* more potent than spirits of the living,
but by detecting projection at work. In order to accommodate their
ambivalent emotions, the murderous sons project their own hostile
impulses onto their victim(s). Thus Caesar's revenging ghost responds
to Brutus' command, "Speak to me what thou art" by attaching itself to
Brutus, naming the mechanism of projection: "Thy evil spirit, Brutus"
(4.3.280–81). Hostility may be disclaimed, but only at the price of
creating a demon; hostility is

> detached from our person and attributed to the other. Not we,
> the survivors, rejoice because we are rid of the deceased, on the
> contrary, we mourn for him; but now, curiously enough, he has
> become an evil demon who would rejoice in our misfortune and
> who seeks our death. The survivors must now defend themselves
> against this evil enemy; they are freed from inner oppression,
> but they have only succeeded in exchanging it for an affliction
> from without. (83)

Freud's assumption of the first person pronoun is telling,[21] as it is a few
pages later when he normalizes the discovery of hostility:

> The analysis of dreams of normal individuals has shown that
> our own temptation to kill others is stronger and more frequent
> than we had suspected and that it produces psychic effects even
> where it does not reveal itself to our consciousness. (92)[22]

Here, at some distance from the mystification practiced in *The Interpretation of Dreams*, he tacitly acknowledges murderous impulses.

Apparently the disclosure is possible because Freud's aim is to
valorize the ambivalence of Oedipal emotions, as the root cause not
only of social behavior but of inner awareness, of conscience, and of
consciousness itself. "Taboo conscience" he calls the "oldest form" of

"the phenomenon of conscience," that which "we know most surely," that which "in some languages . . . is hardly to be distinguished from consciousness" (89). In guilt and in its presupposing condition, ambivalence, Freud finds the source of self-awareness. Curiously though, as if uneasy with the instability inherent in the very concept of ambivalence, Freud ends by grounding it too in the "father complex." Near the conclusion of the book, expressing "great surprise" that his questions about the origin of society, religion, and culture could be "solved through a single concrete instance, such as the relation to the father," he raises "another psychological problem"—the origin of ambivalence. His answering formulation(s) at once enact ambivalence and further emphasize the scope of Oedipal theory:

> [Ambivalence] may be assumed to be a fundamental phenomenon of our emotional life. But the other possibility seems to me also worthy of consideration: that ambivalence, originally foreign to our emotional life, was acquired by mankind from the father complex, where psychoanalytic investigation of the individual to-day still reveals the strongest expression of it. (202)

Freud manages to have it both ways—to assert the child's independence, his self-creation (ambivalence is "fundamental"), and to pay the parental debt (half of it, anyway) that no human creature can logically deny (ambivalence is attributed to "the father complex").

If Freud's nephew John "was a revenant" when he played the part of Caesar, we might well ask, "whose ghost was he?" and find in the whispered reply, "Thy evil spirit, Brutus," the historical site of *Totem and Taboo*. Freud says his nephew returned from England "as the playmate of my earliest years," but his ghostliness includes his signification, as Caesar, of the father—not simply of Freud's real father, for the point here is not merely biographical speculation, but of that which Lacan (himself adumbrating the views of the father of psychoanalysis) terms the "name-of-the-father" (199). Caesar, more potent in his ghostly than his mortal manifestation, is the Law, the dead Father, he whose significance is predicated on his death. As pure signifier, the name-of-the-father does not exist on the literal level at all. So too with Caesar; Shakespeare shows Caesar the man playing with some discomfiture the role of Caesar the emperor, and in the fragment from Schiller Caesar's existence is entirely posthumous. The ghostliness of Freud's nephew in the remembered drama suggests his surplus of signification; he figures as both his own former and current selves, as Jacob Freud, as Caesar, and as Caesar's ghost. The disjuncture between John and all that he represented and represents opens a space that only a ghost could be powerful enough and free enough to fill, so Freud, like Shakespeare, renders the father a ghost—Caesar's ghost, John's ghost, his own ghost—conquering him, but at the same time attesting to his inescapability.

"Playing the part of Brutus" exerted a deep attraction for Freud, and implicit in the appeal was the literal nature of Brutus' crime. According to the historical myth Freud would propagate, it is the condition of a more primitive society to perform actions that in later civilized society are repressed. The story of Julius Caesar—part myth, part history—exists on the cusp of civilization; the father–son conflict is partly actual and partly symbolic. Yet because Brutus is identified in action, he must fail where Freud, heir to his ambivalence, succeeds: repression of the parricidal wish enables Freud to internalize the father, in the form of taboo law or superego. Brutus' offer to sacrifice himself for Rome as he had sacrificed Caesar (3.2.46–48) signals his attempt to become the father through reenactment. But having once committed himself to the process of history by taking action, Brutus cannot sidestep history's unfolding consequences and choose the world of the symbolic.

The concluding words of *Totem and Taboo* summarize the claim for action's priority over symbol: "'In the beginning was the deed'" (207). Yet in this instance of what Cynthia Chase calls "Freud's chronically oedipal textuality" (67), what seems a valorization of action is undermined by debts of textual reference. Freud quotes Goethe's Faust, who misquotes the Gospel of John ("In the beginning was the Word"). The chain of reference begins not with "the deed" but with "the Word," and Freud seems to devote himself to an unending textuality (Chase 67). The importance for Freud of *Julius Caesar*—and of drama generally—lies in the unique function of the medium of theater to unite text with action, deed with word. Not only is Brutus's action *within* the text literal, but the textual word itself becomes deed in performance, as it did for the young Freud playing the part of Brutus; theater, "acting out" the drama of the psyche, makes manifest much that remains occluded in a text. Freud's mature theater, by contrast, becomes more purely symbolic and internal, and his history becomes the created myth of *Totem and Taboo*. Devoting himself to the world of the text, he can claim any role as his.[23]

NOTES

1. In *Moses and Monotheism*, Freud expresses a commitment to preserving the stages of composition in his text, comparing "the distortion of a text" to "a murder," because the evidence is difficult to erase. "Accordingly, in many instances of textual distortion, we may nevertheless count upon finding what has been suppressed and disavowed hidden away somewhere else, though changed and torn from its context. Only it will not always be easy to recognize it" (43). The text takes on a ghostly existence of its own: in the prefatory note to Part 11 of Chapter III, Freud apologizes for the amount of repetition in the chapter, but professes himself "unable to wipe out the traces of the history of the work's origin." He continues, "actually, it has been written twice.... I determined to give it up; but it tormented me like an unlaid ghost...." (103). See also the analogy between textual distortion and psychic defense mechanisms in "Analysis Terminable and Interminable" (236–37).

2. And rumored to be Caesar's biological son: Plutarch reports that Caesar "persuaded himself that he begat" Brutus (114). As evidence of Shakespeare's familiarity with the story, Robert Miola (85n) cites *2 Henry VI*, 4.4.136–37, Ernest Jones believes that Shakespeare "suppressed the fact that Brutus was the actual, though illegitimate, son of Caesar" (*Hamlet* 124)—confirming, in Jones's estimate, the parricidal wish fueling the play.

3. As T.S. Dorsch notes, "The actual words, *Et tu, Brute*, are not found in any classical writer," but had by the time of Shakespeare's play already "become something of a stage commonplace" (67n). Garber calls the phrase "a quotation of a quotation ... [but] ultimately a quotation of nothing" (55), an example of the idealized, constructed character of Shakespeare's "idea of Rome" (52).

4. See, e.g., Clayton 246, Miola 102, and for a review of comments on resemblances between the two characters, Rabkin 146–47n.

5. Adrien Bonjour, who calls *Julius Caesar* "the drama of divided sympathies" (3), sees ambivalence as the salient trait shared by Brutus and Caesar.

6. See Lynn de Gerenday's discussion of Brutus' use of ritual "as defense against ambivalence" (32). Although she includes

quotations from *Totem and Taboo*, her analysis does not concern Freud as author and hence differs substantially from my own.

7. Garber also discusses this dream (64–65), and although she reaches somewhat different conclusions about it, her sense of what the dream reveals about "the status of the revenant" has influenced my argument. Garber writes that the dream shows that "it is intrinsically the idea of such a person, in contradistinction to his palpable or historical reality, that exercises so powerful an effect upon the memory" (65). Whereas she seems to retain a connection between the ghost and at least "the idea of" the nephew John, I see John as a screen for Freud's father.

8. Strachey's footnote identifies the enacted scene as the "lyric in dialogue form recited by Karl Moor in Act IV, Scene 5, of the earlier version of Schiller's play *Die Räuber*" (460).

9. Jones comments on "the pronouncedly parricidal content" of *Die Räuber*, and on Freud's own failure to mention it (*Life* 23n).

10. Presumably in Plutarch's text, since Charles von Moor mentions Plutarch in his first speech in the play. In Plutarch, of course, reference to the rumor that Caesar was Brutus' biological father raises the Oedipal theme from a symbolic level to that of possible actuality.

11. Freud's nephew John receives important reference in this essay as well.

12. The best example of this would be Freud's dream of a marble tablet commemorating his discovery of dream theory (letter to Fliess, June 12, 1900; qtd. in Willbern 108).

13. Possibly paralleling the suspicion that Brutus was Caesar's illegitimate son.

14. Norman Holland observes that the allusion to Prince Hal confirms the parricidal wish within Freud's identification with Brutus (64).

15. The conclusion of the note—"except in so far as the 'matriarchy' calls for a qualification of this assertion"—opens important issues beyond the scope of this paper. Feminist critics are currently challenging Freud's effacement of matriarchy.

16. So Lévi-Strauss found it: "a vicious circle deriving the social state from events which presuppose it" (491).

17. I am suggesting only that the explicit task of analogizing the individual mind with society founders. *Civilization and Its Discontents*, focusing on the difficulties of civilized group behavior, represents the further development of the argument Freud is at pains to establish in *Totem and Taboo*.

18. I quote from A.A. Brill's translation rather than the Strachey version in the Standard Edition, because Brill reserves more of what Bettelheim calls "the essential humanism" (4) of Freud's style, which figures in this text as a preference for "psychic" where Strachey translates "mental," "cultural" where Strachey puts "civilized," and as a retention of Freud's first-person pronouns at several points that are important to my argument.

19. As René Girard remarks, in another, more general, connection: "Ambivalence, it would appear, is good for patients, but of no use to psychoanalysis" (185).

20. Because of its sociological dimensions, *Julius Caesar* corresponds more closely to *Totem and Taboo* than does *Oedipus the King*, the "conspicuous" absence of reference to which Girard finds "an act of censorship pure and simple" (208, 209), necessary because Freud failed to realize the centrality of the sacrificial act. Since Oedipus already served as Freud's model for "unconscious desires" (209), to present him also as model for the actual parricidal act would "undermin[e]" the standard interpretation upon which psychoanalysis built its case. Girard is building the case for his own theory of mimetic desire, which would demote the father from the position of eminence, as the end toward which Freud strives unavailingly in *Totem and Taboo*.

21. "Nicht wir, die Überlebenden, freuen uns jetzt darüber, dab wir des Verstorbenen ledig sind; nein, wir trauern um ihn . . ." (*Totem und Tabu* 73).

22. "Wenn wir aber der durch die Psychoanalyse—an den Träumen Gesunder—gefundenen Tatsäche Rechnung tragen, dab die Versuchung, den anderen zu töten, auch bei uns stärker und häufiger ist als wir ahnen, und dab sie psychische Wirkungen aubert, auch wo sie sich unserem Bewubtsein nicht kundgibt. . . ." (*Totem und Tabu* 80–81).

23. I would like to express thanks to Marsha Walton and John Traverse for useful comments about this paper, and to Horst Dinkelacker for help with translations.

Works Cited

Bettelheim, Bruno. *Freud and Man's Soul*. New York: Random-Vintage, 1982.

Bonjour, Adrien. *The Structure of Julius Caesar*. 1958. Folcroft, PA: Folcroft Press, 1970.

Brooke, C.F. Tucker. *Shakespeare's Plutarch*. 2 vols. Vol. 1. New York: Duffield, 1909.

Chase, Cynthia. "Oedipal Textuality: Reading Freud's Reading of *Oedipus*." *Diacritics* 9.1 (1979): 54–68.

Clayton, Thomas. "'Should Brutus Never Taste of Portia's Death but Once?': Text and Performance in *Julius Caesar*." *Studies in English Literature 1500–1900* 23.2 (1983): 237–255.

De Gerenday, Lynn. "Play, Ritualization, and Ambivalence in *Julius Caesar*." *Literature and Psychology* 24 (1974): 24–33.

Freud, Sigmund. *The Standard Edition of the Complete Psychological Works of Sigmund Freud*. Trans. James Strachey. 24 volumes. London: Hogarth Press and the Institute of Psychoanalysis, 1955–74.

———. "Analysis Terminable and Interminable." *Standard Edition* 23: 209–53.

———. *Civilization and its Discontents*. *Standard Edition 21*: 59–145.

———. *The Interpretation of Dreams*. *Standard Edition* 4 and 5. New York: Avon, 1965.

———. *Moses and Monotheism: Three Essays*. *Standard Edition* 23:3–137.

———. "Screen Memories." *Standard Edition* 3:301–322.

———. *Totem and Taboo: Some Points of Agreement between the Mental Lives of Savages and Neurotics*. *Standard Edition* 13: ix–xv, 1–162.

———. *Totem and Taboo: Resemblances Between the Psychic Lives of Savages and Neurotics*. Trans. A.A. Brill. New York: Random-Vintage, 1946.

———. *Totem und Tabu: Einise Uberein stimmungen im Seelenlebeen der Wilden und der Neurotike*. Hamburg: Fischer Bucherei, 1940.

Garber, Marjorie. *Shakespeare's Ghost Writers: Literature as Uncanny Causality*. New York: Methuen, 1987.

Gay, Peter. *Freud: A Life for Our Time*. New York: Norton, 1988.

Girard, René. *Violence and the Sacred*. 1972. Trans. Patrick Gregory. Baltimore: Johns Hopkins UP, 1977.

Holland, Norman. *Psychoanalysis and Shakespeare*. New York: McGraw-Hill, 1966.

Jones, Ernest. *Hamlet and Oedipus*. 1949. New York: Norton, 1976.

———. *The Life and Work of Sigmund Freud*. 3 vols. New York: Basic Books, 1953.

Lacan, Jacques. *Écrits: A Selection*. Trans. Alan Sheridan. New York: Norton, 1977.

Lévi-Strauss, Claude. *The Elementary Structures of Kinship*. 1949. Trans. James Harle Bell, John Richard von Sturmer, and Rodney Needham. Boston: Beacon, 1969.

MacCallum, M.W. *Shakespeare's Roman Plays and Their Background*. London: Macmillan, 1910.

Miola, Robert S. *Shakespeare's Rome*. Cambridge: Cambridge UP, 1983.

Rabkin, Norman. *Shakespeare and the Common Understanding*. New York: Free Press, 1967.

Schanzer, Ernest. *The Problem Plays of Shakespeare: A Study of Julius Caesar, Measure for Measure, and Antony and Cleopatra*. London: Routledge & Kegan Paul, 1963.

Schiller, Friedrich von, *Early Dramas*. Trans, Samuel Taylor Coleridge, R.B. Boglau, et al. Edition De Luxe. 8 Vols. Vol. 6. New York: Amaranth Society, 1901.

Shakespeare, William. *Julius Caesar*. Ed. T.S. Dorsch. New Arden Edition. London: Methuen, 1955.

Siemon, James R. *Shakespearean Iconoclasm*. Berkeley: U of California P, 1985.

Willbern, David. "Freud and the Inter-penetration of Dreams." *Diacritics* 9.1 (1979): 98–110.

LADY CHATTERLEY'S LOVER
(D.H. LAWRENCE)

~~~

"1925–30"
by Frank Kermode, in *D.H. Lawrence* (1973)

INTRODUCTION

Due to its sexually explicit scenes, vulgar language, and depiction of a scandalous affair between an aristocratic lady and a working class man who is her husband's gamekeeper, *Lady Chatterley's Lover* was banned in the United States and England and was not available legally in unabridged form until 32 years after its initial printing in Florence, Italy. As Frank Kermode indicates, Lawrence intended to shock his audience with his exploration of these and other taboos. However, according to Kermode, rather than merely seeking to create a shocking piece of literature, Lawrence also crafted an explicit critique of society in his novel, calling for "cultural and economic reform." For Kermode, rather than a prurient work qualifying as pornography, *Lady's Chatterley's Lover* presents the taboo within a highly moral framework.

~~~

Kermode, Frank. "1925–1930." *D.H. Lawrence.* New York: Viking Press, 1973.

In letters written when he was halfway through *Lady Chatterley's Lover*, Lawrence called it "the most improper novel ever written," but denied that it was pornography. "It's a declaration of the phallic reality" (*Collected Letters*, 1028). He knew no English printer would handle it, and arranged for a private edition to be printed and published in Florence, "the full fine flower with pistil and stamens standing" (1046). He talked a great deal about this reassertion of the phallic as against "cerebral sex-consciousness" (1047), asserting that, while "nothing nauseates me more than promiscuous sex," he wanted, in this novel, "to make an *adjustment in consciousness* to the basic physical realities" (IIII). His attitude, as he admitted, was Puritan; he respected natural impulses but hated "that pathological condition when the *mind* is absorbed in sex . . . It is true that Lawrence himself was possessed by the subject of sex—but in what a different way! His possession was like that of a doctor who wishes to heal."[1] He was perfectly aware of the trouble he would bring on himself by this last effort "to make the sex relation valid and precious instead of shameful" (972). There is no doubt that Lawrence, although he was later to be ill with bitterness against his countrymen for their response to this and other late works, intended to shock; that was part of the therapy.

He wanted to call the book *John Thomas and Lady Jane*, though sometimes he preferred *Tenderness*. Tenderness, as he explained in a letter already quoted, was to replace leadership as the quality most necessary to the health of the world. But first it was necessary to purge the very lexicon of sex. The four-letter words (which were still occupying so much attention at the trial of 1960) were obscene, he argued, only because of "unclean mental associations": the important task, then, was to "cleanse the mind," to end the associations of fear and dirt, to get rid of the taboo on such words.

> The Kangaroo is a harmless animal, the word shit is a harmless word. Make either into a taboo, and it becomes most dangerous. The result of taboo is insanity. And insanity, especially mob-insanity, massinsanity, is the fearful danger that threatens our civilisation. . . . If the young do not watch out, they will find themselves, before so very many years are past, engulfed in a howling manifestation of mobinsanity, truly terrifying to think of. It will be better to be dead than to live to see it (Introduction to *Pansies, Complete Poems*, 420).

The change in consciousness which would make *Lady Chatterley's Lover* acceptable as "tenderness" rather than "obscenity" is one that the book itself desperately advocates, though at the same time taking it to be impossible without the intervention of the "bad time" that it announces as on the way. It seems certain that the changes of consciousness which have in fact occurred to allow the free publication of the book are not of a kind that Lawrence would have approved; I expect he would have campaigned against the unrestricted use of a word such as *fuck* in books and conversation. They can hardly be said to have acquired a tender, let alone a numinous quality; acceptable in common use, whether as expletives or as part of a genuinely sexual language, they have no doubt also been restored to the bourgeois bedroom; but they remain part of sex-in-the-head, or as instruments of the wrong kind of letting go, which Lawrence detested equally, as a betrayal of the self. Hence Mellors' use of them, though it may impress liberal bishops, strikes most people as a bit comic, doctrinaire almost—at best the language of a lost paradise.

It may be that the whole attempt was misguided. The need, as Lawrence saw it, was to avoid euphemisms which are in themselves evidence of the sell-out of the passional to the intellectual; to restore the words which belong to the old blood-consciousness. But insofar as these words were secret and sacred, they had value as ritual profanities; and so they became a part of the culture, proper to the expansive movements of constricted lives—a fact reflected in the heavy use made of them by soldiers and sailors, poor men in circumstances of sexual privation. Perhaps a good society would use them only with great semantic purity; but the history of our society, as Lawrence knew, and the history of the words, also, were such that a lexical could not induce a spiritual purgation. Lawrence must, as he wrote and rewrote his story, have been partly conscious of this. The vile press reaction to the book, as represented by the hysteria of his old enemy *John Bull*, cannot have surprised him; nor, I suspect, would the knowledge that for thirty years after publication this innocent work was converted, by the minds of furtive purchasers, into precisely the pornography that he so abhorred. More recently we have come, now that it has sold its paperback millions, to find it tame, a reaction which would certainly have shocked him just as much.

Lady Chatterley's Lover is about the need for a rebirth of phallic consciousness, and this is conceived, in a familiar Lawrencian way, as the only means to regeneration both personal and national. The approaching death of the English, which he had prophesied in the war years, was an aspect of the final extinction of that old consciousness. The war had announced the Last Days, the bad time that would come, whether or not there was a rebirth. Constance Chatterley in part becomes like Ursula, at moments a representative of England as a sleeping beauty, only to be revived by the *grosbaiser* of a phallic prince. Always apocalyptic when he wrote of regeneration, Lawrence made this prophetic novel absorb much of the last version of his apocalyptic theory. There is the sexuality of death—the impotence of Chatterley, the "loving" of Michaelis—and there is something else, so far beyond it that the word sex barely applies to it, which is why, when he thought of Mellors, Lawrence habitually spoke not of sex but of the phallus as beyond sex. The sense of sexual experience as something to be passed through, as the prelude or initiation into a more satisfactory condition of life on the other side, is strong in him; so are the ideas of renunciation and chastity. A man who admits to having been in his youth enraged by the idea of a woman's sexuality ("I only wanted to be aware of her personality, her mind and spirit" [Phoenix II, 568]) might well feel that the only good chastity must come after the restoration of the "natural life-flow." It is a further charge against the mother, that a son should regard sex as an improper secret; Lawrence's mother thought it indecent that there should be a seduction in *The White Peacock*: "To think that my son should have written such a story."[2] *Lady Chatterley's Lover* retains traces of the puritanism inherited from the mother, as well as evidence of a desire to take a last revenge on her, and on all the women who have ruined England; to them Connie will be the Scarlet Woman, to him she is the Woman Clothed with the Sun; Saint John took them apart, and Lawrence puts them together again as an emblem of a virtually impossible restoration

Although Chatterley regards sex as an atavistic organic process (I), his impotence is a direct result of the war. The second sentence of the book places the story firmly in the postwar era: "The cataclysm has happened, we are among the ruins." It is a world of death and impotence; the melancholy park, the ruined countryside, the unmanned colliers, Chatterley in his mechanical chair. This is the background against which Connie's rebirth will be described. In the old world of death, women use sex as an instrument by means of which to gain power over men. We recall that Kate, in *The Plumed Serpent*, had to forego orgasm;

Lawrence seemed to think that a woman, holding back orgasm until after her partner's ejaculation, was merely asserting herself, preferring the quasi-masturbatory pleasure of clitoral orgasm, induced by pelvic friction, to unassertive submission, or vaginal orgasm. In the end, even the patient and skillful womanizer Michaelis, who let Connie get her satisfaction in this way, condemns her for it ("You couldn't go off at the same time as a man, could you? You'd have to bring yourself off! You'd have to run the show!" [IV]); and full vaginal orgasm is a stage along the way to life in the affair with Mellors. "Beaked" sex (clitoral orgasm) belongs in a world out of order; it is not distinct from the blighted countryside, from the ruined miners and their wives, who have lost even the sense of subordination, or from the lifeless, nervous stories of Chatterley.

The marriage of the Chatterleys is, of course, a sexless relationship quite unlike the positive chastity of Connie and Mellors at the close; far from being "valid and precious," it is simply death. Connie's affair with Michaelis is another aspect of the profound degeneracy that Lawrence nearly always associated with race; Michaelis is Irish, but he has the look of "a carved ivory Negro mask. . . . Aeons of acquiescence in race destiny, instead of our individual resistance. And then a swimming through, like rats in a dark river" (III). This is the Lawrencian imagery of degenerate corruption, *fin de la race*; he returns to it, finding in Michaelis "that ancient motionlessness of a race that can't be disillusioned any more, an extreme, perhaps, of impurity that is pure. On the far side of his supreme prostitution to the bitchgoddess he seemed pure, pure as an African ivory mask that dreams impurity into purity" (V). He stands for the fascinating racial corruption of the Last Days. And at this point the only voice that speaks of the need for a deeper blood consciousness, a transformation of sex, is the somewhat implausible voice of Dukes: "Real knowledge comes out of the whole corpus of the consciousness; out of your belly and your penis as much as out of your brain and mind . . . once you start the mental life you pluck the apple" (IV). He gives a potted account of Lawrence's own views on this Fall and extends it to cover the whole world crisis; but set down as conversation with the skeptical Chatterley it is all thin and unconvincing; deliberately so, for we are to learn under a more gifted teacher.

The gamekeeper looks back to Annable in *The White Peacock*; the educated gamekeeper who has dropped out of civilization into what is left of the natural world, that "greenwood" into which E. M. Forster in *Maurice* dispatches his drop-out bourgeois with another gamekeeper. He is related to Lawrence's Indians and gipsies (*The Virgin and the Gipsy* was written only a short time before the novel), but the difference is important; he has found his way *out* of the white consciousness. This is why Lawrence makes him an educated man and an ex-officer, and why he gives him two dialects, middle class and peasant. To the latter belong the famous four-letter words; spoken in the Chatterley dining room they are nasty, here they are "part of the natural flow" (*Phoenix II*, 570). Mellors is also part of that flow; we see that when he pushes Chatterley's mechanical chair as well as when he goes about his gamekeeper's business; we see it in his difference from his social superiors. He inhabits his world alone and chaste; when he has to move into Connie's worn-out world he feels the "bruise of the war" (V) but dreads rebirth; for that is what his relation with her must involve. As for Connie, she has to abandon the impurity of Michaelis, whose way is only down and out, for the way of Mellors, which is a passage through the gates of life and death (*Etruscan Places*, which also celebrates this mystical journey, is contemporary with the novel).

Mellors might have been a lay figure, representing Lawrencian opinions; he calls his little daughter a "false little bitch" for crying dishonestly (VI) and holds the right views about marriage. In many ways he differs little from Dukes, with his prophesying of the end: "Our old show will come flop; our civilization is going to fall. It's going down to the bottomless pit, down the chasm. And believe me, the only bridge across the chasm will be the phallus" (VII). But Connie, though moved by this talk of "the resurrection of the body" and a "democracy of touch" finds more than words in Mellors; even as she deeply senses "the end of all things," she is capable of receiving "in her womb" the shock of the vision of the gamekeeper's body as he washed: "the pure, delicate, white loins, the bones showing a little, and the sense of aloneness" (VI). She goes to him not in frustrated desire but in the need to be reborn in the last days—a harsh ecstasy, unlike that of Chatterley's surrender of his solar plexus (no stimulus possible to *his* lumbar ganglia) to Mrs. Bolton.

What follows is Connie's initiation and mystic rebirth, as in the original plot of Apocalypse; and Lawrence is suggesting that the novel itself mimes this process, for "it can inform and lead into new places the flow of our sympathetic consciousness, and it can lead our sympathy away in recoil from things gone dead. . . . The novel, properly handled, can reveal the most secret places of life: for it is in the *passional* secret places of life, above all, that the tide of sensitive awareness needs to ebb and flow, cleansing and freshening" (IX). Thus the novel fleshes out the scheme provided by the metaphysic. Lawrence, for example, knows better than to make Mrs. Bolton a caricature or diagram, or neglect the broader social context. There must be flow and recoil, density. The newborn chick is a natural object, though Connie sees it "eyeing the Cosmos" (X), and her crying at the sight is the recognizable reaction of a sensitive woman as well as the sign of "her generation's forlornness."

When they first make love, Connie is content without orgasm. It is enough that in the mechanized, frictional world, rebirth may be on the way. Later, Lawrence has to try to find a prose capable of representing genuine orgasm; and, later still, after a few backslidings, a few profanations, she must move into the next stage of passional knowledge, an awareness of the phallic mystery which includes a proper awe of man. Meanwhile, the world seems even more horrible in its irrelevent excesses, its dissociation from the authenticities of the bloodstream; but Connie goes on with her initiation and is "born: a woman" (XII). Remembering *Women in Love* once more, Lawrence allows her to say that "it was the sons of god with the daughters of men." Her dread of maleness is all but overcome; though she still can't quite break herself of the habit of talking about love, that alienating irrelevance. Life has returned; but the process is not complete. The book represents Connie's initiation into mystery as having seven stages, like the seven stages in the mystery-religion behind Revelation. She progressively comes alive; she can dance in the unspoiled part of the wood, and tell her husband that the body, killed by Plato and Jesus, will be reborn: "It will be a lovely, lovely life in the lovely universe, the life of the human body" (XVI) she says, echoing the Lawrencian view that eternity is a fourth-dimensional apprehension of the life of the body here and now. "My dear, you speak as if you were ushering it all in!" says Chatterley. But there remains an ultimate stage of purgation, the sensuality which is "necessary . . . to burn out the false shames and smelt out the heaviest ore of the body into purity"—the exploration by the phallus of "the last and deepest recesses of organic shame." They must go beyond tenderness, though when the experience is over Connie begs Mellors not to forget tenderness forever.

Chapter XVI of *Lady Chatterley's Lover* contains what has become the most controversial passage in all of Lawrence's novels. The fact that it describes anal intercourse was long ignored; nobody mentioned it at the 1960 trial. The question has now been argued at length,[3] and the discussion need not be repeated here. As in *Women in Love*, the climactic sexual act is an act of buggery, conceived as a burning out of shame. The invasion of the genital by the excremental, the contamination of joy by shame and life by death, was a strategy for the overthrow of the last enemy. We have seen that Lawrence had earlier thought of these polarities as reconcilable only by a third force, his Holy Ghost; the phallus, its representative, will bridge the flows of dissolution and creation, which, coming together in the genitalia, also come together in history, at this moment. The metaphysic is very complicated, not least because Lawrence is less candid at such moments than in describing more ordinary sexual activity; but he is again fighting the woman-inspired *pudeur* which has blanched sexconsciousness, made women "fribbles" and emasculated men.

In *Women in Love* he tried to distinguish between buggery which was wholly dissolute and buggery that was initiatory, the symbolic death before rebirth, the cracking of the insect carapace. Culturally, the parallel is this: we have to get to the point where nothing is left of our mistaken civilization, and the Holy Ghost can institute the third Joachite epoch. The forbidden acts of Gerald and Gudrun, or Birkin and Hermione, or Mellors and Bertha, are merely corruption within the rind; the same acts committed by Birkin and Ursula, Connie and Mellors, are the acts of healthy human beings. When "no dark shameful things are denied her" Ursula is "free" (*Women in Love*, XXX). The next step for Gudrun is death. For Connie it is a ritual death, with the phallus as psychopomp. She experiences what is "necessary, forever necessary, to burn out false shames" (XVI). No need ever to do it again; now there can be tenderness, and even chastity.

This is the climactic sexual encounter, for the last, described in Chapter XVIII, is a kind of marital epilogue and belongs to initiated tenderness, not to the harsh intiatory experience we are talking about. To Chatterley, Mellors' reputation (there is talk of his buggering his wife) was merely an illustration of man's "strange avidity for unusual sexual postures" (XVII); but Lawrence wasn't as a rule of Chatterley's opinion, and clearly does not want us to be.

This was a bold thing to have done, and obviously it was a matter of importance to Lawrence. One thinks of Milton's necessary audacity in describing the love-making of the angels; each writer, we may think, could well have avoided the course he follows. But Milton could not think his interpenetrating angels redundant; they were of the stuff of the imagination. Lawrence was equally committed to this reconciliation of dissolution and creation in anal sex. Mellors, in the England of Lloyd George, is the Saint George who kills the dragon (the serpent of corruption, of shame at defecation) and sets the lady free; an act as apocalyptic as that of Spenser's Saint George. And he also opened her seven seals to initiate her. In the end, as Lawrence Chatterley's paralysis, "Whether we call it symbolism or not, it is, in the sense of its happening, inevitable" (*Phoenix II*, 514). What made it so was the force of Lawrence's belief in the phallus as the Comforter, the reconciler, the agent of rebirth. And just as Lawrence himself recognized, when he read his first draft, that Chatterley's lameness symbolized "the paralysis, the deeper emotional or passional paralysis, of most men of his sort and class today" (514) so we recognize the symbolism of Connie's rebirth. Both symbolisms belong to a metaphysic which Lawrence had long since internalized, and which the tale had, in its own way, to make objective.

Lady Chatterley's Lover, like most of Lawrence's novels, has astonishing lapses; he occasionally allows himself risqué sexual punning which, in this context, obviously constitutes a dangerous mistake; and occasionally he lapses into the jeering viciousness of some of the work of the preceding years. But it remains a great achievement, not only in itself but in the change it helped to bring about in Lawrence himself. The book ends on a "long pause," the pause between epochs. Lawrence filled the pause in his own life with poems, pictures, one of the greatest of his stories (which is also about rebirth into creativity) and some of his most impressive and enduring polemical-discursive prose.

PORNOGRAPHY AND OBSCENITY

Under this heading I group the essays *A Propos of Lady Chatterley's Lover, Pornography and Obscenity*, and a few related pieces.[4] Lawrence had fought bruising battles with various censors before, and he must have known his later work would run into trouble, especially when the oppressive Sir William Joynson-Hicks was Home Secretary. *A Propos of Lady Chatterley's Lover*, an expansion of *My Skirmish with Jolly Roger* (1929), was published in the last year of Lawrence's life. It's importance is that Lawrence must here, in the process of justifying his unconventional novel, express his sense of cultural and sexual crisis, and his recommendations as to conduct, with little aid from myth or metaphysic. His "honest, healthy book" (*Phoenix II*, 489)—so he describes *Lady Chatterley*—is a contribution to that evolved culture in which taboo and superstition, obscurity and violence, will have been eliminated from our thinking about sex. Not, he says, that we should necessarily increase sexual activity; but there must be clear thinking about it, even by those whose role is to abstain. And this calls for improvements in sexual education, for the benefit not only of those tragically ignorant of sex, but also of "the advanced youth" who "go to the other extreme and treat it as a sort of toy to be played with, a slightly nasty toy" (491). The "perversion of smart licentiousness" is no better than the perversion of Puritanism" (492). We live in a world of fake sexual emotion; only true sex can change it. "When a 'serious' young man said to me the other day: 'I can't believe in the regeneration of England by sex, you know,' I could only say, 'I'm sure you can't.' He had no sex anyhow. . . . And he didn't know what it meant, to have any" (496). To such young people sex is at best the "trimmings," thrills and fumbling. Real sex seems to them barbaric.

Lawrence believes in fidelity as essential to good sex, and therefore in indissoluble marriage; the sacramentality of marriage is the greatest boon of the Church, a recognition of a balance and a rhythm which is reflected in the liturgy and binds sex to the seasons. But the marriage has to be phallic, the column of blood in the valley of blood, the remaking of Paradise. It is not to be a union of "personalities," a nervous indulgence, "frictional and destructive" (*Phoenix II*, 507). Such sex will certainly not regenerate England. What is required is not a logos, a Word, but rather a Deed, "the *Deed* of life" (510). Only thus may we be restored to a healthy relation with the cosmos. Buddha, Plato, Jesus cut us off from life; we have to get back to ancient forms, Apollo, Attis, Demeter, Persephone; to the threefold relationship of man and universe, man and woman, man and man. The isolation of "personality" (typified by Clifford Chatterley) "the death of the great humanity of the world" (513) is what must end; the restoration of a phallic language was the means chosen in Lawrence's last novel to bring this about.

That a revolution in the passional lives of men and women must precede the establishment of the good society; and that this change, though in one sense revolutionary, will require a return to mythic origins, to the human condition that prevailed before some aboriginal catastrophe, is not doctrine peculiar to Lawrence. An obvious ancestor, among other, is Nietzsche; but such motions were in the air. The "dissociation of sensibility," to use Eliot's term, is an old doctrine, and Lawrence knew it very early, perhaps as early as 1906, if that was the year in which he told Jessie Chambers that there could never be another Shakespeare, for Shakespeare was the product of an integrated age, whereas "things are split up now."[5] Early in 1929 he wrote an introduction to a projected book on his paintings, and in this extraordinary essay he found occasion to examine the nature of the dissociation in more historical detail. The reason why the English cannot paint is fear, fear of life; and Lawrence, now arguing that this fear is already visible in Shakespeare, dates it from the Renaissance, and specifically from the syphilis epidemic of the sixteenth century. "But with the Elizabethans the grand rupture had started in the human consciousness" (*Phoenix*, 552). The division between mental and physical consciousness was established; sex was associated with terror, and intuitive awareness of other people, and of nature, was lost. The art of the eighteenth century is optical rather than intuitive, the body disappears from painting; even the French Impressionists escaped into light. The chaos of modernism begins in this terror. Lawrence is particularly hard on Significant Form, a Bloomsbury doctrine. What he recounts "is the nauseating and repulsive history of the crucifixion of the procreative body for the glorification of the spirit, the mental consciousness.... The Renaissance put the spear through the side of the already crucified body, and syphilis put poison into the wound made by the imaginative spear.... We ... were born corpses" (569). Cezanne moved the stone from the door of the tomb, but the critics rolled it back; and English artists have reached a condition of death, whether or not this is a prelude to rebirth.

Here we have a new historical version of Lawrence's myth of the lost paradise, of the forfeited blood-consciousness and the closed imaginative eye. Such myths are normally inspired by a strong sense of the desperate need of one's own epoch, and Lawrence's is certainly no exception to the rule. He wrote *Lady Chatterley* and *A Propos* as contributions to an urgently needed passional revolution. His metaphysic

grew increasingly conscious of practical needs of the moment; hence
the restored sexual vocabulary, and hence a further attempt to justify
it in the pamphlet *Pornography and Obscenity*, published in the same
series as one by Joynson-Hicks which stated the opposing case.

Of all Lawrence's writings, this is the work that has kept best as
a contribution to a continuing debate. It states the need for true sex
in art, and the rightness of genuine sexual stimulus; Boccaccio seems
to him less pornographic than *Jane Eyre* or *Tristan und Isolde*. True
pornography, however, ought to be censored; it is what does dirt on
sex. And here Lawrence tames and uses an old theory of his:

> The sex functions and the excrementory functions in the human
> body work so close together, yet they are, so to speak, utterly
> different in direction. Sex is a creative flow, the excrementory
> flow is towards dissolution, de-creation . . . In the really healthy
> human being the distinction between the two is instant. . . .
>
> But in the degraded human being the deep instincts have
> gone dead, and then the two flows become identical. *This* is the
> secret of really vulgar and of pornographical people: the sex flow
> and the excrement flow is the same to them. It happens when
> the psyche deteriorates, and the profound controlling instincts
> collapse. Then sex is dirt and dirt is sex, and sexual excitement
> becomes a playing with dirt (Phoenix, 176).

The clarity of this insight will survive the criticism that it does
nothing to aid a censor's choice between the creative and the excrementatory in literary sex, much less enable unqualified lawyers and
juries to make it. Its survival is a function of its utter seriousness,
its dedication to the idea that life must be kept up, that sex is not a
"dirty little secret," though it can be made so by pornographers and
magistrates alike. Thus the abstractions of the metaphysic prove to be
rooted in life; and this is what people mean when they declare that
Lawrence was always, whatever he might seem to be doing, a most
moral writer.

Lawrence's disgust at pornography depends in a measure upon his
hatred of masturbation, a practical way of turning a procreative into an
excrementatory function. Masturbation is another consequence of the
lies we tell about sex; to be free of the lies would mean to be free not
only of masturbation but of the lies that "lurk under the cloak of this

one primary lie;" for example "the monstrous lie of money . . . Kill the puritylie, and the money-lie will be defenceless" (Phoenix, 185). So once again sexual reform is the key to cultural and economic reform. Lawrence here has the consistency that a fully developed metaphysic affords. And as usual in the midst of death he finds some hope of rebirth; there is a minority, he ends, which "hates the lie . . . and which has its own dynamic ideas about pornography and obscenity" (186–87). One may doubt that the achievement of that minority—the Obscenity Act of 1959 and its successors, the successful defense of *Lady Chatterley's Lover* but also of other books which Lawrence would probably have wanted to censor—would have gratified him. But this is part of the general truth that the revolution which has occurred in our handling of the "dirty little secret" is hardly at all the revolution Lawrence wanted. Our literary sex, like the pill and the modern commune, would have had him once more prophesying the last days and the need for rebirth. He always thought of the movies as a masturbatory medium; he castigated them in *The Lost Girl*, in the late poem "When I Went to the Film," in which the audience is "moaning from close-up kisses, black-and-white kisses that could not be felt" (*Collected Poems*, 444) and in *Pornography and Obscenity*. It is not conceivable that the sex-in-color of our cinema would have pleased him more. The reason why he is so often called a Puritan is that he thought that sex was the key to life and spiritual regeneration, and also that these were solemn matters.

NOTES

1. Earl H. Brewster, in Edward H. Nehls, ed. *D. H. Lawrence: A Composite Biography*, III, 135.
2. Edward H. Nehls, op. cit., I, 62.
3. See George W. Knight, "Lawrence, Joyce and Powys," *Essays in Criticism*, XI (1961) , and in *Neglected Powers: Essays on Nineteenth and Twentieth Century Literature* (New York, 1971) ; J. Sparrow, "Regina vs. Penguin Books," *Encounter*, 101 (1962), pp. 35–43; F. Kermode, "Spenser and the Allegorists," British Academy Warton Lecture, 1962, reprinted in *Shakespeare, Spenser, Donne: Renaissance Essays* (New York, 1971); George Ford, *Double Measure* ; Colin Clarke, *River of Dissolution*; Mark Spilka, "Lawrence Up-Tight," *Novel*, IV (1971), pp. 252–67;

Ford, Kermode, Clarke, Spilka, "Critical Exchange," *Novel*, V (1971), pp. 54–70.

4. Conveniently gathered in Harry T. Moore's collection, *D.H. Lawrence: Sex, Literature, and Censorship* (New York, 1953). This book has a useful introduction recounting Lawrence's dealing with censorship from the prosecution of *The Rainbow* to the suppression of *Lady Chatterley's Lover* and *Pansies*, and the seizure of his paintings at the Warren Gallery in 1929.

5. Harry T. Moore, *The Intelligent Heart*, p. 94.

LOLITA
(VLADIMIR NABOKOV)

"I have only words to play with': Taboo and Tradition in Nabokov's Lolita"
by Samuel Schuman, University
of North Carolina at Asheville

Since it was first published in America in 1958,[1] Vladimir Nabokov's novel *Lolita* has been praised by some as a masterpiece of American literature and condemned by others as an immoral, pornographic, and evil work. Over the years the work has solidified its reputation as a classic, but it still continues to outrage the censorious.[2] At first blush, the novel's plot seems to justify its repute as a racy novel of scandalous content. *Lolita* tells the story of the passionate sexual love affair between a 37 year-old man, Humbert Humbert (the book's narrator), and a 12 year-old girl, Dolores Haze, called "Lolita". Humbert is a cosmopolitan, polyglot middle-aged European; Dolores is a mid-twentieth-century, small-town American pre-teenager. Humbert marries Dolores' mother, Charlotte Haze, solely in order to be close to her daughter. When the hysterical Charlotte is killed in an automobile accident just seconds after discovering Humbert's true affections, Humbert swoops up Dolores from summer camp, consummates his sexual lust (but, he affirms, he wasn't even Dolores' first lover), and the step-father and daughter travel throughout America until Dolores escapes with another middle-aged man, the playboy playwright Clare Quilty (who Humbert eventually murders). To say that *Lolita* focuses upon subject matter which was, and still is, strongly taboo in Western culture is, clearly, a flamboyant understatement.

The novel's notoriety was surely enhanced by the two movie versions that have been made of it. The first, in 1962, was directed by Stanley Kubrick and starred James Mason as Humbert Humbert and Sue Lyon as Dolores, with Shelley Winters playing Charlotte Haze and a madcap performance by Peter Sellers as Quilty. The 1997 version by director Adrian Lyne had Jeremy Irons and the 15-year-old Dominique Swain in the two major roles, and Melanie Griffith as Charlotte. Frank Langella played Quilty in a performance entirely different from Sellers', but equally wild. Nabokov himself actually wrote a script for the earlier film, but Kubrick chose not to use it, a decision that Nabokov himself eventually concluded was wise.

Since Humbert Humbert is the sole narrator of the book, we see all its characters and action through the eyes of a pedophile, and this adds an important level of nuance and complexity to *Lolita*. Moreover, Humbert is telling his story from a jail cell to justify his obsession and to try to make the case that he is not a criminal, much less a pervert, just a devoted lover with a particularly rich imagination. Thus, he constantly addresses the readers of *Lolita* as "Ladies and gentlemen of the jury" (*Lolita* 11). He argues that "the majority of sex offenders that hanker for some . . . girl child, are innocuous, inadequate, passive, timid strangers who merely ask the community to allow them to pursue their practically harmless, so-called aberrant behavior, their little hot wet private acts of sexual deviation without the police and society cracking down upon them. . . . We are unhappy, mild, dog-eyed gentlemen. . . . emphatically, no killers are we. Poets never kill" (89). And yet, as we noted earlier, Humbert does kill his rival Quilty. But is he a "poet"?

What makes Humbert's narration problematic is that, poet or not, he is a consummate wordsmith: learned, witty, full of arguments and examples that support or justify his obsession. His words are always fascinating, even mesmerizing (Nabokov even considered naming the character "Mesmer Mesmer"). Consider just the opening lines of his narration:

> Lolita, light of my life, fire of my loins. My sin, my soul.
> Lo-lee-ta: the tip of the tongue taking a trip of three steps
> down the palate to tap, at three, on the teeth. Lo. Lee. Ta.

> She was Lo, plain Lo, in the morning, standing four feet
> ten in one sock. She was Lola in slacks. She was Dolly at
> school. She was Dolores on the dotted line. But in my arms she
> was always Lolita. (*Lolita* 11)

Rather like Satan in Milton's *Paradise Lost*, Nabokov and Humbert have been seen by some readers as making the case that vice is so much more interesting than virtue, that there is a kind of repellent attraction that can make evil irresistible.

Lolita invites thoughtful readers to ponder a series of questions, not just about the novel itself, but about the process of experiencing and understanding challenging and controversial works of literary art. Among those questions remains the obvious: Is *Lolita* a dirty book?

As a quick internet search makes appallingly clear, the word "Lolita" has entered the English language with the meaning of a sexually precocious young girl. Many more people have heard at least something about *Lolita* than have actually read the book. The novel's racy public image guarantees that its sexually suggestive reputation confronts most readers before they have a serious encounter with Nabokov's actual words. Of course, in some respects, the work's repute is helpful: many students and others are relatively eager to read the book, because its reputation precedes it. After a few chapters, though, readers are going to recognize that Nabokov does not present what the author characterizes as typically pornographic action, "limited to the copulation of clichés" (*Lolita* 305). To Nabokov, "the term 'pornography' connotes mediocrity, commercialism, and certain strict rules of narration. Obscenity must be mated with banality because every kind of aesthetic enjoyment has to be entirely replaced by simple sexual stimulation ..." ("On a Book Entitled *Lolita*" 315). Even the harshest critics of Lolita, at least those who have read any of the novel, would not suggest that it is mediocre, commercial, predictable, or banal.

The "dirty book" question, however, does invite thoughtful readers to consider the difference between a book in which sex is an important motif (which is surely the case in *Lolita*, and in life) and a work of pornography, which, as I believe Nabokov accurately suggests, has as its primary, usually sole, function as the predictable sexual stimulation of the reader. Actually, by contemporary standards, and even by those of the mid-twentieth century, this novel is remarkably prim and discrete when it comes to depicting the mechanics of physical passion. *Lolita* is full of colorful, even lurid, prose, but none of it is devoted to describing acts of lust. Even Humbert Humbert observes, immediately after the first time he and Dolores make love, "I am not concerned with so-called 'sex' at all. Anybody can imagine those elements of animality" (*Lolita* 136). Clearly, Lolita is not a book about sex; it is a book about a man who is sexually obsessed. This leads to a second, worthwhile, query: Is Vladimir Nabokov a pervert, a pedophile, a sex maniac, or what?

This is a simple question, but one that opens the door to an important set of issues in literary study. It is easy to forget that sometimes readers, particularly relatively inexperienced readers, habitually confuse the narrative voice with the authorial perspective. (This is perhaps one reason such readers tend to refer to the author, and often the characters, of literary works as "they," as in "What do they mean at the end of *Hamlet* by calling him a 'sweet prince'?") The difference between the narrative mask and the authorial consciousness seems so obvious to more experienced readers that we often forget how crucial the discovery of that gap is to literary understanding. *Lolita* is an ideal book to teach, or reinforce, that lesson. Initially, the novel's narrative voice is beguiling and seems to be presenting a strong legalistic case justifying Humbert's lust for Dolores. Because Humbert is trying so hard, with such intellectual heavy artillery, to suggest that his thoughts and actions are not evil, it can be easy at first to imagine that his creator is making that case.

This confusion can be amplified by the fact that in some aspects of their lives, Humbert Humbert and Vladimir Nabokov seem similar: both are European and cosmopolitan, living in a more simple, suburban America. Both have been college teachers. Both are multilingual, and both are enormously widely read. But a second look at the biographies of the fictional hero, and his real creator, make it very clear that they are wholly different people. Humbert is from Switzerland, Nabokov from Russia. The former's parents were the proprietors of a resort hotel, the latter's were intellectual Russian aristocrats. Humbert Humbert comes to America because he has inherited a business from his uncle; Vladimir Nabokov came in flight from Nazis who were overrunning Europe in 1940. Humbert entered into marriage only to be near the child daughter of his short-lived wife; Nabokov married Vera Slonin in 1925, they had a son Dmitri, and remained wed together for the rest of their lives. Most importantly, of course, Humbert is a pedophile, and Nabokov is most certainly not.

A careful reading of *Lolita* demonstrates the underlying ethical soundness of the work and its author. The novel moves increasingly away from the narrator's pathetic efforts at moral justification, and attentive readers, even if inexperienced, come to realize that Nabokov and Humbert are totally different entities. Anyone who reads *Lolita* attentively from cover to cover is going to realize that the author does not agree with, or even much like, his main character. In his preface to the English translation of another novel, *Despair*, Nabokov speaks of "the rhetorical venom I injected into the narrator's tone" in *Lolita*, and unambiguously describes Humbert as a "neurotic scoundrel" ("Foreword" 9).

Well, then, if Lolita isn't a dirty book, and Nabokov is not a sex maniac, is Humbert Humbert a pervert? This is another valuable question. It invites us to consider Shakespeare's words in *A Midsummer-Night's Dream*: "The lunatic, the lover, and the poet / Are of imagination all compact" (5.1.7–8). Questions about Humbert's morality are considerably less naïve than those about Nabokov's, and do not admit glib answers. Humbert certainly claims he is a poet and a lover. Sometimes he also seems to see himself as a madman. In the remark cited earlier, Humbert compares "sex offenders" to "poets." How can that be? This question takes us to the heart of *Lolita*, and to much of Nabokov's work.

Throughout most of this novel, Humbert Humbert does not so much love, nor lust after Dolores Haze: his passion is for his *idea* of this girl. He certainly seeks to possess her physically, but the "her" here is not so much the actually flesh and blood kid as the fantasy of childhood sexuality that he has grafted unto her. It is not that Humbert finds his lover; it is that he creates her.

This is actually clear to Humbert himself. Soon after moving into the home of Charlotte and Dolores, Humbert has a one-sided sexual encounter with his Lolita. This occurs when, in a rather grotesque parody of fatherly affection, she is sitting in his lap and he is singing to her, both are fully clothed, and he manages to achieve a sexual climax without her knowing it. At this point, he declares, tellingly, "Lolita had been safely solipsized." "Solipsism" is the philosophy that only the self can be known, only the self is real. Humbert only truly possesses Dolores when he makes of her a figment of his own fevered imagination. When she is "solipsized" into a creation all his own, then, and only then, he is her lover. Humbert can thus claim to be a "poet" in that he is a creator, and his creation is the object of his affection and passion, his Lolita, not Dolores Haze.

The problem with this interpretation of events, presented so compellingly by their principal actor, is that, in the context of the fictional events of the novel, Dolores Haze is not just a creation of Humbert's fevered imagination: she is a real little girl, and one he abuses. At the very end of the novel, Humbert himself realizes this: he is standing on a hillside, overlooking a small town, and he hears the sounds of a group of children at play. At that point, and only at that point, he comes to understand "that the hopelessly poignant thing was not Lolita's absence from my side, but the absence of her voice from that concord" (*Lolita* 310).

Some readers of *Lolita* find Humbert to be pathetic; others believe he is a dangerous criminal. Some say they find him likable, in a repellent sort of way; others find him disgusting. These are all, I believe, legitimate reactions, and they make for animated and worthwhile discussion. They also invite us to ask even more questions, such as: What is the difference between a criminal imagination and an artistic one? What do we mean by "madman?" If a person understands exactly what he is doing, can he be a lunatic? Can we like someone, and still find that person disgusting? And perhaps the most important and interesting question of all: Can a book dominated by a powerful, perverse, and dark voice be an attractive and even uplifting work of fiction?

It also leads to questions about the role of females in the book, and whether the book is degrading to women because it treats them as objects of the male fantasy instead of real people. Many reads question whether the women in Lolita are full characters, or whether they are simply animated stereotypes. If the latter is true, to what extent does this actually represent the final position of the novel (or even its author) and to what degree is it a manifestation of Humbert's deformed vision? Should modern readers view Charlotte Haze, Lolita's mother, as a degrading representative of women? What about other female characters in the work? And, of course, what about Dolores herself? This is an issue on which many thoughtful students and critics have taken opposite sides (in itself, a valuable lesson and observation). My reading of the novel is that it is Humbert who has turned three-dimensional female characters into reductive and simplistic versions of women, not Nabokov. Certainly, Humbert's efforts to "solipsize" Dolores preclude his allowing himself to notice or acknowledge that she has feelings and thoughts of her own, independent of his imagination, that she can have beliefs and moods that are not in harmony with his, that she can have an independent existence that has no relation to his whatsoever. Indeed, one of the things that makes Humbert a monster is that he similarly transforms everyone with whom he comes in contact—male or female. Other people are, to this character, appendages of, or supplements to, his own personality, not discrete individuals in their own right. This is a mode of living in the world which is not only inaccurate, but also dangerous, even frightening.

Lolita is a novel which exploits the sexual taboos of our culture in order to explore, in a complex and fascinating narrative structure, a number of issues and themes which have nothing whatsoever to do with sexual behavior. For example, *Lolita* serves as a splendid case study proving T.S. Eliot's thesis that every work of literature builds upon the works of the past and the literary tradition of which it is merely the latest manifestation. One of the characteristics which makes Nabokov's prose so dense and sometimes difficult is the way in which his works are saturated with references to a diverse cluster of artistic predecessors, American, European, and Russian. I certainly do not, after over a dozen readings of the novel, "catch" all these references, and first time readers are likely to miss most of them. However reading and re-reading such a densely allusive novel helps us to begin to understand the ways in which modern works of literary art build upon their precursors. Just noticing many of the references to Poe and to Shakespeare, probably the two most accessible authors from which *Lolita* mines, heightens our awareness of the richness and the vitality of the novelistic tradition.

Another valuable insight that Nabokov imparts, especially for younger or relatively inexperienced readers, is that good literature doesn't really teach lessons. Many of us were encouraged, especially in high school English courses, to see literature as a kind of repository of simplistic moral aphorisms (e.g., the moral of *Othello* is "don't be jealous"). *Lolita* will lead us away from such readings. I have sometimes asked students questions such as "what is the theme or moral of *Lolita*?" just to launch a discussion which will inevitably lead to the conclusion that the initial query was wrong. Nabokov does not give us a choice on this. Nobody can read the novel seriously and decide that the point of the book is "don't sleep with people a quarter of your age," or "don't marry your girlfriend's mother," or "don't murder your rival for the affections of a child."

The "moral" or "theme" of *Lolita* is to be found in its magical prose. To read Lolita, or to re-read it, is to heighten one's sense of the power of words, to see them dance and hear them sing. It is certainly not impossible to have read *Lolita* carefully and still write sloppy prose. But I believe it is not possible to read *Lolita* with care and not recognize poor writing, one's own and that of others. At the beginning of the novel, its protagonist laments that he has "only words to play with" (*Lolita* 34). Nabokov's novel teaches us that we might as well play with the best.

NOTES

1. The novel was first published in 1955, in Paris, by the Olympia Press, a somewhat shady concern, which printed both legitimate authors and naughty novels.
2. For example, *Lolita* made *Time* magazine's list of the 100 best English language novels written between 1923 and 2005. On the other hand, when it was first published, the editor of the *London Sunday Express* described it as "the filthiest book I have ever read."

WORKS CITED

Nabokov, Vladimir. *The Annotated Lolita*. Ed. Alfred Appel, Jr. New York: McGraw-Hill, 1970.

———. "Foreword." *Despair*. New York: Capricorn Books, 1966.

———. "On a Book Entitled *Lolita*." *The Annotated Lolita*. Ed. Alfred Appel, Jr. New York: McGraw-Hill, 1970.

LORD OF THE FLIES
(WILLIAM GOLDING)

ᘒᗅ ᗅᘒ

"Men of a Smaller Growth: A Psychological
Analysis of William Golding's *Lord of the Flies*"
by Claire Rosenfield, in
Literature and Psychology (1961)

INTRODUCTION

In her psychological analysis of William Golding's *Lord of the Flies*, Claire Rosenfield focuses on the way Golding dramatizes Freudian theory. Rosenfield argues that without the structuring and repressive influence of traditional authority figures, the boys on the island are free to create a new culture, which reflects "the genuine primitive society, evolving its gods and demons (its myths), its rituals and taboos (its social norms)."

ᗑᗢᗒ

When an author consciously dramatizes Freudian theory—and dramatizes it successfully—only the imaginative re-creation of human behavior rather than the sustaining structure of ideas is apparent. In analyzing William Golding's *Lord of the Flies*, the critic must assume that Golding knows psychological literature and must then attempt to

---

Rosenfield, Claire. "Men of a Smaller Growth: A Psychological Analysis of William Golding's *Lord of the Flies*." *Literature and Psychology* 11.4 (Autumn 1961): 93–101.

show how an author's knowledge of theory can vitalize his prose and characterization. The plot itself is uncomplicated, so simple, indeed, that one wonders how it so effortlessly absorbs the burden of meaning. During some unexplained man-made holocaust a plane, evacuating a group of children, crashes on the shore of a tropical island. All adults are conveniently killed. The narrative follows the children's gradual return to the amorality of childhood, and it is the very nature of that state of non-innocence which makes them small savages. Or we might make the analogy to the childhood of races and compare the child to the primitive. Denied the sustaining and repressing authority of parents, church, and state, they form a new culture the development of which reflects that of the genuine primitive society, evolving its gods and demons (its myths), its rituals and taboos (its social norms). On the level of pure narrative, the action proceeds from the gradual struggle between Ralph and Jack, the two oldest boys, for precedence. Ralph is the natural leader by virtue of his superior height, his superior strength, his superior beauty. His mild expression proclaims him "no devil." He possesses the symbol of authority, the conch, or sea shell, which the children use to assemble their miniature councils. Golding writes, "The being that had blown . . . [the conch] had sat waiting for them on the platform with the delicate thing balanced in his knees, was set apart." Jack, on the other hand, is described in completely antithetical terms; he is distinguished by his ugliness and his red hair, a traditional demonic attribute. He first appears as the leader of a church choir, which "creature-like" marches in two columns behind him. All members of the choir wear black; "their bodies, from throat to ankle, were hidden by black cloaks."[1] Ralph initially blows the conch to discover how many children have escaped death in the plane crash. As Jack approaches with his choir from the "darkness of the forest," he cannot see Ralph, whose back is to the sun. The former is, symbolically, sun-blinded. These two are very obviously intended to recall God and the Devil, whose confrontation, in the history of Western religions, establishes the moral basis for all actions. But, as Freud reminds us, "metaphysics" becomes "metapsychology"[2]; gods and devils are "nothing other than psychological processes projected into the outer world."[3] If Ralph is a projection of man's good impulses from which we derive the authority figures—whether god, king, or father—who establish the necessity for our valid ethical and social action, then Jack becomes an externalization of the evil instinctual forces of the unconscious. Originally, as in the more primitive religions, gods and devils were one; even Hebraic-Christian tradition makes Satan a fallen angel.

The temptation is to regard the island on which the children are marooned as a kind of Eden, uncorrupted and Eveless. But the actions of the children negate any assumption about childhood innocence. Even though Golding himself momentarily becomes a victim of his Western culture and states that Ralph wept for the "end of innocence," events have simply supported Freud's conclusions that no child is innocent. On a third level, Ralph is every man—or every child—and his body becomes the battleground where reason and instinct struggle, each to assert itself. For to regard Ralph and Jack as Good and Evil is to ignore the role of the child Piggy, who in the child's world of make-believe is the outsider. Piggy's composite description not only manifests his difference from the other boys; it also reminds the reader of the stereotype image of the old man who has more-than-human wisdom: he is fat, inactive because asthmatic, and generally reveals a disinclination for physical labor. Because he is extremely near-sighted, he wears thick glasses—a further mark of his difference. As time passes, the hair of the other boys grows with abandon. "He was the only boy on the island whose hair never seemed to grow. The rest were shock-headed, but Piggy's hair still lay in wisps over his head as though baldness were his natural state, and this imperfect covering would soon go, like the velvet on a young stag's antlers" (81). In these images of age and authority we have a figure reminiscent of the children's past—the father. Moreover, like the father he counsels common sense; he alone leavens with a reasonable gravity the constant exuberance of the others for play or for play at hunting. When they scamper off at every vague whim, he scornfully comments, "Like a pack of kids." Ungrammatically but logically, he tries to allay the "littluns" fear of a "beast." "'Life is scientific, that's what it is. . . . I know there isn't no beast—not with claws and all that, I mean—but I know there isn't no fear, either'" (105). He has excessive regard for the forms of order: the conch must be held by a child before that child can speak at councils. When the others neglect responsibility, fail to build shelters, swim in the pools or play in the sand or hunt, allow the signal fire on the mountain to go out or to get out of hand and burn up half the island, he seconds Ralph by admonishing the others vigorously and becomes more and more of a spoil-sport who robs play of its illusions, the adult interrupting the game. Ralph alone recognizes his superior intelligence but wavers between what he knows to be wise and the group acceptance his egocentricity demands. Finally, Piggy's role—as man's reasoning faculties and as a father—derives some of its complexity from the fact that the fire which the children foster and guard on the mountain in the hope of communicating with the adult world is lighted with his glasses. In mythology, after all, the theft of fire brought civilization—and, hence, repression—to man. As the new community becomes more and more irrational, its irrationality is marked by Piggy's progressive blindness. An accident following an argument between Ralph and Jack breaks one of the lenses. When the final breach between the two occurs and Piggy supports Ralph, his remaining lens is stolen in a night raid by Jack. This is a parody of the traditional fire theft, which was to provide light and warmth for mankind. After this event Piggy must be led by Ralph. When he is making his final plea for his glasses—reasoned as always—he is struck on the head by a rock and falls. "Piggy fell forty feet and landed on his back on that square, red rock in the sea. His head opened and stuff came out and turned red. Piggy's arms and legs twitched a bit, like a pig's after it has been killed" (223).

The history of the child Piggy on the island dramatizes in terms of the individual the history of the entire group. When they first assemble to investigate their plight, they treat their island isolation as a temporary phenomenon; they want to play games until they are rescued—until their parents reassert the repressive actions of authority. This microcosm of the great world seems to them to be a fairy land.

> A kind of glamour spread over them and the scene and they were conscious of the glamour and made happy by it. (33)

> The coral was scribbled in the sea as though a giant had bent down to reproduce the shape of the island in a flowing, chalk line but tired before he had finished. (38)

> "This is real exploring," said Jack. "I'll bet nobody's been here before." (35)

> Echoes and birds flew, white and pink dust floated, the forest further down shook as with the passage of an enraged monster: and then the island was still. (37)

They compare this reality to their reading experiences: it is Treasure Island or Coral Island or like pictures from their travel books. This initial reaction conforms to the pattern of play which Johan Huizinga establishes in *Homo Ludens*.[4] In its early stages their play has no cultural or moral function; it is simply a "stepping out of real life into a temporary sphere of activity."[5] Ironically, the child of *Lord of the Flies* who thinks he is "only pretending" or that this is "only for fun" does not realize that his play is the beginning of the formation of a new society which has regressed to a primitive state, with all its emphasis upon taboo and communal action. What begins by being like other games in having a distinct "locality and duration"[6] apart from ordinary life is—or becomes—reality. The spatial separation necessary for the make-believe of the game is represented first by the island. In this new world the playground is further narrowed: the gatherings of the children are described as a circle at several points, a circle from which Piggy is excluded:

> For the moment the boys were a closed circuit of sympathy with Piggy outside. (29)

> They became a circle of boys round a camp fire and even Ralph and Piggy were half-drawn in. (92)

Piggy approximates the spoil-sport who "robs the play of its illusion."[7]

The games of the beginning have a double function: they, first of all, reflect the child's attitude toward play as a temporary cessation from the activities imposed by the adult world; but like the games played before the formation of civilization, they anticipate the ritual which reveals a developing society. So the children move from voluntary play to ritual, from "only pretending" to reality, from representation to identification. The older strictures imposed by parents are soon forgotten but every now and then a momentary remembrance of past prohibitions causes restraint. One older child hides in order to throw stones at a younger one.

> Yet there was a space round Henry, perhaps six yards in diameter, into which he dared not throw. Here, invisible yet strong, was the taboo of the old life. Round the squatting child

was the protection of parents and school and policemen and the law. (78)

Jack hesitates when, searching for meat, he raises his knife to kill his first pig.

> The pause was only long enough for them to understand what an enormity the downward stroke would be. Then the piglet tore loose from the creepers and scurried into the undergrowth. . . .
> "Why didn't you—?"
> They knew very well why he hadn't: because of the enormity of the knife descending and cutting into living flesh; because of the unbearable blood. (40–1)

The younger children first, then gradually the older ones, like primitives in the childhood of races, begin to people the darkness of night and forest with spirits and demons which had previously appeared only in their dreams or fairy tales. Now there are no comforting mothers to dispel the terrors of the unknown. They externalize these fears into the figure of a "beast." Once the word "beast" is mentioned, the menace of the irrational becomes overt; name and thing become one. At one critical council when the first communal feeling begins to disintegrate, Ralph cries, "'If only they could send us something grown-up . . . a sign or something'" (117). And a sign does come from the outside. That night, unknown to the children, a plane is shot down and its pilot parachutes dead to earth and is caught in the rocks on the mountain. It requires no more than the darkness of night together with the shadows of the forest vibrating in the signal fire to distort the hanging corpse with its expanding silk 'chute into a demon that must be appeased. Ironically, the fire of communication does touch this object of the grown-up world only to foster superstition. Security in this new situation can be achieved only by establishing new rules.

During the first days the children, led by Jack, play at hunting. But eventually the circle of the playground extends to the circle of the hunted and squealing pig seeking refuge—and it is significant that the first animal slain for food is a nursing sow—which itself anticipates the circle of consecrated ground where the children perform the new rites of the kill.

The first hunt accomplishes its purpose: the blood of the animals is spilled; the meat, used for food. But because Jack and his choir undertake this hunt, they desert the signal fire, which is dictated by the common-sense desire for rescue, and it goes out and a ship passes the island. Later the children reenact the killing with one boy, Maurice, assuming the role of the pig running its frenzied circle. The others chant in unison: "'Kill the pig. Cut her throat. Bash her in.'" At this dramatic representation each child is still aware that this is a display, a performance. He is never "so beside himself that he loses consciousness of ordinary reality."[8] Each time they reenact the same event, however, their behavior becomes more frenzied, more cruel, less like representation than identification. The chant then becomes, "'Kill the beast. Cut his throat. Spill his blood.'" It is as if the first event, the pig's death, is forgotten in the recesses of time; a new myth defines the primal act. Real pig becomes mythical beast.

Jack's ascendancy over the group begins when the children's fears distort the natural objects around them: twigs become creepers, shadows become demons. I have already discussed the visual imagery suggesting Jack's demonic function. He serves as a physical mani-festation of irrational forces. After an indefinite passage of time, he appears almost dehumanized, his "nose only a few inches from the humid earth." He is "dog-like" and proceeds forward "on all fours" "into the semi-darkness of the undergrowth." His cloak and clothing have been shed. Indeed, except for a "pair of tattered shorts held up by his knife-belt, he was naked." His eyes seemed "bolting and nearly mad." He has lost his ability to communicate with Ralph as on the first day. "He tried to convey the compulsion to track down and kill that was swallowing him up" (65). "They walked along, two continents of experience and feeling, unable to communicate" (70). When Jack first explains to Ralph the necessity to disguise himself from the pigs he wants to hunt, he rubs his face with clay and charcoal. At this point he assumes a mask, begins to dance, is finally freed from all the repressions of his past. "He capered towards Bill, and the mask was a thing on its own, behind which Jack hid, liberated from shame and self-consciousness" (80). At the moment of the dance the mask and Jack are one. The first kill, as I have noted, follows the desertion of the signal fire and the passage of a possible rescue ship. Jack is still reveling in the knowledge that he has "outwitted a living thing, imposed their will upon it, taken away its life like a long and satisfying drink" (88).

Already he has begun to obliterate the distinctions between animals and men, as do primitives; already he thinks in terms of the metaphor of a ritual drinking of blood, the efficacy of which depended on the drinker's assumption of his victim's strength and spirit. Ralph and Piggy confront him with his defection of duty.

> The two boys faced each other. There was the brilliant world
> of hunting, tactics, fierce exhilaration, skill; and there was the
> world of longing and baffled common-sense. Jack transferred
> the knife to his left hand and smudged blood over his forehead
> as he pushed down the plastered hair. (89)

Jack's unconscious gesture is a parody of the ritual of initiation in which the hunter's face is smeared with the blood of his first kill. In the subsequent struggle one of the lenses of Piggy's spectacles is broken. The dominance of reason is over; the voice of the old world is stilled. The primary images are no longer those of fire and light but those of darkness and blood. The link between Ralph and Jack "had snapped and fastened elsewhere."

The rest of the group, however, shifts its allegiance to Jack because he has given them meat rather than something useless like fire. Gradually, they begin to be described as "shadows" or "masks" or "savages" or "demoniac figures" and, like Jack, "hunt naked save for paint and a belt." Ralph now uses Jack's name with the recognition that "a taboo was evolving around that word too." Name and thing again become one; to use the word is to incite the bearer. But more significant, the taboo, according to Freud, is "a very primitive prohibition imposed from without (by an authority) and directed against the strongest desires of man."[9] In this new society it replaces the authority of the parents. Now every kill becomes a sexual act, is a metaphor for childhood sexuality.

> The afternoon wore on, hazy and dreadful with damp heat; the
> sow staggered her way ahead of them, bleeding and mad, and
> the hunters followed, wedded to her in lust, excited by the long
> chase and dropped blood. . . . The sow collapsed under them and
> they were heavy and fulfilled upon her. (167–68)

Every subsequent "need for ritual" fulfills not only the desire for communication and a substitute security to replace that of civilization, but also the need to liberate both the repressions of the past and those imposed by Ralph. Indeed, the projection of those impulses that they cannot accept in themselves into a beast is the beginning of a new mythology. The earlier dreams and nightmares can now be shared as the former subjectivity could not be.

When the imaginary demons become defined by the rotting corpse and floating 'chute on the mountain which their terror distorts into a beast, Jack wants to track the creature down. After the next kill, the head of the pig is placed upon a stake to placate it. Finally one of the children, Simon, after an epileptic fit, creeps out of the forest at twilight while the others are engaged in enthusiastic dancing following a hunt. Seized by the rapture of reenactment or perhaps terrorized by fear and night into believing that this little creature is a beast, they circle Simon, pounce on him, bite and tear his body to death. He becomes not a substitute for beast but beast itself; representation becomes absolute identification, "the mystic repetition of the initial event."[10] At the moment of Simon's death, nature speaks; a cloud bursts; rain and wind fill the parachute on the hill and the corpse of the pilot falls or is dragged among the screaming boys. Both Simon and the dead man, beast and beast, are washed into the sea and disappear. After this complete resurgence of savagery in accepted ritual, there is only a short interval before Piggy's remaining lens is stolen, he is intentionally killed as an enemy, and Ralph, the human being, becomes hunted like beast or pig.

Simon's mythic and psychological role has earlier been suggested. Undersized, subject to epileptic fits, bright-eyed, and introverted, he constantly creeps away from the others to meditate among the intricate vines of the forest. To him, as to the mystic, superior knowledge is given intuitively which he cannot communicate. When the first report of the beast-pilot reaches camp, Simon, we are told, can picture only "a human at once heroic and sick." During the day preceding his death, he walks vaguely away and stumbles upon the pig's head left in the sand in order to appease the demonic forces they imagine. Shaman-like, he holds a silent colloquy with it, a severed head covered with innumerable flies. It is itself the titled Lord of the Flies, a name applied to the Biblical demon Beelzebub and later used in Goethe's *Faust, Part I*, to describe Mephistopheles.[11] From it he learns that it is the Beast, and the Beast cannot be hunted because it is within. Simon feels the advent of one of his fits and imagines the head expanding, an anticipation or intuition of the discovery of the pilot's corpse. Suddenly Golding employs a startling image, "Simon was inside the mouth. He fell down and lost consciousness" (178). Literally, this image presents the hallucination of a sensitive child about to lose control of his rational faculties. Metaphorically, it suggests the ritual quest in which the hero is swallowed by a serpent or dragon or beast whose belly is the underworld, undergoes a symbolic death in order to gain the elixir to revitalize his stricken society, and returns with his knowledge to the timed world as a redeemer. Psychologically, this narrative pattern is a figure of speech connoting the annihilation of the ego, an internal journey necessary for self-understanding, a return to the timelessness of the unconscious. When Simon wakes, he realizes that he must confront the beast on the mountain because "what else is there to do?" He is relieved of "that dreadful feeling of the pressure of personality" which had oppressed him earlier. When he discovers the hanging corpse, he first frees it in compassion although it is rotting and surrounded by flies, and then staggers unevenly down to report to the others. Redeemer and scapegoat, he becomes the victim of the group he seeks to enlighten. In death—before he is pulled into the sea—his head is surrounded by flies in an ironic parody of the halo of saints and gods.

Piggy's death, soon to follow Simon's, is foreshadowed when the former proclaims at council that there is no beast. "'What would a beast eat?'" "'Pig.'" "'We eat pig,'" he rationally answers. "'Piggy!'" (104) is the next word. At Piggy's death his body twitches "like a pig's after it has been killed." Not only has his head been smashed, but also the conch, symbol of order, is simultaneously broken. A complex group of metaphors unite to form a total metaphor involving Piggy and the pig, hunted and eaten by the children, and the pig's head which is at once left to appease the beast's hunger and is the beast itself. But the beast is within, and the children are defined by the very objects they seek to destroy.

In these associated images we have the whole idea of a communal and sacrificial feast and a symbolic cannibalism, all of which Freud discussed in *Totem and Taboo*. Here the psychology of the individual contributes the configurations for the development of religion. Indeed, the events of *Lord of the Flies* imaginatively parallel the patterns which Freud detects in primitive mental processes.

Having populated the outside world with demons and spirits which are projections of their instinctual nature, these children—and primitive men—must then unconsciously evolve new forms of worship and laws, which manifest themselves in taboos, the oldest form of social repression. With the exception of the first kill—in which the children still imagine they are playing at hunting—the subsequent deaths assume a ritual form; the pig is eaten communally by all and the head is left for the "beast," whose role consists in sharing the feast. This is much like the "public ceremony"[12] described by Freud in which the sacrifice of an animal provided food for the god and his worshippers. The complex relationships within the novel between the "beast," the pigs which are sacrificed, the children whose asocial impulses are externalized in the beast—this has already been discussed. So we see that, as Freud points out, the "sacrificing community, its god [the 'beast'], and the sacrificial animal are of the same blood,"[13] members of a clan. The pig, then, may be regarded as a totem animal, an "ancestor, a tutelary spirit and protector"[14]; it is, in any case, a part of every child. The taboo or prohibition against eating particular parts of the totem animal coincides with the children's failure to eat the head of the pig. It is that portion which is set aside for the "beast." Just as Freud describes the primitive feast, so the children's festive meal is accompanied by a frenzied ritual in which they temporarily release their forbidden impulses and represent the kill. To consume the pig and to reenact the event is not only to assert a "common identity"[15] but also to share a "common responsibility" for the deed. None of the boys is excluded from the feast. The later ritual, in which Simon, as a human substitute identified with the totem, is killed, is in this novel less an unconscious attempt to share the responsibility for the killing of a primal father in prehistoric times, than it is a social act in which the participants celebrate their new society by commemorating their severance from the authority of the civilized state. Because of the juxtaposition of Piggy and pig, the eating of pig at the communal feast might be regarded as the symbolic cannibalism by which the children physically partake of the qualities of the slain and share responsibility for their crime. (It must be remembered that, although Piggy on a symbolic level represents the light of reason and the authority of the father, on the psychological and literal level of the story he shares that bestiality and irrationality which to Golding dominate all men, even the most rational or civilized.)

In the final action, Ralph is outlawed by the children and hunted like an animal. Jack sharpens a stick at both ends so that it will be ready to receive the severed head of the boy as if he were a pig.

Jack keeps his society together because it, like the brother horde of
Robertson Smith[16] and Freud, "is based on complicity in the common
crimes."[17] In his flight Ralph, seeing the grinning skull of a pig, thinks
of it as a toy and remembers the early days on the island when all were
united in play. In the play world, the world of day, he has become a
"spoil-sport" like Piggy; in the world based upon primitive rites and
taboos, the night world where fears become demons and sleep is like
death, he is the heretic or outcast. This final hunt, after the conch is
broken, is the pursuit of the figure representing law and order, the
king or the god. Finally, Jack, through misuse of the dead Piggy's
glasses, accidentally sets the island on fire. A passing cruiser, seeing the
fire, lands to find only a dirty group of sobbing little boys. "Fun and
games,' said the officer. . . . 'What have you been doing? Having a war
or something?'" (246–47).

But are all the meanings of the novel as clear as they seem? To
restrict it to an imaginative re-creation of Freud's theory that children are little savages, that no child is innocent whatever Christian
theology would have us believe, is to limit its significance for the adult
world. To say that the "beasts" we fear are within, that man is essentially irrational—or, to place a moral judgment on the irrational, that
man is evil—that, again, is too easy. In this forced isolation of a group
of children, Golding is making a statement about the world they
have left—a world, we are told, "in ruins." According to Huizinga's
theory of play, war is a game, a contest for prestige which, like the
games of primitives, or of classical athletes, may be fatal. It, too, has
its rules, although the modern concept of total war tends to obscure
both its ritualistic and its ennobling character. It, too, has its spatial
and temporal limitations, as the new rash of "limited" wars makes very
clear. More than once the children's acts are compared to those of the
outside world. When Jack first blackens his face like a savage, he gives
his explanation: "For hunting. Like in war. You know—dazzle paint.
Like things trying to look like something else'" (79). Appalled by one
of the ritual dances, Piggy and Ralph discuss the authority and ratio-
nality of the apparently secure world they have left:

> "Grown-ups know things," said Piggy. "They ain't afraid of
> the dark. They'd meet and have tea and discuss. Then things 'ud
> be all right—"
> "They wouldn't set fire to the island. Or lose—"

"They'd build a ship—"

The three boys stood in the darkness, striving unsuccessfully to convey the majesty of adult life.

"They wouldn't quarrel—"

"Or break my specs—"

"Or talk about beasts—"

"If only they could get a message to us," cried Ralph desperately. "If only they could send us some thing grown-up . . . a sign or something." (117)

The sign does come that night, unknown to them, in the form of the parachute and its attached corpse. The pilot [is] the analogue in the adult world to the ritual killing of the child Simon on the island; he, like Simon, is the victim and scapegoat of his society, which has unleashed its instincts in war. Both he and Simon are associated by a cluster of visual images. Both are identified with beasts by the children, who do see the truth—that all men are bestial—but do not understand it. Both he and Simon attract the flies from the Lord of the Flies, the pig's head symbolic of the demonic; both he and Simon are washed away by a cleansing but not reviving sea. His position on the mountain recalls the Hanged or Sacrificed god of Frazer; here, however, we have a parody of fertility. He is dead proof that Piggy's exaggerated respect for adults is itself irrational. When the officer at the rescue jokingly says, "'What have you been doing? Having a war or something?'" this representative of the grown-up world does not understand that the games of the children, which result in two deaths, are a moral commentary upon the primitive nature of his own culture. The ultimate irrationality is war. Paradoxically, the children not only return to a primitive and infantile morality, but they also degenerate into adults. They prove that, indeed, "children are but men of smaller growth."

NOTES

1. William Golding, *Lord of the Flies* (London, 1958), p. 25. Subsequent references to this work will be noted parenthetically by page numbers in the text.
2. Sigmund Freud, *Psychopathology of Everyday Life*, as quoted by Ernest Jones, *The Life and Works of Sigmund Freud* (New York, 1957), III, 53.

3. Ibid.

4. Johan Huizinga, *Homo Ludens* (Boston, 1955).

5. Ibid., p. 8.

6. Ibid., p. 9.

7. Ibid., p. 7.

8. Ibid., p. 14.

9. Sigmund Frued, "Totem and Taboo," in *The Basic Writings of Sigmund Freud*, trans. A.A. Brill (New York, 1938), p. 834.

10. Ibid.

11. Ibid.

12. There are further affinities to Sartre's *Les Mouches*.

13. *Totem and Taboo*, p. 878.

14. Ibid., p. 808.

15. Ibid., p. 914.

16. William Robertson Smith, *Lectures on the Religion of the Semites*, 3rd ed., with introduction by Stanley A. Cook (New York, 1927).

17. *Totem and Taboo*, p. 916.

"THE MILLER'S TALE"
(GEOFFREY CHAUCER)

$\mathscr{D}\!\!\swarrow\,\,\searrow\!\!\mathscr{C}$

"Social and Religious Taboos in Chaucer's *The Miller's Tale*"
by Robert C. Evans,
Auburn University at Montgomery

Although the word "taboo" did not exist in Geoffrey Chaucer's fourteenth-century English culture, the general concept of taboo behavior certainly did. Indeed, the broad notion of behavior (including speech) that is forbidden, condemned, prohibited, and/or proscribed by society as improper or unacceptable has probably existed in every human culture, even if precise definitions of taboo topics, objects, conduct, or forms of speech have varied widely from place to place and across time. Cultures define themselves, in large part, in terms of what they prohibit, condemn, or find unacceptable, and thus the study of taboo behavior is, paradoxically, one of the best ways of comprehending a culture's deepest and most cherished standards as well as its most widely shared assumptions and beliefs. By understanding what a culture condemns, we can understand what it values. Like a photographic negative that can provide a positive image, the study of taboo thoughts, behavior, and speech can illuminate a culture's most fundamental ideals.

Probably no character in Chaucer's *The Canterbury Tales* violates more taboos—both in conduct and in speech—than the Miller. Indeed, people long after Chaucer's era have had trouble dealing with the Miller's abrasive personality and his scandalous tale [V 12–26].[1]

Chaucer himself seems to have anticipated that *The Miller's Tale* might offend many members of his original audience, and so his narrative alter-ego in the tales invites any reader who might take offense to "Turne over the leef, and chese [i.e., choose] another tale," and he even warns such readers, "Blameth nought me if that ye chese amis" (*Introduction*, ll. 69, 73). Of course, having been admonished in such a tantalizing fashion, few readers can resist the temptation to read the tale, but the Miller's pride in violating taboos is evident long before he begins telling the story that bears his name.

Nearly all the taboos the Miller flouts can be defined, to one degree or another, as religious taboos—rules rooted in a strong sense of what was proper, sacred, and holy, particularly in Christian terms. Christian ideals and beliefs were a tremendously strong influence on Chaucer's culture, even if those ideals and beliefs were (inevitably) not always perfectly or universally practiced. Chaucer and his audience lived in a society in which basic Christian teachings were taken for granted and in which most thinking and conduct was judged in Christian terms. Chaucer himself seems to have been strongly convinced of the merits of Christian thought, and, in creating characters such as the Miller (as well as the various persons who populate the Miller's tale), he seems to have intended to teach Christian truths by depicting people who fail to lead exemplary Christian lives. *The Miller's Tale*, in other words, seems to have been intended as an elaborate exercise in extended (and often quite humorous) irony. Readers are expected to supply the moral and spiritual values so obviously lacking in the Miller himself and in the people he describes, and readers are also expected to use those values to judge the thinking and conduct the tale presents. Chaucer and his audience would have had a very strong sense of all the social, intellectual, and behavioral taboos that the Miller and his characters violate, and they would have recognized that all the transgressed values—both in the *Introduction* and in the *Tale* itself—were ultimately grounded in Christian thought. By showing so many people living in direct contradiction of Christian teachings, Chaucer reminds his readers of the kinds of lives that they themselves were expected (but often failed) to lead.

Modern scholarship has documented many of the taboos the Miller and his characters reflect, but rarely have the transgressions been discussed comprehensively or conveniently in a relatively brief space. Providing such a survey, therefore, is the chief purpose of the present essay. One of the first of the Miller's violations, for instance, appears in the very first line in which he is mentioned in the *Introduction*, where we are immediately told that he is drunk and can thus sit only with difficulty upon his horse (ll. 12–13). His drunkenness, of course, already violates standard Christian teachings (see, for instance, Proverbs 23: 29–35, Ephesians 5:18, 1 Corinthians 6:12, and 2 Peter 2:19), while the fact that he sits unsteadily on his horse would have been a standard symbol of loss of moral self-control [B&G 630], since the image of a rider controlling a horse was an age-old representation of reason controlling passion. In addition, the fact that the Miller will doff his hat to no one and will give preference to no one out of courtesy (ll. 14–15) shows that he is behaving with uncharitable disrespect to other persons; like all the sinners depicted in *The Canterbury Tales* (and indeed like all sinners at all times and places, according to standard Christian teachings) he is guilty of the fundamental sin of selfishness or pride. Thus it is not surprising when we are told that he speaks in the voice of Pilate (l. 16), who was often depicted in medieval writings, including morality plays, as boastful, tyrannical, ruthless, cruel, melodramatic, and bombastic [B&G 484; V120]. The fact that Pilate had a major hand in the death of Christ is, of course, also highly significant, for the Miller is himself the embodiment of anti-Christian discord, exemplified by his profane references to Christ's body [V121]. His vow to "quite" (i.e., requite) the Knight's tale (l. 19) is thus often seen as evidence of his highly competitive spirit [M66; V119]. Here and everywhere, the Miller violates the central Christian taboo against self-centered, egotistical thought, feelings, and behavior.

Given the fact that the Miller is so consumed by pride, it is a tactical mistake for the Host to ask that the Miller wait until "Some better man"—perhaps the Monk—should first tell a tale (l. 22). The Miller, of course, instantly feels insulted, and Chaucer not only has him swear obscenely again, but also has him heavily stress the key pronoun "I" by placing it firmly at the end of a line (l. 24). Like an egotistical child throwing a very public tantrum, the Miller vows that he will speak now "or elles go my way" (l. 25). The Host, in response, speaks more accurately than he realizes when, in frustration, he replies that the Miller should speak in the devil's name (l. 26); this is ironic, since the Miller does in fact embody some of the same kind of pride and rebelliousness as Satan himself [B&G 630]. The Miller is indeed a "fool", as the Host says, precisely because his "wit" (or reason) truly *has* been "overcome" (l. 27) not only by the effects of his drinking but also (and more significantly) by his essential egotism. The Miller violates a basic taboo against engaging in unreasonable and belligerent social behavior, especially when dealing publicly with other people, and particularly when dealing with social superiors (such as the Knight and the Monk). His basic willingness to break taboos, however, promises to be all the more shocking when he begins his drunken tale by announcing that he will "telle a legende and a lif / Bothe of a carpenter and of his wif" (ll. 33–34). This announcement would have made many of the other pilgrims nervous, since the words "legende" and "lif" (i.e., "life") were terms commonly associated with stories of saints, and the most famous saintly carpenter was Joseph, whose wife was the Blessed Virgin Mary [B&G 533, see also 558, 622, 624, 639, and 653; in addition, see V123]. The drunken Miller, then (partly, perhaps, as a way of getting in a dig at the Monk [V123]) seems about to launch into a probably highly profane tale about the Holy Family—a tale that would almost inevitably violate numerous Christian taboos. Fortunately, however, it eventually turns out that the carpenter and wife whom the Miller has in mind are residents not of the Holy Land, but of nearby Oxford.

The carpenter in question is a rich (some would even say avaricious [V30; V131]) old man named John, who has violated a standard social taboo of the time [V139] by marrying a much-younger and highly attractive wife. Living as a boarder in John's home is a young, handsome, and spunky clerk named Nicholas—a student at Oxford University who seems, however, to be transgressing many of the ideals expected of students at that time [V136; B&G 138]. Technically Nicholas is supposed to be preparing for service to the church, but most of his interests seem to involve the pursuit of selfish and sensual pleasures. He also shows a superstitious interest is astrology—an interest that was often condemned by medieval theologians [B&G 491; V132]. In numerous ways, in fact, Chaucer's Nicholas is the exact opposite of his namesake, holy St. Nicholas, although there are also many points of ironic contact between the career of Chaucer's Nicholas and the life of the Christian saint [B&G 540, 562, 570, 579; V32, V134, V150]. The fact that Nicholas spends much of his time alone in his room singing Christian hymns, and particularly the fact that one of those hymns is titled *Angelus ad Virginem* (or "The Angel to the Virgin"; l. 30), seems full of irony. Not only (as practically every commentator notes) does the title of the hymn remind us of the story of the angel Gabriel announcing to the Blessed Virgin that she would give birth to the Prince of Peace [B&G 533; M68], but it also ironically foreshadows Nicholas's own interest in John's wife, Alison, later in the tale. Just as one medieval tradition suggested that the biblical carpenter Joseph suspected his wife Mary of infidelity when he learned that she was pregnant [B&G 572], so the carpenter John in Chaucer's tale will soon have real reason to suspect (although, ironically, he doesn't) that his own wife is cheating with Nicholas. By continually alluding to Christian lore and legend throughout the tale, Chaucer constantly reminds us of all the taboos being broken by Nicholas as well as by practically all of the other characters.

One of those characters, of course, is Alison herself, whose very name in the middle ages was a common name for a witch [B&G 510], the name of a noted literary prostitute [V33], a name shared with Chaucer's own notorious and highly-sexed Wife of Bath [V34], and also a name that may ironically echo the famous liturgical phrase "kyrie eleyson" ("Lord, have mercy"; [V172]). The famous description of Alison's body is a parody of descriptions of beautiful ladies in courtly romances of Chaucer's time [B&G 518], but whereas most of those descriptions begin with the lady's head and face, the Miller immediately focuses (as does Nicholas later) on Alison's middle [B&G 637; V142–43]. Although her dress and appearance are repeatedly associated with the holy colors of black and white [V142] (colors which were often used in the habits on nuns), many details of the description foreshadow Alison's later sinful behavior. Her embroidered underwear, for instance (ll. 52–53), was associated with "vanity, extravagance, and sensuality" [V145], while her pulled black eyebrows were not only fashionable at the time [V146] but were also considered by some physiognomists to be a sign of "a lecherous nature" [B&G 504; however, for a dissenting view, see B&G 539 and V146]. Repeatedly Alison is described in terms that liken her to different kinds of animals (thus already suggesting her potential violation of ideal standards of human conduct), and perhaps the most memorable of all these comparisons is the simile likening her body to that of a "wesele" (l. 48). Weasels, as it happened, were thought in the middle ages to have a "lustful nature. . . . The creature was associated with shape-shifting, sexual trickery, storms, showers and bad young women"

[B&G 510]. The weasel was "supposed to conceive in its ear [like the Blessed Virgin] and give birth through its mouth" [B&G 648; see also V143]. The "weasel's colors are Alison's, black and white; furthermore, the appearance of the weasel precedes rain"—a fact that ironically foreshadows the later deception of John in Nicholas's prophecy of a second flood [V143]. In folklore, moreover, the weasel was considered "unclean [and] afflicted with abnormal sexual desires" [V143]. In all these ways, then, various aspects of the Miller's description of Alison would have alerted Chaucer's readers to her potential as a violator of various sexual and religious taboos.

Other details have the same effect. Thus, when Alison is compared to a blossoming pear-tree (l. 62), we are reminded that this was a standard "symbol of sexual awakening" [V147]. The purse (tasseled with silk and decorated with brassy spangles) that hangs from her belt (ll. 64–65) not only seems "slightly pretentious" [V148] but may also symbolize "cupidity" [B&G 540]. In various ways, particularly in the allusion to her soft skin (which is softer than wool), she is ironically compared to the Virgin Mary [V147], and other details used in her description may allude to the biblical Canticles, or Song of Songs [V150]. Meanwhile, the fact that she is compared to a swallow may have reminded Chaucer's first audience that swallows were not only associated "'with sexual licence'" [B&G 628] but that such birds could also sense when their nests were about to fall [B&G 492 and 628]—a fact that may seem ironic in light of later developments in the present tale. The images that associate Alison with the potential for lechery and infidelity are too numerous (and often too obvious) to mention, but one last detail seems worth noting: she is compared to the plant called the "piggesnye" (i.e., pig's eye; l. 82), a term that not only seems comically incongruous but may also have reminded some of Chaucer's readers that this particular plant was sometimes considered a remedy for "maladies of the groin" [V152]. Nicholas, in fact, will soon try to use Alison as just such a remedy himself, thus violating not only the obvious Christian taboos against adultery and fornication but also transgressing the common cross-cultural taboo stipulating that a guest should not mistreat a host.

Nicholas's incredibly comic "courtship" of Alison (which quickly involves his forthrightly grabbing her between the legs; l. 90) demonstrates in practically every way possible (both ironic and unironic) why he is so often described as "hende" (or "handy"; l. 86), a term which could mean "near, at hand; handy, ready or skilful with the hand; pleasant in dealing with others; courteous, gracious; 'nice'" [V134]. Nicholas violates numerous common Christian taboos: committing a kind of idolatry in his fevered pleas to Alison; taking God's name in vain in highly inappropriate circumstances ("'Lemman, love me al at atones [i.e., at once], / Or I wol die, also God me save'"; ll. 94–95); and misusing his obvious intelligence for improper purposes (thus abusing his God-given gift of reason). He is indeed the embodiment of intellectual pride (the worst kind of pride; see V31), and when Alison quickly promises to commit adultery with him, we cannot help but notice the extremely ironic terms in which her promise is phrased: she swears an oath "by Saint Thomas of Kent" (one of the greatest of all Christian martyrs; see V158) that she will be at Nicholas's "commandement" (thus violating, it goes without saying, numerous commandments from God; ll. 105–06). The fact that she is then immediately described as heading for "the parrissh chirche, / Criste's owene werkes for to wirche" (ll. 121–22)—a phrase that refers to "liturgical worship" [V160]—is just more ironic icing on the cake. Nicholas and Alison may not yet be fully guilty of physically violating the taboo against adultery (although both have already committed adultery in their hearts), but both are clearly transgressing taboos against hypocrisy and sacrilegious conduct. They assume that they can keep their sinful plans secret from John, but those plans are, of course, already apparent to God, from whom no taboo behavior (or even any taboo thoughts or impulses) can ever be hidden.

Perhaps the most obviously ironic character in the entire tale, however, is the prim, affected dandy named Absolon, whose very name and long, flowing hair clearly allude to the Old Testament figure Absolom, who revolted against his father in the Bible and suffered severe punishment as a result. Absolom's rebellion was long considered a symbol of any rejection of God, and Chaucer's Absolon is clearly a breaker of many social and religious taboos. He is, of course, another prospective adulterer (he courts Alison far more flagrantly than Nicholas does; ll. 170–83), and in fact he considers himself—despite his high voice and effeminate appearance—quite a ladies' man. He scopes out women while ostensibly serving as a minor cleric in the local church (l. 156), and various details of his grooming, costuming, physiognomy, and behavior link him to such flaws as pride, pomp, lechery, luxury, deceit, and fleshly excess [B&G 483, 495, 522; V162–63; V166]. His fashionable dress is typical of the kind of behavior condemned by medieval churchmen [B&G 502] as well as by university authorities (he is, after all, a clerk) [V33], and the mere fact that he fails to wear a tonsure (not to mention his pride in his abundant hair) would by itself have made him suspect [V33, V162]. That he has actually played the role of Herod in local mystery plays (l. 198), combined with the fact that he even dresses like the stage Herod in his everyday life [V43], associates him symbolically with an obvious enemy of Christianity. It is his undeniably irreligious conduct both in and out of church, however, that makes this sort of symbolism almost unnecessary [B&G 557]. It seems especially ironic, for instance, that Absolon walks up and down the aisles of the local church with a "censer," which was "an instrument of symbolic purificiation" [V168], especially since he lecherously eyes women as he does. Both when he is inside and outside the church, Absolon (like Nicholas and Alison as well) violates numerous social and religious taboos. In introducing all four of his main characters, then, Chaucer comically teaches valuable lessons about Christian ideals by showing us how those ideals are violated.

Nicholas, in fact, is able to implement his scheme to sleep with John's wife primarily because John is ignorant of the Bible and of basic Christian teachings. If John had only remembered God's promise never to destroy the earth again by a flood (Genesis 9:11), John would never have fallen for Nicholas's false prophecy of just such a calamity. The flood imagery, however, is ironically appropriate to Chaucer's tale for several other reasons. Thus, medieval commentators believed that the original flood had been sent largely as a punishment for just the sort of lechery exhibited by many of the characters in the Miller's tale [B&G 617; V196]. In addition, the biblical flood was also considered a prefiguration of precisely the kind of spiritual baptism from which all of these characters would benefit [B&G 519, 536]. Thanks, then, to John's ignorance of the Bible, as well as to John's own idolatry of his wife (ll. 336–38) and to his avarice (ll. 395–96; V205), Nicholas is able to persuade John to rig up the elaborate mechanism of the three hanging tubs—a detail that ironically echoes a famous episode from the life of the truly virtuous Saint Nicholas, who saved three men from death in pickling tubs [B&G 562, 570, 624].

The denouement of Nicholas's scheme is, of course, hilarious, and it is just as full of ironic details as is the rest of the story. Inevitably these details remind us of all the social and religious taboos being broken by Nicholas, Alison, and Absolon, as when Nicholas and Alison are described as making "melodye" (i.e., having sex; l. 466) not only in John's own bed (a violation of the taboo against mistreating a host and husband) but also while friars in a nearby church are literally singing praises of God (l. 469–70). At that very same moment, of course, Absolon is also up and about and is full of renewed hopes of adulterous success with John's wife. The language he uses in attempting to court Alison (ll. 512–21) is full of ironic echoes of the Biblical Song of Songs [B&G 498, 507, 550, 553, 615, 626], and it is also a parody of the language of courtly love [B&G 602], but the irony of his conduct would be perfectly obvious from one line alone: the line in which he begs Alison to commit adultery "For Jesus love and for the love of me" (l. 531). Alison herself, of course, also take's God's name in vain (l. 523), and she is also either very cynical or very naïve when, explaining to Absolon why she cannot grant him his wishes, she says, "I love another, and elles I were to blame" (l. 524). Her threat to cast a stone at Absolon is an ironic reminder of the story of the Biblical woman taken in adultery (John 8:7; B&G 615, 626), while Absolon's kneeling position as he engages in his misdirected kiss (l. 537) not only symbolizes his idolatry of Alison but also puts him in a posture more appropriate for worship of God or the Virgin Mary [B&G 574]. When he inadvertently kisses Alison's "naked ers [i.e., arse]" (l. 548), he unwittingly engages in an act associated in the middle ages with worship of the devil [B&G 558]—a fact that makes his later vicious anger ("'My soule betake I unto Satanas'; l. 564) all the more significant. As if to underline all the ironic points he is making, Chaucer fills this whole section of the tale with numerous explicit religious references (e.g., ll. 557, 581–83, 585, 596, 606). These come to a point when Absolon, right before he scalds Nicholas on (and also apparently in) the rear, once more takes God's name in vain (l. 609). Nicholas's scream for water is, typically, accompanied by ironic profanity ("'for Goddes herte!'" (l. 629), and the emphasis on water at the end of the tale has been linked once more to the need all the characters exhibit for both literal and figurative baptism [B&G 512].

The Miller himself, of course, has no lofty moral purpose in telling his tale; for him its main function is to shock, titillate, and entertain—and perhaps also to mock the Knight, the Reeve, and also the Clerk. The Miller, in his own way, is just as much a violator of various social and religious taboos as any of the characters he describes, and in fact the three male sinners (Nicholas, John, and Absolon) have each been linked, respectively, with three distinct sins (lechery, avarice, and pride [B&G 507]). These sins are all exhibited by the Miller himself, so that Absolon in particular, who also combines all three sins, can be seen (with perfect irony!) as the Miller's representative within the Miller's own tale [B&G 522]. Thus, while the Miller probably sets out to mock other pilgrims, as well as to burlesque the conventions of "serious" tales of love, and while the Miller seems to take Christian ethics and values no more seriously than do his main characters, Chaucer contrives the work in such a way that by telling the tale, the Miller inadvertently makes a mockery of his own crude ethics and unchristian conduct. *The Miller's Tale* is a work that brims with violations of assorted social and religious taboos, but it is also a work that inevitably reminds us of the very standards and ideals that its characters (and teller) transgress.

NOTES

1. For ease of reference, I will use abbreviations to refer to several sources. Thus, V = Thomas R. Ross's *Variorum* edition, where the cited numbers refer to page numbers; B&G = the Burton and Greentree bibliography, where the cited numbers refer to item numbers; and M = MacLaine, where the cited numbers refer to page numbers. When quoting Chaucer's poetry, I will cite from the Donaldson edition.

WORKS CITED OR CONSULTED

Burton, T.L. and Rosemary Greentree, eds. *Chaucer's* Miller's, Reeve's, *and* Cook's Tales. Toronto: University of Toronto Press, 1997.

Donaldson, E.T., ed. *Chaucer's Poetry: An Anthology for the Modern Reader*. New York: Ronald Press, 1958.

MacLaine, Allan H. *The Student's Comprehenive Guide to* The Canterbury Tales. Woodbury, NY: Barron's Educational Series, 1964.

Ross, Thomas W., ed. *The Miller's Tale: A Variorum Edition of the Works of Geoffrey Chaucer*. Norman, OK: University of Oklahoma Press, 1983.

"THE MOTHER"
(GWENDOLYN BROOKS)

"The Taboo in Gwendolyn Brooks' 'the mother'"
by Kate Falvey, New York City College of
Technology of the City University of New York

Gwendolyn Brooks' elegiac and hauntingly ruthless poem, "the mother," was controversial at the time of its composition. Brooks had to insist on its inclusion in her 1945 collection, *A Street in Bronzeville,* over the objections of her literary advocate, Richard Wright. The poem has a rare power to ignite conflicting responses and to slyly compel readers to question and qualify a too-sure initial reading. Certainly, the poem conjures the powerlessness and straitened socioeconomic conditions that compel the mother-narrator's extreme response and ultimate self-victimization. Also at stake in the poem is the meaning of motherhood itself, both as an identity and identifier—with the ferocity, the losses, the self-pity and self-justification, the guilt, and despair that comprise such a vexed, singular experience. That the poem is spoken by a non-mother, one who has aborted her children out of necessity, in defiance, with tremendous ambivalence, is the central—and perhaps misleading—irony of this lyrically charged poem.

The poem is a dramatic monologue spoken by a Bronzeville woman who has had multiple abortions. She perceives these aborted fetuses as physical facts, as children, and sees the lives they might have lived had she not intervened and "killed" (11) them. She addresses her "dim dears" (13) and offers a litany of what she stole from them and denied herself: "If I stole your births and your names, / Your straight baby tears and your games, / Your stilted or lovely loves, your tumults, your marriages, aches, and your deaths . . ." (17–19). She asks them to understand that though she is responsible for having these abortions, her choice was an equivocal one: "Believe that in my deliberateness I was not deliberate"(21). She haltingly tries to find words to convey the complexity of her choice and its aftermath: "But that too, I'm afraid, / Is faulty: oh, what shall I say, how is the truth to be said?" (27–28). The speaker concludes with a mournful and desperate adjuration: "Believe me, I loved you all" (31).

The speaker, doubtless poor, lives in Bronzeville, a black neighborhood located on Chicago's South Side. Bronzeville was a mecca for southern blacks, especially during the 1940's, when mechanization made agricultural jobs scarce. The swelling population in Bronzeville made for a cultural vitality as well as all the urban ills associated with substandard housing and overcrowding. Brooks lived in Bronzeville and gave poetic voice to the experience of marginalized blacks whose chances and choices were limited by poverty and racism. She surveyed her South Side community from a window in a small "kitchenette" apartment and found poems "walking or running, fighting or screaming or singing" wherever she looked ("Part One" 69). "[T]he mother" exposes the hard reality of many women's lives by breaking the silence and making the private, often shameful act of abortion dramatically public, while confronting the taboo subject of women's sexuality and lack of reproductive control. Brooks read "the mother," still a provocative choice in 1980, when she was invited by President Jimmy Carter and Rosalynn Carter to the White House for "A Salute to Poetry and American Poets," which, writes D.H. Melhem with some understatement, "one might interpret as a feminist gesture" (14).

There is no delicacy of expression, no euphemistic tact, no way of broaching the subject of abortion without conjuring a politicized psycho-spiritual hornet's nest. The poem begins with a bald declaration: "Abortions will not let you forget"—an unnervingly confessional statement, aggressive in its shocking matter-of-factness. The mother gives voice to what is still considered by many to be publicly unspeakable. A 2004 article in the *New York Times*, for example, calls abortion "television's most persistent taboo," even given the unbridled sexual content on hosts of mainstream programs (Aurthur 27). In 1945, the subject and the act were avowedly taboo—and certainly not likely matters for poetic treatment. Richard Wright, who was asked to review *A Street in Bronzeville* for Harper and Brothers, praised the collection, but recommended leaving out "the mother" because of its non-poetic subject matter. In a 1961 interview with Studs Terkel, Brooks says: "This poem was the only poem in the book that Richard Wright, who first looked at it, wanted to omit, and he felt that a proper poem could not be written about abortions, but I felt otherwise, and I was glad that the publishers left it in" (5). D.H. Melhem explains that Brooks' emphasis was, she felt, "not the abortion but the poverty that made for ambivalence in the mother, thwarting her maternal desire" (17).

Ungratified maternal desire finds outlet in the wrenchingly poignant evocation of the imagined lives of the children this mother "got" but "did not get" (2). Absence—the not-getting—is a befuddling keynote of the mother's monologue. She has, for herself, only the not-having and she holds this airy construction as vehemently as if she held the substance of "[t]he singers and workers that never handled the air" (4). "Not having" is a searing thematic motif that spreads throughout *A Street in Bronzeville*, with its modernist echoes of T.S. Eliot's "The Wasteland" and "The Love Song of J. Alfred Prufrock." The hard, barren ground of the Bronzeville streets stunts growth and makes for a paltry harvest. *Bronzeville* begins with these lines from "the kitchenette": "We are things of dry hours and the involuntary plan, / Grayed in, and gray. 'Dream' makes a giddy sound, not strong / Like 'rent,' 'feeding a wife,' 'satisfying a man'." In his introduction to *The Essential Gwendolyn Brooks*, James Merrill recognizes the "universal questions" within Brooks' "keen and satisfying specificity," noting that "Brooks took especially seriously the inner lives of young black women: their hopes, dreams, aspirations, disappointments." Brooks' poems ask: "How do people tend their dreams in the face of day-to-day struggle?.... How do black communities grapple with the problems of materialism, racism, and blind religiosity?" (xvii). The voice of "the mother" resonates with the voice of all motherhood, sounding the primal chords of hope and unrelenting love even in the face of unremitting losses.

Yet this mother also exhibits a darker side of motherhood as she feasts on the deliciousness of her unborn children while intimating that, had they lived, she may have harmed them: "You will never neglect or beat / Them.... You will never leave them, controlling your luscious sigh, / Return for a snack of them, with gobbling mother-eye" (5, 9, 10). The grim irony of these contradictory impulses in the wake of the speaker's abortions is disturbingly multi-layered. John Gery asserts that Brooks' title "demonstrates both the importance and impotence of conventional motherhood for a woman in the ghetto" (51). She is prey to her own ungovernable inner forces as well as to the pressures of poverty. "Yet," Gery argues, "what emerges, in both the poem's imagery and its voice, is more deeply ironic, in that the speaker is in fact a parody of 'the mother' to the extent that she expresses exactly the emotions archetypally associated with motherhood" (51). These emotions, says Gery, culminate in "the poem's horror [which] registers not only the vacuum left by abortion but also, in a grotesquely condensed manner, the delusion of power every mother is liable to experience, and then inevitably suffer from, at the loss of a child at whatever stage of its life" (51). The true horror of this poem reveals itself in the mother's self-absorption. This is *her* story and is titled as such. This mother archetype can never know her children as beings individuated from herself—which may well be a fundamental existential dilemma, an irony at the heart of all mother-child relationships.

The mother in this poem is symbolic of a more insidious taboo that Brooks' poems expose and break: our societal refusal to see members of our underclasses as fully sentient, fully human, and fully credible. Brooks gives this mother an achingly self-reproachful maternal fortitude and a hungry solicitude for her destroyed children that belie her (presumably) childless state and status. The poem moves through pregnancy, childbirth, and the lives and deaths of the speaker's imagined children, encapsulating the flux of the street life in Chicago's Bronzeville where many an aborted life is ineffectually mourned. The mother of the poem is wistful, appropriately self-recriminatory, perhaps self-serving, and jarringly insistent on her sacrificial love. In the contemporary wake of Toni Morrison's 1987 Pulitzer Prize-winning horror story, *Beloved*, a backward glance at Brooks' Bronzeville mother gives evidence of a woman who has been forced (as she suggests when she asks herself: "Though why should I whine, / Whine that the crime was other than mine?" 23–24) to abort her children, perhaps to save them from a life of grinding poverty and despair. Brooks herself wrote of the persona in her poem: "Hardly your crowned and praised and 'customary' Mother; but a Mother not unfamiliar, who decides that *she,* rather than her *World,* will kill her children. The decision is not nice, not simple, and the emotional consequences are neither nice nor simple" (Part One 184).

For too many chilling years, women subjected themselves to substandard, illegal procedures, risking their future reproductive health and their very lives in order to relinquish their pregnancies. Sought and performed in secret, abortion was an extreme, invasive, potentially agonizing and lethal route to reproductive control. The operation was not widely sanctioned by feminist decree or sanitized by medical license. Poor women with less access to medical care often attempted to self-abort by using anything sharp, scalding, or caustic. Abortions were not legal in all of the United States until the 1973 landmark Roe vs. Wade Supreme Court decision. In 1945, the Bronzeville woman of Brooks' poem, would have had recourse to few assuaging sentiments. Her multiple abortions would have been deliberate, desperate remedies induced by dire need. She would have, doubtless, been unable to care for her children. She might have been compelled to live child-free by a demanding man. Brooks offers no explanations beyond the complex of emotions voiced by the mother and offers no moral judgment. Abortion is the unabashed, unapologetic, unsentimentalized focal point of this poem, but it is the mother's sentimental apology and suffering that demands attention and scrutiny.

The first obvious question must be: can a woman who has had her pregnancies terminated claim to be a mother? Brooks declares the speaker to be a mother in both the title and the placement of the work at the forefront of the collection, just after "the old-marrieds" and "kitchenette building" and just before "southeast corner." This quartet of poems moves from the pregnant "crowding darkness" (1, 6) of "the old-marrieds," with their unvoiced possibilities, their passivity and inevitable distance from each other to the routine measly "hope" of "lukewarm" bath water ("the kitchenette" 13). The sexuality of the mother in the next poem at once upbraids and underscores the dispassionate resignation of the couple in the first poem. The mother was first a lover in order to "get" her pregnancies. She refuses her children's births only to reclaim their ghosts, her voice hopeless but filled with passion. Yet passion is not inviolate and memory will be desecrated by desertion or disinterest, so suggests the next poem, the ballad "southeast corner." The passion of building a "School of Beauty" (1) succumbs, of course, with the death of the school's proprietor—her status, her fortune gone to dust and her enterprise transmuted into a corner "tavern" (1). Madam made a splash of color in a drab world—suspect in terms of Brooks' concern with white images of beauty and the color line—but a feat no less impressive for all its ambiguities. Yet the corner still yields to the soporific of drink and the false ease it brings, the School of Beauty supplanted by the school of hard knocks, as in the preceding poem, and fertility is supplanted by the false relief of barrenness.

The second poem, "the kitchenette building," then, provides both backdrop and vantage point to the Bronzeville street scene. Reading the mother's lament within the context of the collection makes plain that abortion and squandered fertility are not only the speaker's literal experience but also emphatic metaphors for a lusterless, meager existence. The pathos of the mother "mothers" the vignettes in "Bronzeville," showing the aborted "dreams" of "the kitchenette" and the lives laid waste by "gray" and hopeless happenstance. In "the kitchenette," incipient dreams vie with the insistent, unromantic drama of survival:

> But could a dream send up through onion fumes
> Its white and violet, fight with fried potatoes
> And yesterday's garbage ripening in the hall,
> Flutter, or sing an aria down these rooms,
>
> Even if we were willing to let it in,
> Had time to warm it, keep it very clean,
> Anticipate a message, let it begin?

The unrealized "dream" in these stanzas becomes in "the mother" the dream of giving birth and mothering a child, a child who the disconsolate mother couldn't "warm" or "keep clean" and who will never "sing an aria" or even be allowed to "begin."

With the sober pronouncement of "the mother's" opening lines, Brooks' narrator signals her need to unburden herself, to dignify herself with the story of her perpetual remorse and grief. The "abortions" here, as the rest of the poem makes plain, refer to the fetuses as well as to the procedure of removing the fetuses. In the whole of the first stanza, the narrator refers to herself in the second person as a distancing "you"—a device that has the effect of implicating others as well as suggesting the mother's initial reluctance to lay complete claim to her irrevocable actions: "You remember the children. . . ." / "You will never neglect or beat / Them. . . . / You will never wind up the sucking-thumb . . . . . / You will never leave them. . . ." (1–9). The line "You remember the children you got that you did not get" (2) has an unmistakable echo of Billie Holiday's blues classic, "God Bless the Child" (written in 1939 by Holiday and Arhur Herzog, Jr.): "Them that's got shall get." The rest of Holiday's verse provides a gloss for the mother's dilemma: she "got" but only sexually and ironically. She is among the "losers" and knows her children won't ever be blessed with having their "own": "Them that's not shall lose / So the Bible said and it still is news / Mama may have, Papa may have / But God bless the child that's got his own."

Readers are often moved to acquit Brooks' mother, to empathize with her inner city struggle and to avoid stigmatizing her for her self-preserving actions, to recognize her capitulation, her need, her despair. Abortion as a solution to unwanted pregnancy, even given a post-feminist, pro-choice awareness of female marginalization and empowerment, is a strained, stultifying act, one that decries a Pyrrhic victory for women's self-determination. Brooks' Bronzeville woman makes clear that her aborted children live in her psyche, as they have lived in her body. They have become ghosts of her own longing for motherhood, and they swirl into consciousness, tangling their unlived lives with her own: "I have heard in the voices of the wind the voices of my dim killed children" (11). The poem is part cathartic vindication of the narrator's unspoken predicament: for her own unexpressed reasons, she has chosen multiple abortions. Not-mothering has become her burdensome identity in a world that sanctifies images of motherhood. Especially on the South Side of Chicago in the post-war years, the special province of motherhood was sacrosanct and immutable. Mothers, as in the culture at large, try to hold it all together as best they can, even if they are often times ineffectual. Women could be reproached, scorned, defiled, victimized—but mothers, then as now, stand on hallowed ground.

The next lines exert the palpable physicality of her pain, which is personified in the startling image of "damp small pulps with a little or with no hair" (3)—the embryonic children who have remained eternally indeterminate. "I have contracted" (12), the speaker announces—an obvious reference to labor or to her experience of the abortion. Yet coming after the line in which she mentions the wind-borne voices of the aborted children, "contracted" also implies a "shudder"—or to shrink. In the sense of compact or an obligation, as in to contract a debt, the word offers a further shade of meaning. The image of the woman holding empty air to her breasts emphasizes the theme of insufficiency and "not-having": "I have eased / My dim dears at the breasts they could never suck" (12–13). There is a hint of a rationale for the abortion in "breasts they could never suck." Of course, there were no children born so there were no nursing babies, but the woman may also be aware that she would not have been able to be a source of sustenance. The guilty, importunate, emotionally intense plea for absolution is abruptly halted with a flat, matter-of-fact observation: "Since anyhow you are dead" (24)—the sobering, inescapable truth, expressed more graphically in the harrowing closing lines of Anne Sexton's later poem, "The Abortion" (1962): "Yes, woman, such logic will lead / to loss without death. Or say what you meant, / you coward . . . this baby that I bleed" (Sexton 20).

The mother's closing exhortation—"Believe me, I loved you all. / Believe me, I knew you, though faintly, and I loved, I loved you / All"—is, writes Lillian S. Robinson, "all the more [passionate] for having no object outside her own emotions" (286). The dramatic repetition of "all" recalls well-known lines from Eliot's "The Love Song of J. Alfred Prufrock": "'I am Lazarus, come from the dead, / Come back to tell you all, I shall tell you all'" (94–95), a poem having to do with time, impotence, and isolation. That Brooks' woman *has* loved—however imperfectly, becomes her defining appeal and release. Lois Spatz, an English Professor, used both Brooks' and Sexton's poems on abortion in a seminar with medical professionals unaccustomed to thinking about the human significance of literature. The response to "the mother" was mixed and heated: "I," writes Spatz,

> full of my own white liberal guilt, was willing to sympathize and blame society for the persona's problem. But the black doctor did not sympathize with the feelings in the poem because of her own anger against the type of ghetto woman the persona represents. She represented what she considered wallowing in self-pity; she [the doctor] rejected summarily any person who would keep having abortions and rationalizing them away instead of preventing conception and taking her own life in hand. (681)

It's worth noting that the Comstock laws, which prevented the sale of any birth control and the dissemination of information about birth control, were only invalidated in 1938. Birth control methods, when available, were still very much unreliable, compounding and frustrating women's bids for reproductive control.

Abortion remains a perpetually controversial taboo. Later poems such as Sexton's and Jan Beatty's "An Abortion Attempt by My Mother" (1995) are more blatant, graphic, and personal than Brooks' earlier poem. Yet Brooks' work supplies a hard-hitting, taboo-breaking exposure of the same issues that plague women today and remains a testament to her bravery and uncompromising poetic resolve. When Studs Terkel asked Brooks in 1961 if Richard Wright might, "in later years," have reconsidered his position on omitting "the mother" from Brooks' collection, she replied, "I'd rather think he might have changed later" (5).

Works Cited

Aurthur, Kate. "Television's Most Persistent Taboo." *New York Times* July 18, 2004, sec. 2: 27.

Beatty, Jan. "An Abortion Attempt by My Mother." *Mad River*. Pittsburgh: University of Pittsburgh Press, 1995. 29.

Bloom, Harold, ed. *Gwendolyn Brooks*. Philadelphia: Chelsea House, 2000.

Brooks, Gwendolyn. *The Essential Gwendolyn Brooks*. ed. Elizabeth Alexander. New York: Library of America, 2005.

———. *The World of Gwendolyn Brooks*. New York: Harper & Row, 1971.

———. *Report from Part One*. Detroit: Broadside Press, 1972.

———. "The Mama and the Papa." Reading "the mother." *Poetry Off the Shelf: Online Journal and Podcast*. (9/16/08). http://www.poetryfoundation.org/journal/audioitem.html?id=577

Flynn, Richard. "'The Kindergarten of New Consciousness': Gwendolyn Brooks and the Social Construction of Childhood." *African American Review* Vol. 34 (Fall 2000): 483–99.

Gery, John. "Subversive Parody in the Early Poems of Gwendolyn Brooks." *South Central Review* 16.1 (Spring 1999): 44–56.

Guy-Sheftall, Beverly. "The Women of Bronzeville." *Sturdy Black Bridges: Visions of Black Women in Literature*. Ed. Roseann P. Bell, Bettye J. Parker, and Beverly Guy-Sheftall. Garden City, NY: Anchor Books. 1979. 157–70.

Johnson, Barbara. "Apostrophe, Animation, and Abortion." Diacritics 16.1
    (Spring, 1986): 29–47. Letherby, Gayle and Catherine Williams. "Non-
    Motherhood: Ambivalent Autobiographies." Feminist Studies 25.3
    (Autumn 1999): 719–28.

Kent, George E. *A Life of Gwendolyn Brooks*. Lexington: University Press of
    Kentucky, 1989.

Melhem, D.H. *Gwendolyn Brooks: Poetry and the Heroic Voice*. Lexington:
    University Press of Kentucky, 1987.

Merrill, James. "Introduction." *The Essential Gwendolyn Brooks*. ed. Elizabeth
    Alexander. New York: Library of America, 2005.

Reagan, Leslie. *When Abortion Was a Crime: Women, Medicine and Law in the United
    States, 1897–1973*. Berkeley: University of California Press, 1997. 11–12.

Robinson, Lillian S. *Sex, Class and Culture*. Bloomington: Indiana University
    Press, 1978.

Sexton, Anne. "The Abortion." *All My Pretty Ones*. Boston: Houghton Mifflin,
    1962. 20–21.

Shaw, Harry B. *Gwendolyn Brooks*. Boston: Twayne Publishers, 1980.

Smith, Gary. "Gwendolyn Brooks's *A Street in Bronzeville*, the Harlem
    Renaissance and the Mythologies of Black Women." MELUS 10.3
    (Autumn 1983): 33–46.

———. "Paradise Regained: The Children of Gwendolyn Brooks's Bronzeville."
    A Life Distilled: Gwendolyn Brooks, Her Poetry and Fiction. Ed. Maria
    Mootry and Gary Smith. Urbana: University of Illinois Press, 1987.
    128–39.

Spatz, Lois S. "Six Women: A Demonstration of the Uses of Poetry in a Health
    Science Curriculum." College English 44.7 (November 1982): 674–84.

Spillers, Hortense. "Gwendolyn the Terrible: Propositions on Eleven Poems."
    1979. *A Life Distilled: Gwendolyn Brooks, Her Poetry and Fiction*. Ed.
    Maria Mootry and Gary Smith. Urbana: University of Illinois Press,
    1987. 224–35.

Terkel, Studs. "A Conversation with Gwendolyn Brooks." 1961. *Conversations
    with Gwendolyn Brooks*. Ed. Gloria Wade Gayle. Jackson: University Press
    of Mississippi, 2003.

Wheeler, Leslie. "Heralding the Clear Obscure: Gwendolyn Brooks and
    Apostrophe." Callaloo 24.1 (Winter 2001): 227–35.

Willis, Ellen. "Putting Women Back into the Abortion Debate." *Current Issues
    and Enduring Questions: A Guide to Critical Thinking and Argument, with
    Readings*, 6th ed. Eds. Sylvan Barnet and Hugo Bedau. Boston: Bedford/
    St. Martin's, 2002. 464–70.

MOURNING BECOMES ELECTRA
(EUGENE O'NEILL)

❦

"'I Forgive Myself!': Escaping the Ever-Present Past in Eugene O'Neill's *Mourning Becomes Electra*"
by Scott Walters, University of North Carolina at Asheville

It is fitting that Eugene O'Neill's 1931 epic, multi-part family drama *Mourning Becomes Electra* should appear in a volume of essays focused on taboos in literature, for the play contains more prohibited desires and forbidden acts per page, I suspect, than just about any work of dramatic literature in the Western canon. Indeed, by the time the three parts of the play have reached an end, the tally of taboos is impressive indeed: one Electra Complex (Lavinia and her father, Ezra), two Oedipus Complexes (Orin and his mother, Christine; and perhaps more obliquely, Adam and the mother-daughter duo of Christine and Lavinia, both of whom closely resemble Adam's mother, Marie Brantome), one instance of near brother-sister incest (Orin and Lavinia), two murders (Christine kills her husband, Ezra; and Orin and Lavinia kill their mother's lover, Adam Brant), and two suicides (Christine and Orin). In fact, at the end of the play there is only a single major character left standing: O'Neill's titular Electra-figure, Lavinia. And even she, as the curtain falls, is about to lock herself inside the family mansion never to return, a sort of living suicide, if you will.

However, don't be overly distracted by this festival of the forbidden. O'Neill's play is not "about" the taboos themselves, any more than

Sophocles' *Oedipus Rex* is "about" patricide and incest (Freud to the contrary) or *Hamlet* is "about" fratricide and regicide. Rather, the sensationalist events of the plot are the outward manifestations of a toxic and extreme belief system that permeates the characters' past, present, and future. It is this worldview, which O'Neill ascribes to the Puritan values of the New England patrician family of Mannon, that is the focus of O'Neill's play and the true antagonist of *Mourning Becomes Electra*. This worldview is characterized by an obsessive focus on sexuality and past actions, one's own and those of others. Like the Greek gods from whose rivalries and curses the characters of ancient tragedies struggled to free themselves, the dour and oppressive Puritan God likewise dominates the future of the Mannons by chaining them to the past.

Their past, like that of the House of Atreus which serves as the source material for O'Neill's modern variation, is dominated by a curse the nature of which differentiates the ancient story from the modern. As Barrett H. Clark notes, "externally, [*Mourning Becomes Electra*] is a retelling of the tragic tale of Agamemnon and Clytemnestra, Orestes and Electra . . . [but] here no mortal has offended a divinity; it is an American New Englander who has transgressed the moral code of his time and people . . ."(Clark 123). Just so, and yet the contrast goes deeper than that, for in O'Neill's quest to write a "modern psychological drama using one of the old legend plots of Greek tragedy," (Clark 128) he has not only secularized the curse, but he has moved its source from an external action to an internal belief, which has the effect of making the curse more powerful because more inescapable. In order to make this contrast plain, an examination of the backstories for *The Orestia* and *Mourning Becomes Electra* might be helpful.

The central conflict between Aeschylus' brothers Thyestes and Atreus, like that between O'Neill's David and Abe Mannon, is centered on sexual rivalry. Among other things, Thyestes has an affair with Atreus' wife, and is banished; David, however, had an affair not with his brother Abe's wife but with "the Canuck nurse girl who was taking care of father's little sister who died, and [he] had to marry her because she was going to have a baby." Abe, perhaps reacting with moral fervor fueled by jealousy, "put them both out of the house . . ."(O'Neill 239). However, this is where the stories diverge. When Atreus finds out about his wife's affair with Thyestes, he seeks revenge: pretending forgiveness, Atreus invited Thyestes and his young sons to return for a banquet. When Thyestes accepts, Atreus extracts his revenge by killing Thyestes' sons and serving them to his unsuspecting guest as the main course of the homecoming feast. When Thyestes discovers this abomination after having eaten his fill, he curses Atreus and his descendents, thus setting up the events that make up *The Oresteia*. The curse, then, is based not only on an act of extreme violence, the killing of a man's progeny, but on the horrible violation of the taboo against cannibalism. In short, this is no ordinary offense! In addition, the curse comes from the victim of this act, not the perpetrator.

For Abe Mannon, however, there is no similar violent transgression, nor is there an actual curse, for that matter. Rather, David and his paramour Marie are banished to "the West," apparently with little resistance, after which Abe cheats David out of most of his inheritance, leaving him destitute. In a final act of disgust and rejection, Abe proceeds to tear down his own home and build a new one "because he wouldn't live where his brother had disgraced the family." (O'Neill 239). The house he built resembles, to Christine, the "whited sepulcher" of the Bible, "which indeed appear beautiful outward, but are within full of dead men's bones, and of all uncleanness." (Matthew 23:27). It is, Christine says, a "temple for [Abe's] hatred," with its "pagan temple front stuck like a mask on Puritan gray ugliness!" (O'Neill 237). In summary, the House of Mannon has been poisoned not by any curse laid upon it by the victim, David Mannon, but rather by Abe Mannon himself, and his Puritan hatred which is passed down from generation to generation through the familial mansion itself.

Another revealing departure from the Aeschylean tragedy is O'Neill's treatment of the Furies, ancient gods whose role is to punish those who violate long-standing taboos. Much of the third part of *The Oresteia* is taken up with Orestes' trial for matricide, in which the Furies serve as prosecutor. In *Mourning Becomes Electra*, in contrast, the Furies take the form of ancestors whose paintings hang in the mansion, and whose way of viewing the world has been passed from generation to generation as internalized guilt. The accusations that would be spoken by the Furies in Aeschylus' play are spoken by the Mannons themselves in O'Neill's play, accusations that are as likely to be directed at the self as at others. And unlike the blood-thirsty Furies, from whom Orestes is freed at the end of the trial and who are ultimately transformed into the benevolent Eumenides, the overwhelming guilt of the Mannons seems to be inescapable, because they are themselves prosecutor, defense, judge, and jury. Heredity is destiny in O'Neill's world; the past is the future, and the present is poisoned by it. There is no escape.

The central role played in O'Neill's play by the Electra-character, Lavinia, is also a significant departure from the source material, and demands further investigation. Electra appears in only the middle play of *The Oresteia*, and after she gains Orestes' commitment to murder Clytemnestra, she virtually disappears. She is not present for the return of her father, Agamamenon, from the Trojan War in part one, nor is she brought to trial along with her brother Orestes for murdering Clytemnestra in part three. Even in the play Euripides wrote that is named after her, Electra's ultimate fate is to be forced to marry Orestes' friend, Pylades, a rather tepid end to such an important character. O'Neill seems to have agreed, writing in his notebook about his own play, "have given Yankee Electra tragic end worthy of her" (Floyd 401). That end, as noted previously, is to be the only surviving Mannon. As O'Neill's biographers, Arthur and Barbara Gelb, write "Finally Lavinia condemns herself to a life locked away from the world—bound, as she declares, 'to the Mannon dead' . . ." This is significant, the Gelbs assert, because it paralleled O'Neill's own life. Like Lavinia, they argue, "O'Neill felt himself bound to and haunted by his own dead. "I'm the last Mannon," says Lavinia at the end of the play, echoing O'Neill's mournful cry to a friend, soon after [his brother] Jamie's death, "I'm the last of the O'Neills!" (Arthur Gelb & Barbara Gelb 721).

Arguing that *Mourning Becomes Electra* was "yet another examination of the emotional fabric of the O'Neill family"—an observation made by other critics as well—the Gelbs go on, in a statement that is as daring as it is insightful, to say that "As [O'Neill] conceived it, the legend [of the House of Atreus] now fitted into his own specific frame of reference. Lavinia (*here a symbolic representation of O'Neill himself*) loses, in rapid succession (and in the same order as O'Neill) first her father, then her mother, then her brother." Indeed, they continue, "Although Lavinia is a woman, she is, in many ways, one of the most personally revealing characters O'Neill ever created, and her final speech is one of the most soul-baring O'Neill ever wrote; it incorporates both his consuming preoccupation with the act of suicide and his mordant belief in the inevitability of an even crueler self-punishment." (Arthur Gelb & Barbara Gelb 721).

In this speech of Lavinia's, the Gelbs argue, O'Neill "forecasts his own fate in the last years of his life" when he was facing his own dead as he wrote his autobiographical *Long Day's Journey Into Night*. "I'm not going the way Mother and Orin went," Lavinia asserts in the final speech to which the Gelbs refer, meaning she will not commit suicide, because

> That's escaping punishment. And there's no one left to punish me. I'm the last Mannon. I've got to punish myself. Living alone here with the dead is a worse act of justice than death or prison! I'll never go out or see anyone! I'll have the shutters nailed closed so no sunlight can ever get in. I'll live alone with the dead, and keep their secrets, and let them hound me, until the curse is paid out and the last Mannon is let die! (O'Neill 376)

Such an autobiographical interpretation is hard to resist, especially given how much of O'Neill's oeuvre has roots in his own experience, and the Gelbs' interpretation certainly makes sense of Lavinia's central role as the play's protagonist. And indeed, other critics have also taken an autobiographical view, but have found O'Neill hiding in other characters than Lavinia. Richard F. Moorton, Jr., for instance, in his essay "The Author as Oedipus in *Mourning Becomes Electra* and *Long Day's Journey Into Night*," argues that Ezra represents O'Neill's father, James, Christine is his mother, Mary, and O'Neill is the mother-obsessed Orin. But who, then, is Lavinia, who stands at the play's center? She is, rather improbably given Lavinia's defiant character, "a younger version of O'Neill's mother." (Moorton 312). And the biographical identifications don't stop there. What of Marie Brantome, whose pregnancy sets off the Mannon curse? O'Neill's mother, too. And Adam Brant, Brantome's sailor-son who is Chistine's and Lavinia's lover? Why, O'Neill himself, in his former life as a sailor. In Moorton's interpretation, we soon find ourselves in a familial house of mirrors baffling in its labyrinthine complexity.

However, while finding a one-to-one correspondence between real people and fictional characters can be confusing and, in my opinion, not very helpful in understanding the play itself, Moorton's more general observation that "All the Mannon men look alike, as do all the Mannon women" is illuminating. (Moorton 319). O'Neill repeatedly makes this family resemblance explicit through his stage directions and dialogue, even extending it outside the immediate family to Adam Brantome, who looks like Ezra and Orin, and his mother, Marie, who has the same seductive hair as Christine and Lavinia. Even Seth, the family gardener, has taken on the mask-like characteristics of the Mannon family! "Ultimately," Moorton summarizes insightfully, "the Mannons may be reduced to the same tragic couple." (Moorton 319). The effect of this marked physical resemblance between characters is to erase their individual identities and replace them with that of archetypes.

To understand this, we must go back to roots of the play in the curse that has been passed down from father to son, husband to wife, parent to child. Each generation is desperately trying to escape the curse of the Puritan mores that have shaped their approach to life, a worldview that values Thanatos over Eros, death over life; that thrives on hatred rather than love, and, perhaps most importantly, that rejects sexuality as sinful and damning. "That's always been the Mannon's way of thinking," Ezra says. "They went to the white meeting-house on Sabbaths and meditated on death. Life was dying. Being born was starting to die. Death was being born." (O'Neill 269). To embrace death means to reject life, and thus to reject the sexuality that leads to new life, which is at the very heart of the Mannon curse, and is the cause of all of the violence and hatred that fills the play. Sex is the catalyst for every condemnation, every act of violence, every rejection.

Each grouping, each identical tragic couple, makes their own attempt to escape the Mannon curse, but none are successful until finally, after multiple murders, suicides, and emotional self-destruction, only one character is left to claim the final, ironic victory over the past. O'Neill takes us through a process of spiritual exorcism that begins in punishment, proceeds to flight, and is ended by defiant resignation.

The first attempts to break the curse use condemnation, punishment, and destruction as their primary weapon. Confronted with sexuality in the form of the "foreign" French Canuck nurse and his smitten brother, Abe Mannon, like the Old Testament God faced with the sin of Adam and Eve, condemns his brother's act, punishes the guilty with banishment and poverty, and destroys the very house in which the sin occurred to prevent infection. But despite the seeming clean sweep, the curse remains. Children must be sired to further the Mannon line, which means sexuality must be enjoined, with the attendant Puritan disgust. In short, for the House of Mannon to survive, it must re-embrace the curse.

Thus, the next generation begins anew. Ezra, Abe's son, marries another exotic wife—Christine is French and Dutch—but their love turns to hate, predictably, on their wedding night when, as Christine tells Ezra, "You filled me with disgust." (O'Neill 275). Her disgust leads to a new form of banishment and impoverishment: during the time she is pregnant with Orin, Ezra goes off to fight the Mexican War. When Orin is born in Ezra's absence, she creates a new world for herself and Orin to inhabit together. When Ezra returns from the war, he complains "I was hardly alive for you anymore." (O'Neill 270). Banished from his wife's love, Ezra turns to his professional life—fittingly for a Mannon, he becomes a judge.

Meanwhile, David Mannon's son, Adam, who physically resembles both Ezra and Orin Mannon, has seen his father, a violent alcoholic, commit suicide. Adam escapes to sea, but returns to find his mother destitute and starving. Desperate for money, she had appealed to Ezra for financial help, but the appeal was met with silence. When she dies in Adam's arms, he vows revenge. Returning to New England, Adam falls in love with Christine and she with him, and an affair ensues. When Ezra returns from being a General in the Civil War, they have decided to kill him. Christine provokes a heart attack in Ezra, and then substitutes poison for his heart medicine. Thus, the punishment for Ezra Mannon's wedding night sexuality is, like David Mannon before him, first banishment, and then death.

Lavinia however, has discovered her mother's affair with Adam, and so is suspicious of her father's sudden death. When Orin returns from the Civil War to find his father dead, Lavinia proves to him that their mother has been unfaithful. Orin, who has a classic mother fixation, feels betrayed by her affair. Once again, the pattern is played out: sexuality leads to death. Orin and Lavinia kill Adam.

As with *The Oresteia*, the reader has a sense that this pattern could continue indefinitely with a recurring cycle of discovery, condemnation, punishment and death, each character resembling every other, each reaction to sexuality mirroring every other reaction. Aeschylus, however, breaks the cycle by substituting a trial for personal revenge. Indeed, that is the point of Aeschylus' story: to promote Athens' new legal mode of resolving conflict. But O'Neill purposely avoids this option by making certain that the murders are designed so as not to draw the attention of the police (Adam, for instance, is killed by Orin on his boat in what looks like a robbery). Without an outside force to provoke change, breaking the pattern must come from one of the Mannons themselves.

Christine, a Mannon by marriage, is the first to make the attempt. Faced with the sense that the Puritanism of the Mannons is going to destroy any chance of happiness that she has available to her, Christine seeks the ultimate escape: like David Mannon before her, she commits suicide. She *chooses* death, rather than waiting for it to be imposed from without. In this, she exercises her freedom, which puts her outside the determinism of the Mannon curse.

Orin, tormented by a not unfounded belief that by killing Adam he also killed his mother, is ready to follow his mother's example. However, Lavinia seizes control and, through sheer force of will, forces them both to take another route: she and Orin leave the poisoned atmosphere of the family estate entirely, and travel to the South Sea Islands.

These islands, according to O'Neill, represent all that Puritan New England is not: "release, peace, security, beauty, freedom of conscience, sinlessness, etc." (Falk 121) The effect on Lavinia is powerful. Her severe, angular image and all-black clothing ("I was dead then," she says of her previous mode of dress [O'Neill 345]) has given way to curves, sensuality, and color. In fact, she has come to look like her mother, and Orin his father. Her attitude has changed as well. "I loved those islands," she tells her would-be fiancé Peter.

> They finished setting me free. There was something there mysterious and beautiful—a good spirit—of love—coming out of the land and sea. It made me forget death. There was no hereafter. There was only this world—the warm earth in the moonlight—the trade wind in the coco palms—the surf on the reef—the fires at night and the drum throbbing in my heart—the natives dancing naked and innocent—without knowledge of sin! (O'Neill 348)

To the surprised and delighted Peter, she blurts out "Oh, Peter, hold me close to you! I want to feel love! Love is all beautiful! I never used to know that! I was a fool!" And then she "kisses him passionately." (O'Neill 348). Having once escaped the power of the Mannon estate and its curse, she never wants to return. "We'll be married soon, won't we," she asks Peter, "and settle out in the country away from folks and their evil talk. We'll make an island for ourselves on land, and we'll have children and love them and teach them to love life so that they can never be possessed by hate and death! . . . I want to be rid of the past." (O'Neill 349).

But it is not to be. Orin, consumed by guilt, has written all the crimes of the Mannons into a book, a confession of the Mannon sins, including his and Lavinia's murder of Adam. He will destroy it only if she agrees to give up Peter and, as a way of making sure she never leaves him, consent to have sex with him. "You would feel as guilty then as I do!" he reasons. (O'Neill 365). Lavinia reacts with disgust and rage at his suggestion, and rejects his plea that they confess their crimes and accept their punishment. "I hate you!" she shouts. "I wish you were dead! You're too vile to live!" And she concludes, "You'd kill yourself if you weren't a coward!" (O'Neill 365). Seeing the escape hatch open, Orin accepts her directive, following his mother's path and forgiving her trespasses along the way.

But Lavinia is not so easily beaten. "I'm not asking God or anybody for forgiveness," she cries defiantly. "I forgive myself!" (O'Neill 372). Although she resumes wearing mourning clothes following Orin's suicide, and her face and body have once again assumed their angular, masklike look, she is still determined to marry Peter and escape the curse of the Mannons. "Love can't live in it," she says of the house. "We'll go away and leave it alone to die—and we'll forget the dead." (O'Neill 372). But the Mannon ancestors are not to be gotten rid of that easily. Lavinia feels doubt creeping into her relationship with Peter, the shadow of Orin and the Mannon dead coming between them. In desperation, she pleads with Peter to marry her that day, without waiting. "Kiss me! Hold me close! Want me! Want me so much you'd murder anyone to have me! I did that—for you! Take me in this house of the dead and love me! Our love will drive the dead away! It will shame them back into death!" Carried away completely, she cries out "Want me! Take, me Adam!" (O'Neill 374). And in that moment when she calls Peter the name of the man she really wanted, Adam, the man her mother took from her, the spell is broken and she realizes the impossibility of escape. "I can't marry you, Peter," she says numbly to her stunned and baffled beau. "Love isn't permitted to me. The dead are too strong!" (O'Neill 374).

Nevertheless, she will not be defeated by the dead, but instead will remain defiant. In her final speech, quoted above, she takes her stand to defeat the Mannon curse. While she will not be allowed to grasp the paradise she found in the South Seas, not be allowed to find her way to an innocent, healthy love, she will break the curse nonetheless through her isolation. There will be no more Mannons, no more sexuality necessary to bring into being another generation, and thus no more hunted and haunted children polluting the earth with their condemnation, punishment, and destruction. "I'll live alone with the dead, and keep their secrets, and let them hound me, until the curse is paid out and the last Mannon is let to die!" (O'Neill 376).

It is a Pyrrhic victory, but a victory nonetheless, one that, while not restoring life and health, at least ends death and disease. The final sound of the play is the sound of the shutters slamming closed and the door shutting behind Lavinia. Unlike Aeschylus' play, O'Neill's Furies are not transformed into benevolent Eumenides—that would be too easy for a modern audience to accept, and certainly too easy for the tormented O'Neill to do so—but they are confronted, and they do, at last, die.

And perhaps that, for O'Neill, is the best that one can hope for.

Works Cited

Clark, Barrett H. *Eugene O'Neill: The Man and His Plays*. 1926. New York: Dover, 1947.

Falk, Doris V. *Eugene O'Neill and the Tragic Tension*, 2nd ed. Staten Island, NY: Gordian Press, 1981.

Floyd, Virginia. *The Plays of Eugene O'Neill, A New Assessment*. New York: Frederick Ungar, 1985.

Gelb, Arthur, and Barbara Gelb. *O'Neill*. New York: Harper & Row, 1974.

Moorton, Richard F. "The Author as Oedipus in *Mourning becomes Electra* and *Long Day's Journey Into Night*." *Papers on Language and Literature* 25 (Summer 1989): 304–25.

O'Neill, Eugene. *Three Plays of Eugene O'Neill*. New York: Vintage Books, 1958.

OEDIPUS TYRANNUS
(SOPHOCLES)

❧

"Chapter Nine"
by Friedrich Nietzsche,
in *The Birth of Tragedy* (1872)

INTRODUCTION

In this short excerpt from his influential study of tragedy, German philosopher Friedrich Nietzsche contemplates the many roles Oedipus fulfills in Sophocles' *The Theban Plays*. Oedipus blindly transgresses the most powerful familial taboos–patricide and incest–and this blindness becomes his punishment. But, as Nietzsche observes, Oedipus is a truth seeker, an Apollonian figure who redeems his society. Thus the taboo and Oedipus' desire for knowledge constitute, for Nietzsche, a single act against nature, an "extraordinary counter-naturalness." "Broken by prophetic and magical powers," the "spell of nature" is broken by Oedipus, and audiences are made to "glance at the abyss."

∝

Whatever rises to the surface in the dialogue of the Apollonian part of Greek tragedy, appears simple, transparent, beautiful. In this sense

Nietzsche, Friedrich. "Chapter Nine." *The Complete Works of Friedrich Nietzsche, Vol. 1: The Birth of Tragedy, or, Hellenism and Pessimism.* 1872. Ed. Oscar Levy. Trans. William August Hausmann. London: George Allen & Unwin, 1923. 72–75.

the dialogue is a copy of the Hellene, whose nature reveals itself in the dance, because in the dance the greatest energy is merely potential, but betrays itself nevertheless in flexible and vivacious movements. The language of the Sophoclean heroes, for instance, surprises us by its Apollonian precision and clearness, so that we at once imagine we see into the innermost recesses of their being, and marvel not a little that the way to these recesses is so short. But if for the moment we disregard the character of the hero which rises to the surface and grows visible—and which at bottom is nothing but the light-picture cast on a dark wall, that is, appearance through and through,—if rather we enter into the myth which projects itself in these bright mirrorings, we shall of a sudden experience a phenomenon which bears a reverse relation to one familiar in optics. When, after a vigorous effort to gaze into the sun, we turn away blinded, we have dark-coloured spots before our eyes as restoratives, so to speak; while, on the contrary, those light-picture phenomena of the Sophoclean hero,—in short, the Apollonian of the mask,—are the necessary productions of a glance into the secret and terrible things of nature, as it were shining spots to heal the eye which dire night has seared. Only in this sense can we hope to be able to grasp the true meaning of the serious and significant notion of "Greek cheerfulness"; while of course we encounter the misunderstood notion of this cheerfulness, as resulting from a state of unendangered comfort, on all the ways and paths of the present time.

The most sorrowful figure of the Greek stage, the hapless *Oedipus*, was understood by Sophocles as the noble man, who in spite of his wisdom was destined to error and misery, but nevertheless through his extraordinary sufferings ultimately exerted a magical, wholesome influence on all around him, which continues effective even after his death. The noble man does not sin; this is what the thoughtful poet wishes to tell us: all laws, all natural order, yea, the moral world itself, may be destroyed through his action, but through this very action a higher magic circle of influences is brought into play, which establish a new world on the ruins of the old that has been overthrown. This is what the poet, in so far as he is at the same time a religious thinker, wishes to tell us: as poet, he shows us first of all a wonderfully complicated legal mystery, which the judge slowly unravels, link by link, to his own destruction. The truly Hellenic delight at this dialectical loosening is so great, that a touch of surpassing cheerfulness is thereby communicated to the entire play, which everywhere blunts the edge of the horrible presuppositions of the procedure. In the "Oedipus at Colonus" we find the same cheerfulness, elevated, however, to an infinite transfiguration: in contrast to the aged king, subjected to an excess of misery, and exposed solely as a *sufferer* to all that befalls him, we have here a supermundane cheerfulness, which descends from a divine sphere and intimates to us that in his purely passive attitude the hero attains his highest activity, the influence of which extends far beyond his life, while his earlier conscious musing and striving led him only to passivity. Thus, then, the legal knot of the fable of Oedipus, which to mortal eyes appears indissolubly entangled, is slowly unravelled—and the profoundest human joy comes upon us in the presence of this divine counterpart of dialectics. If this explanation does justice to the poet, it may still be asked whether the substance of the myth is thereby exhausted; and here it turns out that the entire conception of the poet is nothing but the light-picture which healing nature holds up to us after a glance into the abyss. Oedipus, the murderer of his father, the husband of his mother, Oedipus, the interpreter of the riddle of the Sphinx! What does the mysterious triad of these deeds of destiny tell us? There is a primitive popular belief, especially in Persia, that a wise Magian can be born only of incest: which we have forthwith to interpret to ourselves with reference to the riddle-solving and mother-marrying Oedipus, to the effect that when the boundary of the present and future, the rigid law of individuation and, in general, the intrinsic spell of nature, are broken by prophetic and magical powers, an extraordinary counternaturalness—as, in this case, incest—must have preceded as a cause; for how else could one force nature to surrender her secrets but by victoriously opposing her, *i.e.*, by means of the Unnatural? It is this intuition which I see imprinted in the awful triad of the destiny of Oedipus: the very man who solves the riddle of nature—that double-constituted Sphinx—must also, as the murderer of his father and husband of his mother, break the holiest laws of nature. Indeed, it seems as if the myth sought to whisper into our ears that wisdom, especially Dionysian wisdom, is an unnatural abomination, and that whoever, through his knowledge, plunges nature into an abyss of annihilation, must also experience the dissolution of nature in himself. "The sharpness of wisdom turns round upon the sage: wisdom is a crime against nature": such terrible expressions does the myth call out to us: but the Hellenic poet touches like a sunbeam the sublime and formidable Memnonian statue of the myth, so that it suddenly begins to sound in Sophoclean melodies.

THE PICTURE OF DORIAN GRAY
(OSCAR WILDE)

❧

"Taboo in *The Picture of Dorian Gray*"
by Arundhati Sanyal, Seton Hall University

Oscar Wilde's novella *The Picture of Dorian Gray* (1890) explores the relationship between an artist, Basil Hallward, and the subject he paints: a beautiful young man named Dorian Gray who is obsessed with preserving his youth. Under the influence of Lord Henry Wotton, who sees life's purpose as the pursuit of beauty and sensual fulfillment, Dorian wishes that the portrait painted by Hallward will age while Dorian does not. Ultimately, as Dorian engages in hedonistic acts, the image in the portrait ages, gradually becoming more and more disfigured, allowing Dorian to retain his unaffected youth and beauty. As the novel's characters interact and as Dorian changes, a profound discussion of art and its relationship to our moral, ethical, and psychological selves ensues. From this discussion, Dorian Gray emerges as both an innocent upon whom Hallward and Wotton impose meaning and also a Faustian figure championing the taboo.

In his work *The Hero with a Thousand Faces*, Joseph Campbell quotes James Frazer's words connecting the sacred and the taboo within the heroic figure:

> Apparently holiness, magical virtue, taboo, or whatever we may call that mysterious quality which is supposed to pervade sacred or tabooed persons, is conceived by the primitive philosopher as a physical substance or fluid, . . . it is necessary in the interest of the general safety to keep it within narrow bounds, lest

breaking out it should blast, blight, and destroy whatever it comes into contact with. (Campbell 224–25)

Dorian is both a figure representing the sacred virtues of art and also a hedonist, dedicated to gratifying his senses. The word "taboo" can refer both to Dorian's prohibited actions that require concealment as well as his "sacred" pursuit of artistic beauty. Dorian's portrait symbolizes the sacred and taboo experiences he shares with Basil, Henry, and Sybil.

The novel is primarily about the relationship between the artist, his subject, and the created work of art. To that end, the first few chapters give us a glimpse of the complex relationship between Basil Hallward and his subject Dorian Gray. At the beginning of the novel, Basil is protective of his painting as well as his subject, because he fears he has revealed too much of himself: "The reason I will not exhibit this picture is that I am afraid I have shown with it the secret of my own soul" (Wilde 188). The relationship between Basil and Dorian has subsumed that of the artist and his subject, so much so that Basil feels overwhelmed with love for him. Basil's reticence to paint Dorian is overcome by this affection: "I knew that I had come face to face with some one whose mere personality was so fascinating that, if I allowed it to do so, it would absorb my whole nature, my whole soul, my very art itself" (Wilde 189). In confronting Dorian as a subject of his painting, Basil recognizes that he must confront his innermost feelings. Since the process of creation involves revealing and recreating this self, Basil understands that such a revelation means giving up his own self; hence he feels the need to conceal the painting from the rest of the world. Thus in the first few pages of the novel the painting has become a means of both presenting and concealing the self to and from the rest of the world.

Both Basil and Henry attempt to influence the impressionable young Dorian.[1] While he is the subject of Basil's painting, he also becomes the receiver of Henry's philosophy of "new Hedonism," and there is a struggle between Basil and Henry for Dorian's attention. Henry, in explaining the meaning and danger of such influence, deems it "immoral" because "to influence a person is to give him one's own soul. . . . He becomes an echo of some one else's music, an actor of a part that has not been written for him" (Wilde 198). This is the obverse of Basil's reaction to the painting where he had revealed too much of his own soul through Dorian's likeness. Just as Basil fears losing himself and disclosing the contents of his soul, Henry notes the danger influence poses to Dorian, who risks losing his ability to make his own moral decisions by submitting to the personality of others. In both cases, boundaries between self and "other" are crossed, defiling the sanctity of the self-contained soul. Thus, the powerful effect Basil and Henry have on Dorian's development and, conversely, Dorian's power to influence the art and soul of Basil, are both taboo transgressions that threaten our sanctified notions of individuality.

Dorian's pristine beauty and peculiarly "unconscious" innocence are irresistible to both painter and philosopher. In the second chapter, we are told that his beauty is such that it reminds the spectator of the beginning of things, of an innocent, prelapsarian "candor of youth" as well as "all youth's passionate purity . . . unspotted from the world" (Wilde 197). Both of his admirers are drawn to this state of "blankness," which makes Dorian the perfect receptor to all influence as well as profoundly vulnerable: his personality is not strong enough to counter the influence Henry will bring to bear on him. The chapter where these two characters meet makes the outcome of their encounter clear. In what is clearly a scene of covert seduction, Henry Wotton gets the upper hand over Basil in their struggle to court the affections of Dorian, who is clearly drawn in by the amoral and hedonistic philosophy Henry espouses. Unlike Basil, Henry is fascinated by how easily he is able to cross boundaries of the self and sway Dorian with his ideas. In the following passage Henry revels in the God-like re-creation of Dorian that his influence can bring about:

> There was something terribly enthralling in the exercise of influence. No other activity was like it. To project one's soul into some gracious form, and let it tarry there for a moment; to hear one's own intellectual views echoed back to one with all the added music of passion and youth; to convey one's temperament into another as though it were a subtle fluid or a strange perfume: there was a real joy in that (Wilde: 1891 34).

Henry savors his projection of self onto Dorian's pristine, "unspotted" psyche, and the reader senses erotic undertones in the passage. Just as Dorian plays the part of a destructive tempter in his relationship with Basil, Henry threatens the integrity of Dorian's soul, seducing him with his pleasure-seeking philosophy of life.[2] Henry's education of

Dorian is described in sensual and suggestive metaphors. Such metaphors emphasize the taboo nature of Henry's influence over Dorian.

The relationship Dorian develops between himself and his portrait is a direct consequence of Henry's seduction. Henry makes Dorian conscious of his beauty and insists this narcissism is essential to his understanding of the world. Thus Dorian begins to understand himself in terms of the effect his beauty has on the senses of his spectators, so much so that he is able to objectify himself when he gazes at his portrait, becoming enamored with himself. Like the mythic Narcissus, whose tragic fate is sealed when he gazes lovingly at his own reflection for the first time, when Dorian studies the painting, "A look of joy came into his eyes, as if he had recognized himself for the first time. . . . The sense of his own beauty came on him like a revelation" (Wilde 204). Narcissus is driven mad by his dual role as lover and loved; similarly, this moment destroys Dorian's sense of wholeness. He is now able to perceive himself as two distinct selves: one who possesses immutable beauty and the other who has knowledge and soul and consequently is subject to the ravages of time.[3] He has to live a double life. Unlike Narcissus, who instinctively reached out and fell in love with his image, Dorian hates his portrait; it fills him with regret and jealousy ("I shall grow old, and horrid, and dreadful. But this picture will always remain young"). Narcissus wishes to be joined with his image, while Dorian wishes only for the eternal youth that his image seems to possess: "If it was only the other way! If it was I who were to be always young, and the picture that were to grow old!" (Wilde 205). This fracturing of the self into a perfect physical form and a representation of this form that reflects the corruption of Dorian's subsequent life complicates and blurs the boundary between life and art.[4]

Following the dictates of Henry's hedonism, Dorian experiences every form of decadent pleasure and sensation imaginable. Through his journey, the physical form Dorian projects onto the world is the one Basil had been overwhelmed by—a façade of purity, youth, and innocence—while the actual state of his soul and its incessant degeneration is reflected on the painting itself. This allows Dorian the gift of concealment; his experiences are not revealed by his body and thus he is able to lead a life that seemingly denies his debauchery. The metaphor of the painting in the novel, which merges art and life, allows Dorian to violate taboos while avoiding moral consequences. Dorian survives public censure because he remains physically perfect. He alone is able to see the moral degeneration that takes place and is reflected in the painting. Thus, Wilde makes Dorian's self-realization much more personal and psychological than the public "ethics of shame" that Wilde himself had to face in his public trials for homosexual relationships. When Dorian first notices the changing in his portrait, he lays out the implications as follows: "[The picture] held the secret of his life, and told his story. It had taught him to love his own beauty. Would it teach him to loathe his own soul?" (Wilde 228). In other words, because Dorian is allowed to cross the boundary and see his soul as a separate entity from his body, he is able to witness and even appreciate its gradual decay as "a guide to him through life, [it] would be to him what holiness was to some, and conscience to others, and the fear of God to us all" (Wilde 231). At this point, Wilde allows art to be something he had believed all his life it should not: a cautionary tale, a moral beacon that guides character. The rest of Wilde's novel reveals to readers the folly of Dorian's attitude toward art.

Dorian's disastrous relationship with Sybil shows that the changing image of the portrait has not taught him to take responsibility for his decisions. Through Henry's influence, Dorian is able to dissociate himself from every action and relationship by adopting the privileged perspective of an artist. He distances himself from the responsibility that every personal relationship imposes by living his life as though it were a work of art. He loves Sybil not for her personality, but for her ability to successfully become other personae or characters through her acting. The relationship is a test case of the extent to which Dorian has adopted an artistic take on his own life. Ironically, Sybil's love for Dorian spurs her to reject the artificial, unauthentic life she had led before they met. In Sybil's response to Dorian, Wilde is parodying the sentimental and facile treatment of romantic love in literature as a way to reach higher moral ground and reject the artificiality of art. Her intense love for Dorian makes her a bad actress; she loses her protean ability to "be" other people. Dorian can only see this loss of artistic skill in Sybil and fails to understand how she has been transformed by his love to see the world of art and theater as false. Since he loved her because she was a good actress, Dorian ceases to love her when she learns to be herself. So he castigates her with his question, "What are you without your art?" (Wilde 225). Her inability to answer it incites her to commit suicide. Dorian, looking back at this evening, correctly understands his responsibility for this

death: "So I have murdered Sibyl Vane" (Wilde 233). Henry justifies
Sibyl's death as the inevitable result of her lapse in art, which makes
it possible for Dorian to dismiss his guilt and continue his single-
minded life of pleasurable pursuits and no consequences. On the very
same night that he has admitted to having killed one who loved him
deeply, Dorian is able to visit the opera and appreciate the acting skills
of other, better actresses than Sybil.

Sybil's death marks the beginning of Dorian's descent. Like the
legendary Faust, Dorian barters moral responsibility for what he most
desires: pleasure through art, perfumes, exotic music, and forbidden
homosexual love. Wilde also suggests that Dorian's self-destruction
follows his reading of Joris-Karl Huysmans' *A Rebours*. Here Wilde
emphasizes the significant influence of art by indicating how his hero
embarks on a forbidden journey only after having read a book with
a similar character. Rejecting a world of ethical responsibility, Dorian
embraces the world of amoral literature. In a telling commentary on
this influence of amoral literature on Dorian, Wilde states, "There
were moments when he looked on evil simply as a mode through
which he could realize his conception of the beautiful" (270). This
idea is a consistent framework in Oscar Wilde's dialogue, *The Decay of
Lying* where he points out famously, "Life imitates Art far more than
Art imitates Life" (Wilde 337).

Standing in opposition to Henry, Basil confronts Dorian in his
unrelenting journey of amoral passions and unrepentant sins. Basil,
who has stood for the moral dimension of all artistic endeavors, chooses
to counter Henry by becoming a figure of conscience for Dorian. Basil
is also the first and only character in the novel to openly claim his love
for Dorian in an admission of homosexual passion. In certain ways,
Wilde is creating a wish fulfillment in this section of the novel. Unlike
Wilde's own life, where he constantly chose to hide his homosexuality
and went on to marry and have a family of his own, Basil's declaration of his love for Dorian stands as the one single act of honesty
and morality in the novel.[5] It is appropriate that this confession by
Basil frames the other more insidious confession that Dorian makes
as he reveals the degeneration of the portrait to its creator. The first
confession by Basil flagrantly breaks Victorian taboos against homosexual relationships in general; but, ironically, the forthright honesty
of this confession gives Basil the authority to explain to Dorian where
he has gone astray. Basil promises to withhold all judgment against

Dorian until he has seen his soul (274). It is fitting that Dorian leads Basil to his painting for this purpose of revealing his soul, the same painting that Basil himself had refused to exhibit because it would reveal too much of the artist's soul. In acknowledging Dorian's guilt, Basil accepts his own as well when he sees the disfigured painting: "I worshipped you too much. I am punished for it. You worshipped yourself too much. We are both punished" (277). Basil's complicity in Dorian's own painted confession as well as Basil's acknowledgement of guilt in helping to give birth to Dorian's narcissistic double-life lead to his death. Overtaken by murderous "loathing," Dorian kills Basil.

The novel reveals Dorian's degeneration to be irreversible. In his downward spiral, Dorian leaves Henry, who is unable to fathom the debauched depths to which his protégé has fallen, far behind. Eventually, the portrait degenerates murderously, killing the actual Dorian as he attempts to annihilate the image of his moral corruption. Dorian dies, but the painting takes on the youthful and pristine physical characteristics again. In revealing the hero's irreversible and unrelenting end, the narrative becomes an ironic reminder of the moralistic conception of art that Oscar Wilde opposed throughout his creative life.

NOTES

1. Sheldon W. Liebman in his essay "Character Design in *The Picture of Dorian Gray*" points out how Basil and Henry represent two separate and opposed world views that are brought to Dorian's attention. In his words, "Basil believes that the universe is a moral order in which God (or at least fate) punishes evil and rewards good; that the self is (or can be) unitary and autonomous; and that art—as well as human conduct in general—can (and should) be guided by a moral code in which sympathy and compassion are primary values.... Henry's beliefs are based on the assumption that there is no moral order (the universe is purposeless and indifferent to human needs); that the self is not only multiple, but at war with itself and driven by forces beyond its control; and that morality is arbitrary and relative. This moral position leads to a withdrawal from human engagement, the pursuit of pleasure (both sensual and intellectual) as a distraction from

disillusionment, and the manipulation of others for one's own enjoyment and edification" (436–37).

2. Liebman considers Henry to be a serious representation of the scientific character whose understanding of metaphysics makes him a consistent pessimist. In his words, "How does one live in a world in which nothing can be believed and no one can be trusted? Henry's answer is what philosophers call ethical egoism. He encourages Dorian to follow his own example of pursuing his own self-interest, which means seeking pleasure and avoiding pain. Henry's "new Hedonism" is based on the assumption that the quest for pleasure is natural because it is an expression of the quest for life, a response to a basic impulse, . . ." (439).

3. "New Hedonism" is Oscar Wilde's own term for Henry Wotton's amoral philosophy of sensuous enjoyment of life without a moral underpinning. "Carpe Diem" is the theme of "seizing the day or moment" that underlies so many Elizabethan and Romantic poetry. "Doppelganger" is the idea of the "doubling" of a character either in another character or image such as metaphor or symbol.

4. John Paul Riquelme in his essay, "Oscar Wide's Aesthetic Gothic" traces the myth of Narcissus and Echo as parallels to Wilde's own literary relationship with Walter Pater:

"But, in fact, Echo and Narcissus, however different from each other, are counterparts, whose stories consti-tute a single compound myth. Echo as well as Narcissus plays a continuing role in Wilde's novel because of the style's echoic character. By echoing Pater's writings frequently and strategically, Wilde projects the story of a contemporary Narcissus as one truth about Paterian aestheticism. He echoes Pater not in order to agree with the older British writer's views but to present them darkly, in shades of gray, as at base contradictory in destructive and self-destructive ways" (498).

This essay also develops the idea of the *doppelganger* as essential in the Narcissism developed by Wilde and recognizes it to be essentially Modernist: "When Wilde's Narcissus looks into the mirror of his painting, coproduced by his older friends, Basil and Henry, he becomes fascinated first with his own beauty but then with a growing ugliness that he recognizes as also himself" (503).

5. Jeff Nunokawa and Amy Sickels in their biography of Oscar Wilde point out the parallels between Dorian Gray and the author himself:

> The novel's protagonist and the men who surround him are covered in the codes of homosexuality through which Wilde and men like him communicated with one another. Dorian Gray is constantly likened to homosexuals of other times such as Antinous, the emperor Hadrian's lover, or to various other famous and infamous homosexuals from history. Dorian Gray's portrait allows the original to lead a double life, such as the one that Wilde and his friends knew (57).

These biographers also point out that with the publication of this novel where he "invited inevitable comparisons between himself and the characters that he created, Wilde courted the danger of blowing the door off his own closet". They go on to say, the novel "would supply ammunition to his persecutors and prosecutors and thus help bring on the disaster that cost Wilde all but his life" (59).

6. Ellie Ragland-Sullivan in the essay, "The Phenomenon of Aging" takes a different approach in analyzing Wilde's failure to understand or accept the need for secrecy and conformity in his private life: " When the Marquess of Queensberry accused Wilde of sodomy, Wilde insisted, against advice, on prosecuting the Marquess for criminal libel. After his release from prison Wilde, seeking refuge in a Catholic retreat, was refused this courtesy. He was also shunned by friends, wife, and children. Yet despite his own guilty torments, one senses that Wilde could never comprehend how such dire consequences could follow from his pursuit of sensual pleasures and his practice of a kind of love shared by great artists of the past. In Lacanian terms one might say that he never understood that his real crime was to have elevated Desire above Law" (480). One could argue that Basil seems to be having this conversation with Dorian who fails to understand the priority of moral law over desire.

WORKS CITED

Behrendt, Patricia Flanagan. *Oscar Wilde: Eros and Aesthetics*. New York: St. Martin's Press, 1991.

Campbell, Joseph. *The Hero with a Thousand Faces*. Bollingen Series XVII. Princeton: Princeton UP, 1949.

Liebman, Sheldon W. "Character Design in *The Picture of Dorian Gray*." *Studies in the Novel* 31.3 (Fall 1999). Reproduced by Norton Critical Edition. 43–454.

Nunokawa, Jeff, and Amy Sickels. *Oscar Wilde*. Gay and Lesbian Writers. Ed. Leslea Newman. Philadelphia: Chelsea House Publishers, 2005.

Ragland-Sullivan, Ellie. "The Phenomenon of Aging in Oscar Wilde's *Picture of Dorian Gray*: A Lacanian View." *Memory and Desire: Aging—Literature—Psychoanalysis*. Eds. Kathleen M. Woodward and Murray M. Schwartz. Bloomington: Indiana UP, 1986: 114–33. Reproduced in Norton Critical Edition. Oscar Wilde, 470–90.

Wilde, Oscar. *The Picture of Dorian Gray*. A Norton Critical Edition. Ed. Michael Patrick Gillespie. New York: W.W. Norton & Company, 2007.

THE POETRY AND PROSE OF SYLVIA PLATH

❧

"'God's Lioness'—Sylvia Plath,
Her Prose and Poetry"
by Wendy Martin, in *Women's Studies* (1973)

INTRODUCTION

For Wendy Martin, Sylvia Plath is an often-misunderstood writer who, because she courageously explored the taboo of her own emotions, experience, hostility and despair, "challenged the traditional literary prioritization of female experience." Thus, when writing about Plath's autobiographical novel, Martin concludes "*The Bell Jar* chronicles Esther Greenwood's *rite de passage* from girlhood to womanhood, and explores such subjects as sexual initiation and childbirth which are, for the most part, taboo in women's fiction." By focusing on the way Plath forged unapologetic art, Martin illuminates the many ways Plath is "a pioneer and pathfinder."

❧

In recent years, cultists have enshrined Sylvia Plath as a martyr while critics have denounced her as a shrew. Plath's devotees maintain that she was the victim of a sexist society, her suicide a response to

---

Martin, Wendy. "'God's Lioness'—Sylvia Plath, Her Prose and Poetry." *Women's Studies* 1.2 (1973): 191–98.

the oppression of women, and her poetry a choreography of female wounds. Conversely, critics such as Elizabeth Hardwick and Irving Howe complain of her "fascination with hurt and damage and fury."[1] Hardwick can't understand how Plath could persist in her bitterness toward her father years after his death and implies that it was sadistic, or, at best, self-indulgent, to publish *The Bell Jar*.

Echoing Hardwick, Howe accuses Plath of not "caring" or even being "aware of anyone but herself" and asserts that her poetry is "unmodulated and asocial." Complaining that in "none of the essays devoted to praising Sylvia Plath, have I found a coherent statement as to the nature, let alone the value, of her vision," Howe also dismisses Plath's work.[2] This negative and even hostile judgment of Plath's politics obscures the fact that she is one of the most important American women poets since Emily Dickinson; therefore, it is imperative that her work receive attention which is unbiased by sentimentality or authoritarianism.

Born on 27 October 1932 in Boston, Sylvia Plath grew up near the sea in Winthrop, Massachusetts. Her father, a professor of biology at Boston University and author of a respected treatise on bumble bees, died when she was eight; her mother who had been a graduate student in German when she married Otto Plath, taught medical secretarial training at Boston University in order to support the family.

Plath was awarded a scholarship to Smith College where she wrote fiction and prize-winning poetry; as a winner of the *Mademoiselle* College Board Contest, she spent a month in the summer of 1953 in New York City as a guest editor. Later that same summer, she became acutely depressed and attempted suicide. After receiving extensive psychiatric treatment as well as shock therapy, she returned to Smith and graduated *summa cum laude* in 1955. Sylvia was then awarded a fellowship to Newnham College, Cambridge, where she met Ted Hughes, also a poet, in February 1956 and married him in June, a few months before her twenty-fifth birthday.

Sylvia and Ted moved to the United States in the summer of 1957; she taught at Smith College for a year but decided to give up teaching because it took too much time for her poetry writing. The Hugheses then moved to Boston where Sylvia audited Robert Lowell's poetry classes with George Starbuck and Anne Sexton. In December 1959 Sylvia and Ted returned to England and their first child was born in April 1960; she continued to write, alternating the baby-sitting with

Ted. During this time, she began writing her novel, had a miscarriage, an appendectomy, and became pregnant again; her second child was born in January 1962 shortly after their move to Devon. The following year, Sylvia decided to move to London with the children; Ted remained in Devon. When *The Bell Jar* was published in January 1963 under the pseudonym of Victoria Lucas, she was hard at work on her *Ariel* poems. One month later on 11 February 1963 during the coldest winter in London since 1813–14, Sylvia Plath killed herself; she was thirty-one years old.[3]

What is striking about Sylvia Plath's biography is that she was an accomplished writer, wife, and mother; she even described herself as a "triple-threat woman." Friends describe her as energetic, efficient, and cheerful and often express surprise or are shocked by the isolation, confusion, searing pain and anger in *The Colossus* (1960), *Ariel* (1965), *Crossing the Water* (1971), and *Winter Trees* (1972), her four volumes of poetry.[4]

Apparently, Sylvia Plath played her social role so convincingly that few guessed at the intensity of her despair, but her novel, which is largely autobiographical, illuminates the sense of isolation conveyed by her poetry. In spite of the fact that *The Bell Jar* has been on the national best-seller list for over a year, it has received very little serious critical attention; this critical lapse is especially surprising in view of the fact that it is an extraordinary first novel paralleling F. Scott Fitzgerald's *This Side of Paradise* or Hemingway's *In Our Time*.

Not since Kate Chopin's *The Awakening* or Mary McCarthy's *The Company She Keeps* has there been an American novel which so effectively depicts the life of an intelligent and sensitive woman eager to participate in the larger world, who approaches experience with what amounts to a deep hunger, only to discover that there is no place for her as a fully functioning being. Like Chopin's Edna Pontellier and McCarthy's Margaret Sargent, Esther Greenwood struggles to develop the strength to survive in a world where women are alienated from themselves as well as each other (it is this alienation that Doris Lessing explores in *The Golden Notebook* which was published in 1962).

The Bell Jar chronicles Esther Greenwood's *rite de passage* from girlhood to womanhood, and explores such subjects as sexual initiation and childbirth which are, for the most part, taboo in women's fiction. Superficially, Esther Greenwood appears to be the 1950's model college girl, but she feels claustrophobic in the world of ladies' luncheons and fashion shows which she must attend as guest editor for a magazine in New York City.

Esther expects more from life than free complexion and hair care advice and would rather be in a bar than a beauty salon. But her nightclub experiences with her glamorous friend Doreen and disc jockey Lenny Shepard serve only to teach her that in order to live outside the ladies' luncheon circuit, a woman must attract an escort in order to experience the larger world. Sickened by this parasitic femininity, she resolves to get by on her own; she wants to see life for herself: "If there was a road accident or a street fight or a baby pickled in a laboratory jar for me to look at, I'd stop and look so hard I never forgot it."[5]

On her return to Boston, her mother informs her that she hasn't been accepted to a writing program that was important to her, and she resigns herself to writing her thesis while living at home. At this point, Esther's world begins to fall apart; she has rejected the passive femininity of Doreen, but the other women in her life fail to provide her with viable alternative life-styles. Her mother advises her to learn shorthand, but Esther is determined to dictate her own letters. Her resolutions notwithstanding, there are no outlets for her enormous energy and potentially constructive aggression; she turns this energy inward, becomes morbidly depressed, and tries to kill herself.

The "stale and sour" climate of Esther's inner world reflects the stifling conditions of her external life: the bell jar is a symbol for the internal chaos and despair produced by excessive external prohibitions. Ironically, there are carefully detailed rituals and traditions regulating virginity and defloration in Esther's world, but there were insufficient guideposts for intellectual development and creative accomplishment. There was no one in Esther's world to help her break out of her confinement—her boyfriend Buddy demands that she remain a virgin but insists that a poem is a "piece of dust."

Life outside the academy leaves Esther with the choice of being an adjunct to a man and mother to a "big cowy family," or a pioneer in uncharted social and emotional territory. Esther's fear and anxiety get the best of her, and it takes extensive therapy to enable her to emerge "patched, retreaded and approved for the road." When she is finally able to rejoice in pure being, "I am, I am, I am," the external world is still threatening, but at least she is her "own woman," and this hard-won independence enables her to withstand the taunts of people like Buddy: "But who will marry you now?"

In spite of the often grim events of *The Bell Jar*, the novel is frequently humorous: at the elegant luncheon given by wealthy Philomena Guinea, Esther drinks the contents of the fingerbowl, cherry blossoms and all, assuming that it was Japanese after-dinner soup; about to receive her first kiss, she positions herself while her date gets a "good footing on the soil," but does not close her eyes. Plath's narration of Esther's gaffs is brilliant, and her skill provides ample evidence of her commitment to fiction. In an interview with Peter Orr for the British council in October 1962, Plath commented that, unlike poetry, fiction permitted her to luxuriate in details; she also said that she viewed *The Bell Jar* as her apprentice effort and planned to write another novel. In the same interview, she stated that she composed her poems to be read aloud and admitted that *The Colossus* privately bored her because the poems in that volume were not composed for oral presentation.

To hear Sylvia Plath read her own poetry is truly a thrilling experience: her voice was full-bodied, vibrant, and authoritative. Her voice creates the impression that she was not hysterical, timid, or easily subdued. Hearing her read makes it obvious that being a poet was central to her existence—"The actual experience of writing a poem is a magnificent one," she once said, and the immense vitality of her reading underscores the energy of her poems.

Savage anger and bitterness frequently spring from Plath's poems: "Lady Lazarus," "The Applicant," "Daddy," "The Beast," "Zookeeper's Wife," "Magi" are monuments to her rage. "I made a model of you, . . . A man in black with a Meinkampf look . . . And I said I do, I do. . . . So daddy, I'm finally through"; "Daddy" turns on retribution; yet it expresses the release of immense energy that occurs with the decision to break away from emotionally damaging relationships. In *An American Dream*, Norman Mailer experiences the same release when he kills his wife Deborah and metaphorically as well as literally breaks away from her domination: " . . . and *crack* the door flew open and the wire tore in her throat, and I was through the door, hatred passing from me in wave after wave, illness as well, rot and pestilence, nausea, a bleak string of salts. I was floating."[6]

Male writers are permitted to articulate their aggression, however violent or hostile; women writers are supposed to pretend that they are never angry. Sylvia Plath refuses to honor this concept of feminine decorum and dares to express her negative emotions. "Beware . . . Beware . . . Out of the ash . . . I rise with my red hair . . . And I eat men like air" ("Lady Lazarus"). Plath chooses to be true to her experience and to her art rather than to the traditional norms of feminine experience.

Plath's anger gives her strength to face her demons: "Nightly now I flog apes wolves bears sheep . . . Over the iron stile. And still don't sleep." ("Zookeeper's Wife"). But if Plath's poetry is often an exorcism, an effort to stave off madness, it also modulates longing and fear: "I am inhabited by a cry . . . Nightly it flaps out . . . Looking, with its hooks, for something to love. I am terrified by this dark thing . . . That sleeps in me" ("Elm").

Critics frequently point out Plath's love/hate for her father, but they rarely mention her mother. This is a major oversight because the loss of mother-love haunts Plath's poetry and is the basic cause of her profound despair: "Mother, you are the one mouth . . . I would be tongue to" ("Who"); "The mother of mouths didn't love me" ("Maenad"); "Mother of beetles, only unclench your hand" ("Witch Burning").

Born under the sign of Scorpio, Plath speaks of the "motherly pulse of the sea" in an essay entitled "Ocean 1212-W,"[7] and here she again laments her abandonment: "Hugging my grudge, ugly and prickly, a sad sea urchin . . . I saw the separateness of everything. I felt the wall of my skin: I am I. The stone is a stone. My beautiful fusion with the things of this world was over."

Plath was two and a half years old when her brother was born, and like many sensitive children of that age, she felt replaced by her brother and rejected by her mother. Her father's death when she was eight undoubtedly aggravated her already acute sense of loss. The working through of Oedipal and sibling conflicts in Plath's writing is reminiscent of Virginia Woolf, who wrote in her diary, "I used to think of him (her father) and mother daily; but writing the *Lighthouse* laid them in my mind. And now he comes back to me sometimes, but differently. I believe this to be true—that I was obsessed by them both, unhealthily; and writing of them was a necessary act."[8]

In addition to childhood losses, the conflict between domestic and artistic interests, and the lack of financial security as well as health problems undoubtedly left Sylvia Plath extremely vulnerable to depression and suicidal impulses. Lacking favorable or at least serious critical response to her work must have been difficult and painful. Certainly interviews which described her as an "attractive young suburban matron . . . in a neat oatmeal colored suit of wool jersey . . . a living realization of every young college girl's dream" must have been discouraging.

One of Plath's last works "Three Women: A Poem for Three Voices," which appears in *Winter Trees*, is set in a maternity ward and seems to celebrate, in part, fertility, pregnancy, and motherhood along with acceptance, or perhaps resignation, to a women's domestic identity. It concludes, "I am a wife . . . The city waits and aches. The little grasses . . . Crack through Stone, and they are green with life." Again, Plath echoes Virginia Woolf: "And now with some pleasure I find that it is seven; and must cook dinner. Haddock and sausage meat. I think it is true that one gains a certain hold on sausage and haddock by writing them down."[9] Shortly after this 8 March 1941 entry, Virginia Woolf weighted with stones, walked into a tributary of the Thames to drown.

Like Woolf, Plath made desperate efforts to balance on the "razor edge" of the opposing forces of life and death. Kali-like, Sylvia Plath's poetry embodies the profound interrelationship of destruction and creation. Whether or not she could have moved toward a strong affirmation of life as did Anne Sexton in *Live or Die* is a question her readers will never be able to answer.

A. Alvarez in his memoir of Sylvia Plath argues that she was by nature a risk-taker and that her suicide was her last gamble: "Having worked out the odds were in her favor, but perhaps, in her depression, not much caring whether she won or lost. Her calculations went wrong and she lost."[10] Alvarez points out that Plath left the doctor's number near her, that the au pair girl was due to arrive early in the morning, that the man who lived below was an early riser. Plath could not have realized that the gas that suffocated her would sedate him so heavily that he didn't hear the frantic knocking of the au pair girl or that this delay would cost her her life. Yet, the moment she decided to turn on the gas jet, an irrevocable chain of events occurred which caused the "jet blood" of poetry to stop forever.

Sylvia Plath was one of the first American women writers to refuse to conceal or disguise her true emotions; in articulating her aggression, hostility, and despair in her art, she effectively challenged the traditional literary prioritization of female experience. In addition to being a novelist and poet, she was a pioneer and pathfinder.

NOTES

1. Elizabeth Hardwick, "On Sylvia Plath," *The New York Review of Books*, 12 August 1971, 3–6.
2. Irving Howe, "Sylvia Plath, A Partial Disagreement," *Harper's Magazine*, January 1972, 88–91.
3. For useful background, see Lois Ames, "Notes Toward a Biography" in *The Art of Sylvia Plath*, Charles Newman (Ed.) (Bloomington and London: Indiana University Press, 1970), 155–174.
4. Sylvia Plath, *The Colossus and Other Poems* (New York: Random House, 1957), *Ariel* (Harper and Row, 1961), *Crossing the Water* (Harper and Row, 1971), *Winter Trees* (Harper and Row, 1972).
5. Sylvia Plath, *The Bell Jar* (New York: Harper and Row, 1971). This and all subsequent quotations from this edition.
6. Norman Mailer, *An American Dream*, 33–36.
7. Sylvia Plath, "Ocean 1212-W," in *The Art of Sylvia Plath*, 269.
8. Virginia Woolf, *A Writer's Diary*, Leonard Wolf (Ed.) (New York: New American Library, 1968), 138.
9. Virginia Woolf, *A Writer's Diary*, 150.
10. A. Alvarez, "Sylvia Plath: A Memoir," *New American Review*, 312–39.

"A ROSE FOR EMILY"
(WILLIAM FAULKNER)

❧

"Usher, Poquelin, and Miss Emily:
the Progress of Southern Gothic"
by Edward Stone, in *Georgia Review* (1960)

INTRODUCTION

In this study of Faulkner's short story, Edward Stone deals with the elements that make Faulkner's story distinctly taboo: "not only does this obsessed spinster continue for some years to share a marriage bed with the body of the man she has poisoned—she evidently derives either erotic gratification or spiritual sustenance (both?) from these ghastly nuptials. She becomes, in short, a necrophile or a veritable saprophytic organism." By tracing conventions employed by Edgar Allen Poe, Stone articulates what makes the short story emblematic of Faulkner's gothic style, one in which the taboo is wedded with grotesque.

❧

Some years ago Professors Brooks and Warren offered the suggestion in *Understanding Fiction* that we consider William Faulkner's "A Rose for Emily" as akin to Poe's "The Fall of the House of Usher"

Stone, Edward. "Usher, Poquelin, and Miss Emily: the Progress of Southern Gothic." *Georgia Review* 14.4 (Winter 1960): 433–43.

on the grounds that in both "we have a decaying mansion in which the protagonist, shut away from the world, grows into something monstrous. . . ." But to do so, as these critics more or less admit, is to point up as many differences as similarities. Granted that each is "a story of horror": the gloomy corridors of Gothicism are too numerous for such a suggestion to prove more than initially instructive. Without losing sight of the possibilities it may offer, let us extend it and consider Faulkner's spirit-chilling little classic along the additional lines proposed more recently by Professor Randall Stewart—those of Faulkner's relationship to earlier characteristically Southern writers. In particular, let us compare "A Rose for Emily" with George Washington Cable's "Jean-ah Poquelin," to which it is more closely akin, not only in horror, but in that far more important quality defined by Professor Stewart as "a common view of the human condition." Although the situations of these two stories are curiously similar, they are productive of dissimilar results. In comparing them, along with Poe's, accordingly, we can arrive at some conclusion about the direction that Gothic fiction has taken during the past century in its concept of the human personality.

Our first finding is that, unlike "Usher," Cable's and Faulkner's are stories not only of horror, but everywhere of *time* and *place*. Cable sets this down in his first sentence and Faulkner devotes his entire long second paragraph to it. Our imaginations are thus fixed at once in both stories on an *exact* setting. Professor Stewart has pointed out that "a rampant industrialism was transforming the traditional social structure" of the South in the 1920's; similarly, in the years immediately following 1803, the somnolent French province of Louisiana was asked to adapt itself to the American ways of progress. "In the first decade of the present century," Cable begins, with seeming casualness; yet upon reflection this detail becomes a most precise one: merely a decade or two later, during the flood of American immigration into New Orleans, Poquelin's interview with the Governor would have been pathetic, rather than dramatic; and even a decade earlier, there would have been no need for it (the purchase of Louisiana in 1803 being ultimately responsible for Poquelin's desperate situation). Similarly, the coming of garages and gasoline pumps mentioned in the beginning of Faulkner's story places us squarely in the Jefferson of the first decades of the 1900's—a seemingly casual fact that becomes indispensable: it was this change wrought on American life by technology that resulted in the paving of small town sidewalks and streets, which in turn brought the Yankee suitor to Jefferson. And thereby hangs Faulkner's tale. Into both settings of change the author introduces a hero who, fortifying himself in an anachronistic, essentially horrible, and yet majestic stronghold, ignores or defies the insistent encroachments of time and progress. It is the different and yet similar ways in which Poquelin and Miss Emily oppose these encroachments that their creators show their kinship and, after all, their basic difference.

Each curtain goes up on an isolated fortress from bygone days. Jean-ah's is seen as "an old colonial plantation-house" in New Orleans "half in ruin," "aloof from civilization," standing at considerable remove from the smaller, newer houses on the bank of the Mississippi. It is "grim, solid, and spiritless," "its massive build" a reminder of an earlier, more hazardous period of American history. With its "dark" and "weather-beaten" roof and sides, it stands above a marsh in whose center grow two dead cypresses, "clotted with roosting vultures." The Grierson home of Faulkner's story is similarly detached, superseded, and forbidding. It is a "big, squarish frame house that had once been white, decorated with cupolas and spires and scrolled balconies in the heavily lightsome style of the seventies." It too stands alone on the street as a human dwelling, "lifting its stubborn and coquettish decay above the cotton wagons and the gasoline pumps—an eyesore among eyesores."

In the first of these half-ruined homes lives a half-ruined old creole grandee, "once an opulent indigo planter, . . . now a hermit, alike shunned by and shunning all who had ever known him," the last of a prominent Louisiana line. His only relative, a much younger half-brother named Jacques, has not been seen for seven years, two years after Poquelin and he left for the Guinea coast on a slave-capturing expedition and Jean Marie returned alone. ("He must have arrived at his house by night. No one saw him come. No one saw 'his little brother'; rumor whispered that he, too, had returned, but he had never been seen again.") This livelihood Poquelin had descended to after his indigo fields had had to be abandoned, and, after that, smuggling. From the first, there is suspicion of foul play, and with the passing of time "the name of Jean Marie Poquelin became a symbol of witchery, devilish crime, and hideous nursery fictions." His society is avoided, and boys playing in the neighborhood jibe at the old man, who retaliates imperiously with violent but unheeded (and outdated) "French imprecation and invective." All avoid the house after dark. So far as anyone knows, Poquelin lives only with an old African housekeeper, a mute.

Emily Grierson is a similarly sinister relic. The last of a proud line, she lives in her outmoded stronghold, alone but peremptory in her demand for "recognition of her dignity as the last Grierson." Since her father's death she has lived all alone in the big house except for a brief period in her thirties when she went off with a Yankee construction foreman named Homer Barron, presumably to be married. Her lover has since disappeared. ("Within three days Homer Barron was back in town. A neighbor saw the Negro man admit him at the kitchen door at dusk one evening. And that was the last we saw of Homer Barron.") For a period of six or seven years, at the age of forty, Miss Emily resorts to teaching china-painting as a source of income. Then, as years pass and the fashion with it, her pupils disappear and her front door "closed upon the last one and remained closed for good." She lives on into old age in the house "filled with dust and shadows," a place associated in her townsmen's eyes with an unspoken and mysterious horror. The only other inmate, we read, is an old Negro house servant, who does not utter a word during the course of the story.

Progress, in the form of municipal expansion, becomes old Poquelin's adversary. Surveyors give signs of running a new street close to his house and of draining the morass beside it. This is, we note, a Poquelin reverse that the townspeople relish; they too oppose new streets, and will welcome engineering difficulties, but their fearful scorn for Poquelin causes them to look upon his forcible return to the community with pleasure. Poquelin goes directly to the Governor, pleads with him in broken English (after the Governor understandably declines to speak in the French tongue). He pleads on the old, man-to-man basis of the past when informality and the importance of the Poquelin name would have made this kind of interview expectable; does not take kindly to the Governor's suggestion that he deal with the city authorities; and even proposes that the Governor personally intercede with the President on his behalf. To the Governor's innocent query about the stories associated with his house, Poquelin haughtily refuses to answer, and then departs. The city official to whom the Governor has referred him also knows no French and deals with Poquelin through an interpreter. Unsuccessful here too, Poquelin swears abusively and leaves. The new street is cut through, and houses go up near Poquelin's, but still the ugly old ruin remains, to the growing exasperation of the townspeople. Now the newer arrivals plot to persuade, then coerce, the old man to build a new home. Their efforts are rebuffed firmly by Poquelin, who refuses to permit conversation about it with the president of a local Board recently organized. The townspeople renew their pressure on Poquelin and even threaten mob action (a charivari, they say); but on the fateful night they are thwarted, both by the efforts of one of their group (who, on a secret visit to the house, becomes suspicious of a revolting odor about the place, among other things) and by the death of Poquelin himself. His body is brought out of the house by the old African mute, followed by the long-missing Jacques, a leper whose existence he has successfully concealed from all for seven years. Hoisting the coffin on his shoulders, the Negro starts out toward leper soil, Jacques with him. ("[T]hey stepped into the jungle, disappeared, and were never seen again.")

Equally impervious to community pressure, Miss Emily is also menaced in the shabby majesty of her seclusion by the passing of time and by progress. She refuses for days to let the neighbors in when her father dies, and two years later scandalizes them by consorting openly with the crude Yankee, Homer Barron. The neighbors try to thwart the relationship out of mixed feelings, both of resentment at Emily's haughtiness (she is insufferably Grierson, even when fallen on evil days) and of actual sympathy with her (after all, she is one of them, as Homer is not, and the relatives whom they send for turn out to be "even more Grierson" than Emily). She defies society by refusing to identify to the druggist the purposes for which she is buying the arsenic. Shortly afterwards, when Homer apparently deserts her on the eve of their presumed wedding, and an offensive smell develops in her house, there is angry complaining to authority. But the old major intercedes in Emily's behalf, and the only community action that results is the sprinkling of lime around her house (secretly, almost fearfully, at night). She refuses to accept free postal delivery. Finally, thirty years later, when her continued refusals to pay her taxes cause the major himself to write a kind letter to her proposing payment, he "received in reply a note on paper of an archaic shape, in a thin, flowing calligraphy in fading ink" airily rebuffing his proposal. This imperiousness finally causes a deputation of townspeople (mostly younger) to call on her in her dusty, sinister-smelling domain. She turns them away haughtily, claiming an immunity to taxes based on a life-long remission by a mayor long since dead, to whom she refers the deputation. When death finally comes to the old woman herself, the ancient Negro admits the first visitors to the house, then disappears ("He walked right through the house and out the back and was not seen again.") The visitors enter it for the first time in ten years, break down a door abovestairs which no one has been in in forty years, and find the long-decayed corpse of her lover lying in the bed. Only in her death is disclosed the permanence of her conquest a generation before over a man who evidently had no intention of remaining true to her.

Here, then, are two stories presenting a central conflict between a proud and doomed but indomitable last representative of an important family of a bygone era of the South and the progress of an encroaching and usurping civilization. Both Emily Grierson and Jean-Marie Poquelin perpetuate their pristine importance by immuring themselves in a massive, impregnable, outmoded house; and both successfully and secretly conceal in that house until their death a human ghoul who is all that is left to them, the success of the concealment itself recording the triumph of a figure whom time and progress have otherwise relegated to ridiculousness. With plot and characterization parallels like these one might well speculate about the extent to which Cable's story may have inspired Faulkner's. Yet there is a surprising difference in the impressions these two stories create. For, after all the parallels have been itemized, Faulkner has used old materials in an entirely new way and created an effect that is neither Poe's nor even Cable's but entirely his own. And although it is an effect that is derived from the Gothic horror effects of the preceding centuries, it is also characteristically modern and the more horrifying for that reason.

Cable's story and point of view are, after all, in the old fashion. The mysterious and forbidding ruin superseded by time, the proud and isolated owner, a hidden horror—these are the familiar devices of Poe and his Germanic predecessors. What distinguishes "Jean-ah Poquelin" from them is the successful mixture with Gothicism of truly local color and characterization. The scene in which old Poquelin confronts the Governor of Louisiana is one of the memorable ones in American literature. And the stolid, valiant front the old man presents to his suspicious and hostile neighbors over the years, as he harbors a forbidden horror in his home at the risk of his own health, is a masterfully executed effect. Yet, though the story is sophisticated melodrama, it *is* melodrama. Poquelin's gloomy relic of a defunct creole colonialism, with the submarine horrors that guarantee its medieval isolation, is presented as an ugly obstacle to progress; yet, identify though we are encouraged to do with the new villas springing up around it and with the ways of that basically well-intentioned civic group, the "Building and Improvement Company" (one of whose officers, White, even becomes a secondary hero of the piece), primarily and consistently we sympathize with Poquelin and his heroic, if baffling, resistance to them. We do not willingly watch greatness, however faded, vanish from our view, and we all side against the instrument of its obliteration: as the moralist that his century required the serious writer of fiction to be, Cable had to inculcate in his readers attitudes of censure and approbation in viewing the opposing forces of the story.

Faulkner, on the other hand, impassively maintains his (and our) distance, sympathizing with and reproving in turn Emily and her adversary, the Town. The outmoded, mausoleum-like edifice from which she defies society is, to be sure, an eyesore, but to Faulkner it is merely "an eyesore *among eyesores*,"—an unsightly dwelling in the midst of unsightly gasoline pumps. Between the boorish arrogance of Homer Barron and the cultured arrogance of Emily Grierson, can one choose? Or between the testy young alderman who does not recognize old ways and the crusty old judge who does not recognize new ones? Faulkner cares as little (or as much) for the "gross, teeming world" of the New South as he does for the one "monument" to the Old South whose identity it is effacing. His concern is not with the opposition of the forces of Good and Evil. In centering his inquiry on the workings of the morbid mind of his character, he moves beyond the terms of Cable.

Thus it is not surprising to reflect that, unlike Poe's and Cable's, Faulkner's story is not a suspense story at all. Our chief interest in "Usher" eventually focuses on the condition of the hero's sister and our curiosity is solely on what the issue of the last horrible night will be. Almost to an equal degree Cable sets our minds to work on the mystery of Poquelin's insistence on seclusion and on the exact identity of the reported supernatural presence under his roof. Thus it is that when Poe's and Cable's living corpses at last emerge in their shrouds and the mystery of the central situational horror is solved, our minds have an answer—the lady Madeline and Jacques Poquelin had not really died—and need nothing more. Conversely, in "A Rose for Emily" not only do we early anticipate the final outcome with a fair degree of accuracy: *for this very reason* we are imbued with the horror of the heroine's personality at every step throughout the story, and thus in her case the basic mystery outlives the working out of the plot. For Faulkner, so far from withholding all clues to Homer Barron's whereabouts, scatters them with a precise prodigality; since his is a story primarily of character, it is to his purpose to saturate our awareness of Miss Emily's abnormality as he goes, so that the last six shocking words merely put the final touch on that purpose. They do not astound us or merely erase a question mark. If similarities to Faulkner are to be sought in Poe, they will be found not in "Usher," but in "A Cask of Amontillado," whose plot in no way parallels Faulkner's: both stories have a total horror, rather than a climax of horror, for in both we are given at the start a distinct impression of the moral depravity of the central figure, and the ensuing pages heighten that impression rather than merely solve for us a mystery that the opening pages have set forth. We leave Miss Emily as awed by the complexity of her being as when we met her, and therein lies the greatness of Faulkner's story.

But for the most striking evidence of the wide gulf that yawns between Faulkner and his Southern precursor Cable in horror fiction, of the two worlds in which they live, we must turn to the relationships of the two protagonists with their own dead (or living dead) and the effects these create in the reader. The strength of family ties of the Poquelins is emphasized early in Cable's story when we are told that even in old age Poquelin visits his father's tomb in St. Louis Cathedral daily. And the cost of the heart-rending tenderness with which Poquelin spends the years tending his leprous, decaying brother we have abundant evidence of; for as Cable describes him in the interview with the governor, over his entire face is "the imprint of some great grief . . .—faint but unmistakable." It clouds and weights his days and makes each breath a burden. And we, in turn, understand and are moved.

Compare with these conventional touches the effect of change on Miss Emily. When we first inspect her house (in her old age) we incidentally note that there is a portrait of her father "on a tarnished gilt easel before the fireplace" in the parlor. But when, during her early spinisterhood, her father dies and she refuses for three days to hand his putrefying body over for burial, we are shocked by this irrational action, even though in keeping with his standpoint of noncommitment Faulkner tries to minimize it ("We remembered all the young men her father had driven away, and we knew that with nothing left, she would have to cling to that which had robbed her, as people will.") Even more important, by Faulkner's time it was possible for him to defy taboo by substituting a husband for a brother (or, as in Usher's case, a sister) in the concealment theme. But the most frightening detail in Faulkner's story is this: not only does this obsessed spinster continue for some years to share a marriage bed with the body of the man she has poisoned—she evidently derives either erotic gratification or spiritual sustenance (both?) from these ghastly nuptials. She becomes, in short, a necrophile or a veritable saprophytic organism; for we learn that the "slender figure in white" that was the young Miss Emily becomes, as though with the middle-aged propriety that the married state customarily brings, *fat!* "She looked bloated, like a body long submerged in motionless water, and that of parallel hue. Her eyes, lost in the fatty ridges of her face, looked like two small pieces of coal pressed into a lump of dough. . . ." It is in ghoulish inner evolutions like these that Faulkner moves beyond Poe and Cable into the twentieth century, directly into the clinic of Dr. R. von Krafft-Ebing, whose inquries into the psychopathology of sex had revealed that

> When no other act of cruelty . . . is practised on the cadaver, it is probable that the lifeless condition itself forms the stimulus for the perverse individual. It is possible that the corpse—a human form absolutely without will—satisfies an abnormal desire, in that the object of desire is seen to be capable of absolute subjugation, without possibility of resistance.

Not that the appearance of the hero as pathological personality in American fiction had to await the present century, to be sure. He can be found far back in the 1800's, even in minor writers (Simms, for example), not to speak of Hawthorne (stripped of the allegorical veils) or Melville (whose Ahab is as disturbed mentally as Prince Hamlet), or, of course, Poe himself. But in "Usher" or other Poe tales the central character is patently offered to the reader and always received by him as a madman pure and simple; during the time we see him, he has never been sane; and his situation is never even remotely associable with ours—that is, with reality. Roderick Usher is, after all, a shadowy unknown living a bizarre existence in an unidentifiable land and time and suffering from pale preoccupation with a body not-dead from

an equally phantasmal ailment—all details of horror for horror's sake.
And only at first glance is Hawthorne's Gothic intended as much
more than this. To be sure, as we meet Hepzibah Pyncheon, the
"forlorn old maid in her rustling and rusty silks, with her deeply cherished and ridiculous consciousness of long descent," we are reminded
of Professor Stewart's remarks on the parallels between Hawthorne's
time and place and Faulkner's; and we may even be tempted to detect
a foreshadowing of Miss Emily in Hepzibah, who, "though she had
her valuable and redeeming traits, had grown to be a kind of lunatic,
by imprisoning herself so long in one place, with no other company
than a single series of ideas, and but one affection, and one bitter sense
of wrong." But all this Gothic gloom is deepened only to be intruded
upon later by Phoebe and Holgrave until, in the Escape into Life
sequence, it is dispelled utterly, and we see that what Hawthorne has
been striving towards all along is the exact reverse of Miss Emily's
Escape *from* Life. As for Melville's Ahab, he is so much the stuff of
heroes treading the boards of a Renaissance stage that we cannot
consistently believe in him as a nineteenth-century sea-captain at all.
Jean Marie Poquelin, to be sure, is, in terms of verisimilitude, considerably more than this. He is indeed a recognizable character with an
immediate claim to our sympathy and affection. But even he was seen
by Cable through the haze of three quarters of a century, he becomes
alive late in life only, and only the broad outlines of his personality
are set down—a striking animation but blurred as well as endeared by
sentiment and melodrama.

Emily Grierson, on the other hand, not only has a local habitation
and a name: *she is someone we grow up and old with.* In fact, Faulkner's
ubiquitous and omniscient point of view seems used deliberately for
this purpose at the expense of being the only intrinsic artistic flaw in
the story. Her relatives from Alabama and their relationship to the
Mississippi Griersons are made much of, as are the careful distinctions
between the various Protestant sects in the town. With the exception
of the last ten years of her seventy-four, she is represented as living in
a fairly familiar, understandable isolation for an aristocratic Southern
woman, and demonstrating by the very success of her isolation the
majesty and frightfulness of her position. For all that, like other
Gothic characters, she is "impervious" and "perverse"—even to the
point of madness—she is also "tranquil," "inescapable," even "*dear.*"
"All this happened, then," we say to ourselves at the close of her story,

"in our very midst!" It happened, not in the western Germany of several centuries ago, but in the Mississippi of yesterday. Although Faulkner's story is the "logical development" of Edgar Allan Poe, George Snell writes, it is

> brought to a higher degree of force since its action takes place not in some "misty mid region" but exactly and circumstantially in a recognizable South, with all the appurtenances and criticisms of a society which Faulkner knows and simultaneously hates and loves. . . . "A Rose for Emily" shows how little Faulkner has been restrained by the conventions of Southern life which have dictated to many Southern writers how little of reality they could deal with, and at the same time shows his ineluctable kinship with Poe, as technician and as master of the morbid and bizarre.

Furthermore, it would seriously detract from Faulkner's intention and achievement to limit our identification of Emily Grierson's pathological intransigence to the South alone. Appalling though Emily's dealings with the North (Homer Barron) are, far more attention is given to her resistance to her own townspeople. Thus Ray B. West, Jr.'s reminder that "The theme is not one directed at presenting an attitude of Southerner to Yankee. . . . The Southern problem is one of the objective facts with which the theme is concerned, but the theme itself transcends it"; and "Here is depicted the dilemma of our age, not of the South alone nor of the North alone. . . ." How else, for that matter, are we to account for the fact that the surname of the very heroine of Faulkner's story, so far from one of Mississippi or even Southern association, is that of none other than the officer in the *Northern* army who had led so celebrated and devastating a raid throughout the state of Mississippi midway through the Civil War! (And readers of Faulkner will recall how carefully he chooses names for his characters.) In this connection, we might let Van Wyck Brooks, an eminent historian of the literary life in the United States, call our attention to the eccentricities and grotesquerie of the population, both fictional and real, of the other areas of this country during Emily Grierson's decline—of the Midwest, of New England. What! we exclaim, emerging from a prolonged immersion in Faulkner—is this not Yoknapatawpha County, Mississippi?

[It] abounded in men who had once been important and who had no life any longer to shape to their code. . . . They had set the tone for their neighbours and headed their clans. But they had no clans to lead now, and the making of laws was not for them: they were left with the "dusty ruins of their fathers' dreams." They had lost their confidence, as the years went by, and they crept away into their houses and grew queerer and queerer. . . . There were creepers among catacombs, "whose occupation was to die," there were respected citizens who blew their brains out; and one saw them straggling through the town, stumbling over frozen ruts, in the cold white shine of a dreary day. In short, this population was a whole *Spoon River Anthology*, acting out its epitaphs in the world of the living.

Actually, the town described here is Gardiner, Maine.

We are left, then with this irony: in order to identify exactly the weird wizardry that Faulkner has achieved in "A Rose for Emily," to distinguish it chiefly from Poe's, we must borrow a distinction that Poe claimed for himself when he insisted that his particular kind of Gothicism was "not of the Rhine but of the soul."

SABBATH'S THEATER
(PHILIP ROTH)

❧

"The Taboo in Philip Roth's *Sabbath's Theater*"
by Julia F. Klimek, Coker College

When Philip Roth's novel *Sabbath's Theater* won the National Book Award in 1995, readers and critics responded with some ambivalence. Those who found the sexual shenanigans of *Portnoy's Complaint* (1967) offensive and reprehensible were even less amused by Roth's protagonist Mickey Sabbath, whose exploits, both fantasized and realized, surpass Portnoy's by far. According to Mark Shechner, even the award committee was impressed by the abrasive and insulting nature of the novel but decided that art in literature can and should be challenging (Shechner 147). *Sabbath's Theater* challenges the most seasoned Roth reader with its long list of taboos broken, transgressions enacted and imagined, and its general spirit of unapologetic defiance, both in the face of society's morals and of mortality itself. The taboos are manifold: infidelity, phone sex with a student, alcohol smuggled into a recovery clinic, a gleeful rummage through the underwear of a friend's teenage daughter, theft, desecration of a grave (multiple), incest, suicide—Roth's characters behave badly.

Roth ascribes most of the transgressions to his main character, Sabbath, but others participate and collude, and in fact it is Sabbath's aim to draw in fellow transgressors. Sabbath manipulates and corrupts others into joining him in the breaking of taboos. He is driven by a fear of death and a wish to reach beyond its finality. Sabbath is traumatized by losses he cannot accept: first the death of his older brother Morty when he is still a boy, later the disappearance and possible death of his first wife Nikki, and finally the loss of his long-term lover Drenka. Sabbath commits morbid and often offensive acts in his efforts to reconnect with these people, through memories and gestures. When he does succeed, his disregard for his own dignity is oddly touching, and readers empathize with Sabbath, in spite of his transgressions.

Mickey Sabbath is a 64-year-old puppeteer whose hands are crippled by rheumatism and who therefore lives off his second wife Roseanna's income in the small town of Madamaska Falls. His long-term lover is Drenka, the Croatian immigrant wife of the local innkeeper. The novel begins with an argument between Drenka and Sabbath, who regularly meet in a "grotto" outside town. The first sentence sets up the theme of the novel: "Either foreswear fucking others or the affair is over," Drenka essentially demands (3). This sentence roughly translates: contain your chaos and disruption or your life will end. But Sabbath refuses to curb his misbehavior, and it is not his death that follows but Drenka's, leaving Mickey Sabbath at loose ends and in the continued chaos of his own making.

In the first scene, Roth sets up the main tension of the novel: Sabbath breaks taboos specifically to defy death (Safer 61), to remind himself and others that he is an *actor* on his stage, someone who *does* something and has some control over himself and others. Although Drenka's death causes Sabbath great grief, he has "the vital energy to keep going," unlike Kepesh, another of Roth's heroes, who is simply undone by a similar loss (Halio 205). Sabbath's greatest resource is his "energy fueled by eroticism," and as off-putting as this is to some readers, it may also be a redemptive quality (Halio 205). The novel continues to work out the tensions involving death and taboo on several levels: Sabbath's wish to control the stage and manipulate other characters, his memories of loss, and, through these memories, his coming to terms with Drenka's death.

While the novel is set in 1994, Roth shifts between the present and Sabbath's memories. The narrator moves from Sabbath's idyllic childhood on the Jersey shore to his adventures in the merchant marine, his puppeteering career in Manhattan, his first marriage, and finally to his encounters with Drenka. Through Sabbath's memories, Roth establishes the pattern of a man who thrives on controlling the people around him. Sabbath's desire to manipulate begins back in the 1950s, when he performed with his Indecent Theater in Manhattan, reeling in an audience with fingers (rather than actual puppets) and enticing Helen Trumbull, a female audience member, to allow his finger/puppet to unbutton her blouse. Arrested for this initial moral transgression, Sabbath goes to court, where his friends Norman Cowan and Lincoln Gelman help him get off with a fine. He then becomes director of a very small theater group, again controlling the actions of others, and marries a young actress, Nikki, who mysteriously disappears. Sabbath then pursues a second marriage with Roseanna, with whom he is already having an affair.

They move to Madamaska Falls, a small town in the country, where Sabbath holds a teaching position at a college. He has affairs with several female students and is fired when his last affair, with a student named Kathy Goolsbee, becomes public. The scandal drives Roseanna into a rehab clinic, which does not improve the marriage.

The main focus of Sabbath's past 13 years has been his attachment to Drenka Balich, a Croatian immigrant and the local innkeeper's wife. After Drenka, whom he loves and who is clearly more his equal than any of the other women in his life, dies of cancer toward the beginning of the novel, Sabbath's life gets a jolt: Roseanna throws him out of the house, and Sabbath drives to New York to attend Lincoln's funeral. After a visit to Norman, who also throws him out, Sabbath gets sidetracked into searching for his family's graves, visits his ancient cousin Fish, and returns to Madamaska Falls for one last visit to Drenka's grave. At the closing of the novel, Sabbath is still a breaker of taboos, but his reflections and travels seem to have prompted some internal shifts.

Beginning with his Indecent Theater career, all of Sabbath's transgressions are tied in with performances—Sabbath seems to be particularly pleased when others observe his overstepping of boundaries. He depends both on an audience (even if it is only the reader of *Sabbath's Theater*) and on other characters. With his career as a theater director long behind him, unable to manipulate puppets with his now rheumatic fingers, Sabbath instead pulls the strings of those around him: his student Kathy Goolsbee, his wife Roseanna, his old friend Norman, his friend's wife Michelle, his lover Drenka. Each of them in turn he challenges to join him in breaking taboos, but in each case he also loses control over his "puppet." This is most obvious in the case of Kathy, with whom he has a brief affair involving phone sex (its own version of manipulation). Kathy "accidentally" leaves a tape recording of one conversation in a public bathroom, and Sabbath's infraction against the taboo governing professor/student relationships becomes known. Having thus failed to control the secret (and Kathy), Sabbath is judged a second time, and again he loses his job, revisiting the court room scene that effectively shut down his Indecent Theater.

In both cases, the offense he is accused of is not one committed against an individual (the student whose blouse he unbuttoned in Manhattan; Kathy Goolsbee in the small college), as neither one is particularly put out by the experience. At stake is the breaking of the taboo and therefore a matter of principle: one does not take sexual advantage of (young, female) students. Sabbath's point, however, is to overstep the boundaries and to draw others across the line with him. Both these women are game, to a degree, but they cannot prevent Sabbath's punishment by society (the judge, the college administration). They remain shadow figures in the novel, hardly developing their own voice: most of Kathy's voice is reduced to her responses in a footnote, always prompted by Sabbath (215–35); Helen Trumbull is only brought to us second-hand, in a retelling of the event by Sabbath and Norman (312–20). Their voices are appropriated by others: Kathy's by the "Women Against Sexual Abuse, Belittlement, Battering, and Telephone Harassment" committee that makes the tape public; Helen's name is temporarily erased because at first Sabbath cannot remember it (312), then refers to her as Debby, Norman's daughter (321). These undeveloped, quasi-silenced female characters are out-performed by Drenka, a willing participant in Sabbath's performances who begins to stage her own taboo-breaking events.

Drenka is an exception among the novel's female characters as she develops her own identity rather than simply being coaxed into one by Sabbath (Kelleter 176). She easily takes up Sabbath's challenge to break taboos and entice others to do the same. Liberated from an unsatisfying marriage, she happily meets Sabbath for trysts, claiming "I couldn't carry out my responsibilities without you" (19). But she does not stop here: After Sabbath arranges for a threesome with Christa, a woman he first picks up hitchhiking, Drenka not only willingly complies but develops her own relationship with Christa, which quickly slips beyond Sabbath's control: at their first sexual encounter, Sabbath is reduced to looking on "like a medical student observing his first surgical procedure" (63). But further encounters (some kept secret from him) between Drenka and Christa leave him out completely, establishing her as a character in her own right rather than his puppet. She also, encouraged by Sabbath, takes on a string of additional lovers, one of them not only married, but with a pregnant wife at home (certainly another broken taboo), reporting back, in detail, to Sabbath (34–36, 66–68, 74–76).

Debra Shostak describes Drenka as a character who is not quite objectified: while she is indeed an object of Sabbath's sexual desires, and his pupil both in sex and the English language, she is also too alive to be an object: Sabbath is transfixed by her, can't leave her, and allows her to control him. She is her own agent in respect to sex, but, as Shostak continues, in the end her insistence on independence from him is not about sex but language (Shostak, 56). Drenka's voice is distinctly different from Sabbath's, and while he coaches her in American idioms (misinforming her intentionally, at times), she retains the voice of a Croatian immigrant until the end. In the scenes just before she dies in the hospital, Sabbath sneaks in ("It's not allowed, but it is allowed if the nurse allows it," 415) to see her, to speak to her: "I'd show up, we'd talk, I'd sit and watch her breathing through that open mouth" (416). Only the talking remains. Her language is confused, both by the foreign accent and by the morphine she is given, but in contrast to all other relationships, here Drenka and Sabbath are equals—it is their shared memories that define the relationship, and Drenka retains control of her identity, her language, until her death. Reliving a shared memory, her accent even transfers to Sabbath, and she teases him: "'But then it came the full stuff'? You are talking like me! I have made you speak translated Croatian! I taught you, too!" "You sure did," Sabbath agrees (426). In another instance, Sabbath uses one of her phrases ("It takes two to tangle") in conversation with Norman's wife Michelle, showing the presence of her language in his after her death (335). Drenka is Sabbath's valiant collaborator, in language as much as in his taboo-breaking ventures, much more so than Nikki or Roseanna could ever have been. Thus the loss of Drenka prompts Sabbath's descent towards madness (Omer-Sherman 170) as his performance disintegrates.

Everyone around Sabbath becomes part of Sabbath's dramatic performance, and the drama teeters on the verge of insanity. Sabbath only barely controls himself and often fails to control those around him. Mark Shechner has described the novel as a "nervous breakdown" (Shechner 146)—indeed, Sabbath deteriorates mentally and physically. At one point he finds himself mistaken for a homeless beggar as he is reciting Shakespeare's *King Lear* on the subway and terrifies a drama student who prompts him when he forgets his lines (300–03). Sabbath, acting the part of the insane, is mistaken for an insane person, and his confusion between what is real (the subway) and what is imagined (Lear? the heath? the idea that this girl might be Nikki's daughter?) moves Roth's reader to both laugh at and pity Sabbath (Safer 171–72).

Roth illustrates through the character of Lincoln, or Linc, Sabbath's old friend, what happens when a life does get out of control: after a midlife crisis, Linc has become too frightened and unsure to function in society. He is therefore exiled. Fired from his job, and moved to a second apartment by his wife, who only communicates via telephone, he drifts into solitary insanity. When he dies alone, his friends suspect suicide (80). Suicide is "*the* taboo," as Sabbath claims in another context (emphasis his, 285), but once you break that, "you lie in [your coffin] like a good little boy who does what he is told" (307). Suicide appeals to Sabbath as a final gesture of control, but clearly it is also one of submission to society's expectations.

On the opposite end of the spectrum, Roth presents Norman Cowan, Lincoln's former business partner and a man firmly tethered to bourgeois values:

> Norman was the subdued member of the duo, if not the office's imaginary spearhead then its levelheaded guardian against Linc's overreaching. He was Linc's equilibrium. [...] The educated son of a venal Jersey city jukebox distributor, Norman had shaped himself into a precise and canny businessman exuding the aura of quiet strength that lean, tall, prematurely balding men often possess. (79)

Short, fat, untidy, and not respectable by any measure, Sabbath is his opposite in both appearance and attitude: Norman claims to be a happily married man, a claim Sabbath quickly dismisses since every man thinks about killing his wife (343). Sabbath uncovers evidence that all is not well in the Cowan household, but Norman forges ahead, regardless of what he may or may not know about his wife's sexual or monetary infidelity.

To remain functioning in a midlife crisis he compares to Linc's, Norman takes the drug Prozac, which he admits is "not [. . .] a dick-friendly drug" (81). His form of crisis-control is clearly not a viable option for Sabbath, who is fond of all sexual activity, and who takes delight in the crises into which this fervor drives him and others. Thus driven, Sabbath commits two substantial offenses against the respectability and order Norman's household represents: in an ecstatic perusal of Norman's teenage daughter's underwear collection, Sabbath creates complete chaos in the room he has been offered as a guest; he also makes a pass (received favorably) at Norman's wife Michelle. When Norman kicks Sabbath out of the house, Sabbath finds himself aligned with Linc: uncontrollable and therefore exiled—contemplating suicide.

The link between the two types of taboo, sexual transgression and suicide (already suggested by the early death of Roseanna's father), is now moved to Sabbath. Driven from Norman's ordered home, Sabbath begins to contemplate his death (by suicide, as he expects, and in imitation of Linc), and, finding himself at the cemetery where family members are buried, begins to make morbid arrangements for a plot and a head stone (376). But Roth introduces the more general connection between death and taboo much earlier in the novel, in the context of Mickey's first wife Nikki's behavior at the death of her mother.

Nikki—whom Norman has described as "tremendously gifted, extremely pretty, but so frail, so needy, so neurotic and fucked-up. No *way* that girl would ever hold together, none" (83)—has trouble coping with the fact that her mother has died and proceeds to sit with the corpse for days. Sabbath describes both her actions and his response: "the fondling of the dead woman's hands, the kissing of her face, the stroking of her hair—all this obliviousness to the raw physical fact—was rendering her taboo to me" (108). Here even Sabbath, who recognizes few boundaries, draws the line: this, then, is forbidden, "taboo," this ongoing physical attachment to the dead. He calls in authorities (an undertaker, transportation to the morgue) who reestablish order and respectability. Meanwhile, however, Sabbath fails in his own responsibility: Nikki "disappears," only to haunt him for the rest of his life.

Ironically, when he describes Nikki's inappropriate response to *her* mother's death, Sabbath is speaking to *his* mother, who, although dead for many years, seems to retain a physical presence in his life, and not only on long drives in the car: the first time the reader is introduced to her, Sabbath is meeting Drenka in their secret "grotto" outside town and imagines his mother hovering about, noting that "his tiny dynamo of a mother was now beyond all taboos—she could be on the lookout for him anywhere" (29). The dead, in his world, are never far, and contrary to the image of the "good little boy who does what he is told," they seem to be limited by nothing, certainly not by social conventions of propriety.

James M. Mellard claims in his article "Death, Mourning, and Besse's Ghost" that it is the mother's legacy (rather than the father's, as in Roth's *Patrimony*) that is developed in *Sabbath's Theater* (Mellard 119). He points to a direct connection between Drenka and Mickey's mother, established by the mother's presence in the grotto, and to the development of this theme throughout the novel. According to Mellard, Drenka's death not only adds to the series of losses Sabbath has endured (Morty, mother, Nikki), but also returns his mother to him; after all, Sabbath realizes, he is now speaking to her (Roth 15). The mother returns from the dead, breaking yet another taboo, to "restore him to real, ordinary meaningful life" by reconnecting him to his childhood, where his troubles began (Mellard 121).

The absence at the center of the novel—the source of both Sabbath's and his mother's trouble with the boundaries between life and death—is occupied by Morty, Mickey's older brother. Morty, remembered as equally successful at school and sports, handy around the house, and socially adjusted, died in World War II. In response to this loss, their mother becomes unavailable to Mickey, and in one fell swoop his childhood, which Sabbath describes as "endlessness" (31), ends. The term suggests unlimited-ness, perfection, certainly the absence of death. Forever excused from the prosaic and imperfect through his early (and heroic) death, Morty becomes Mickey's ideal and, a symbol of his lost childhood. Mickey's turn toward chaos may also be dated to Morty's death: Mickey's exploits in the merchant marines, a training ground for the sexual libertine, follow closely. Mickey commences a life of challenging propriety, thereby becoming the opposite of his socially adjusted brother.

While we are first introduced to Morty as the son his mother mourns, toward the end Sabbath approaches Morty not simply as an idealized childhood memory but appropriates, or takes on, part of this identity. The means by which this return is accomplished is the contents of a box of objects marked "Morty's things." Sabbath steals, or reclaims, this box from a piece of furniture in his cousin Fish's house. The box, and therefore the gift of Morty's things and the link to the past it represents, is directly tied to his mother. Its discovery conjures her presence: the piece of furniture was his mother's, the labeling on the box is his mother's, and he assumes it was his mother's wish that he, Mickey, should come into Morty's possessions eventually. Driving back to Madamaska Falls with the box beside him, the narrator asks: "How could he kill himself now that he had Morty's things?" (415). It is Morty's "things" that return him to life, rather than his foray into the underwear collection of Norman's daughter Debbie, referred to by Sabbath as "*her things*" (emphasis his, 154).

The letters Sabbath finds in the box give Morty a voice—although a voice that is precariously thin, even with the added significance that they are the last five letters he wrote before being shot down in the Phillippines, and therefore his last words. They are about as ordinary as letters from the war can be, talking about card games and food: "I got some bread from the mess hall and we have grape jelly so we made hot chocolate & ate bread & jelly this evening" (408). More interesting is the American flag that was sent to the family after Morty's death. Along with the track medal and the letters, the flag emphasizes Morty's normality, his society-approved behavior in every situation, up to his death. Then again, going to war and being the hero he was expected to be also got him killed, prompting Mickey to protest his brother's death for the rest of his life in a wild array of taboo-breaking acts. To behave well, in Mickey's eyes, spells death— to behave badly, on the other hand, celebrates, indeed insists on, life. But while Sabbath holds on to this clear division, the novel is not so simple: Nikki's imagined continuation of life, the hovering presence of Sabbath's mother, and Drenka's ongoing presence in the novel already suggest a much more fluid boundary between life and death; Morty's return (via his "things") adds to the suspicion that death is in some ways unreliable—and that Mickey may have less cause for protest than he imagines.

Philip Roth has been aggravating many readers since his debut *Goodbye, Columbus*, and certainly since *Portnoy's Complaint* (1958, 1967). Robert M. Greenberg has pointed out that "Roth's frustration with his subcultural position as a Jew in American society is, in many ways, the irritant that produces his fiction" (81), and he irritates his readers in turn—but he treats the topic of transgression with such nuance that the reader responds with empathy.

While *Sabbath's Theater* is not offensive particularly to his Jewish readership (however, as Shechner reminds us, it takes an extended jab at the Japanese, 151), it may take the cake in its sexual explicitness. Three passages in the novel show Roth on the same path as his hero Mickey Sabbath, breaking taboos and taking his audience with him: the (footnoted) transcription of the telephone sex between Kathy Goolsbee and Sabbath (215–34), a masturbation scene Sabbath imagines Roseanna engaging in (431–33), and a sexual encounter Sabbath and Drenka remember on Drenka's death bed (425–28). All three scenes might have slid into the territory of pornography, and taken out of context they certainly are suggestive enough. But as part of the novel *Sabbath's Theater* they function differently: adding one more turn to the screw, Roth involves his audience on the same level Sabbath involved Helen Trumbull in the performance of Sabbath's Indecent Theater. The sexual content in Sabbath's performance is just as integral to his mission as offensiveness, sexual or other, to Roth's: by probing the limits of his readers' tolerance for difference and explicitness he exposes taboos, offering them up for negotiation and discussion—or just pleasure: as Shechner delights, "The defiance simply is!" (147).

Works Cited

Greenberg, Robert M. "Transgression in the Fiction of Philip Roth." *Philip Roth*. Ed. Harold Bloom. Broomall, PA: Chelsea House, 2003. 81–100.

Halio, Jay L. "Eros and Death in Roth's Later Fiction." *Turning Up the Flame: Philip Roth's Later Fiction*. Ed. Jay L. Halio and Ben Siegel. Newark: University of Delaware Press, 2005. 200–06.

Kelleter, Frank. "Portrait of the Sexist as a Dying Man: Death, Ideology, and the Erotic in Philip Roth's *Sabbath's Theater*." *Philip Roth*. Ed. Harold Bloom. Broomall, PA: Chelsea House, 2003. 163–98.

Mellard, James M. "Death, Mourning, and Besse's Ghost: From Philip Roth's *The Facts* to *Sabbath's Theater*." *Turning Up the Flame: Philip Roth's Later Novels*. Ed. Jay L. Halio and Ben Siegel. Cranbury, NJ: Associated University Presses, 2005. 115–24.

Omer-Sherman, Ranen. "'A Little Stranger in the House': Madness and Identity in *Sabbath's Theater.*" *Philip Roth: New Perspectives on an American Author.* Ed. Derek Parker Royal. Westport, CT: Praeger Publishers, 2005. 169–84.

Roth, Philip. *Goodbye, Columbus.* New York: Houghton Mifflin, 1959.

———. *Patrimony: a True Story.* New York: Simon and Schuster, 1991.

———. *Portnoy's Complaint.* New York: Houghton Mifflin, 1969.

———. *Sabbath's Theater.* New York: Vintage International, 1995.

Safer, Elaine. *Mocking the Age: The Later Novels of Philip Roth.* Albany: State University of New York Press, 2006.

———. "The Tragicomic in Philip Roth's *Sabbath's Theater.*" *American Literary Dimensions: Poems and Essays in Honor of Melvin J. Friedman.* Ed. Jay L. Halio and Ben Siegel. Newark: University of Delaware Press, 1999. 169–79.

Shechner, Mark. *Up Society's Ass, Copper.* Madison: University of Wisconsin Press, 2003.

Shostak, Debra. *Philip Roth—Countertexts, Counterlives.* Columbia: University of South Carolina Press, 2004.

THE SATANIC VERSES
(SALMAN RUSHDIE)

~~~

"Breaking Totems and Taboos:
Rushdie's *The Satanic Verses*"
by Rossitsa Artemis,
University of Nicosia, Cyprus

Few contemporary writers have sparked as much controversy as Nobel prize-winner Salman Rushdie, both for his fiction and non-fiction works, and even more so for his outspoken political views. Undoubtedly, Rushdie's work over the years has had a "rippling" effect on culture and politics worldwide. Rushdie continues to deal with more ominous censors than ungracious reviewers and literary critics: shortly after the publication of his novel *The Satanic Verses* (1988), Iran's Ayatollah Khomeini issued a legal judgment (or "*fatwa*") against the author, effectively sentencing him to death for his allegedly injurious and heretical view of Islam. Having lived under the threat of execution for many years, Rushdie has been made painfully aware not simply of the reception his works receive, but also of the vulnerability of the modern man in a world still governed by religious and political fundamentalism and prejudice.

Acknowledged by many as an extremely gifted writer, rejected by others as an exploiter of situations and contexts, Rushdie is extremely prolific and never leaves readers indifferent. His provocative fiction includes *Midnight's Children* (1981), *Shame* (1983), *Haroun and the Sea of Stories* (1990), *East, West* (1994), *The Moor's Last Sigh* (1995), *The Ground Beneath Her Feet* (1999), *Fury* (2001), *Shalimar the Clown*

(2005), and *The Enchantress of Florence* (2008), as well as non-fiction collected in *The Jaguar Smile* (1987), *Imaginary Homelands* (1992), and *Step Across This Line* (2002). Despite the enormous variety of his settings and plot lines, the common motif in all these literary works is Rushdie's questioning of reality, a preoccupation of what has been christened "postmodern" literature. His fantastic representations make a rather disconcerting point about modernity in all its aspects: social, religious, cultural, and political.

Both Rushdie and his characters are often controversial in their downright rejection of the permanency and stability our common beliefs about life and fiction require. He poignantly speaks about his iconoclastic views in the essay "In Good Faith,"

> I am modern, a modern*ist*, urban man, accepting uncertainty as the only constant, change as the only sure thing. I believe in no god, and have done so since I was a young adolescent. I have spiritual needs, and my work has, I hope, a moral and spiritual dimension, but I am content to try and satisfy those needs without recourse to any idea of a Prime Mover or ultimate arbiter. (1991: 405)

Raised in a liberal Muslim family in Hindu India, Rushdie has been condemned as a religious deserter by his more fanatic enemies, who read his more provocative novels, and especially *The Satanic Verses*, as literally as they can. Rushdie's move to the United Kingdom, a country he so vehemently criticized for its foreign and immigration policies in the '70s and '80s, led him to observe: "[. . . I am] already a mongrel self, history's bastard, before London aggravated the condition" (1991: 404). Rushdie's subsequent visibility on the cultural and academic fronts adds to his portrait as a notorious modern literary figure who thrives on polemics and controversy.

The Satanic Verses is a novel that celebrates the controversies that made Rushdie famous so early in his career: irreverence for the Muslim religion and former British Prime Minister Margaret Thatcher's racist politics. The uncertainties that he values so highly are brought here to their most conspicuous state: an utmost disbelief in the grand narratives of religion and the questionable politics of Western—and Eastern—society, seen through the prism of what cultural theorist Jean-François Lyotard calls "the postmodern condition." Rushdie himself describes the nature of this prism while explaining his intent in writing the novel:

> *The Satanic Verses* celebrates hybridity, impurity, intermingling, the transformation that comes of new and unexpected combinations of human beings, cultures, ideas, politics, movies, songs. It rejoices in mongrelization and fears the absolutism of the Pure. (1991: 394)

With this claim in mind, it is understandable that the novel, with its emphasis on the "mongrelization" of grand narratives, upset many cultural conservatives and religious fundamentalists who felt that their way of life was under attack. *The Satanic Verses* is transgressive on many levels: language and imagery in the novel work together to break sacred taboos of Islam and the demagogical doctrines of Western politics. For the Islamic mullahs, as well as some conservative Westerners, even Rushdie's most obvious novelistic transgressions are unpardonable. Rushdie aptly sums up this situation: *The Satanic Verses* pitted him "against the granite, heartless certainties of Actually Existing Islam," as well as against "some 'friends' [in the West]." (1991: 436)

But how are the rejection of totalizing narratives and their "mongrelization" in *The Satanic Verses* offensive, or, rather, for whom are they offensive? A careful look at Rushdie's literary "transgressions" and their repercussions in the world will help us realize, first of all, the dangers of reading fiction literally. For the Islamic believers, and especially for the Islamic clerics, the number of metaphors—not *a* single metaphor—embedded in *The Satanic Verses* is clearly overwhelming and offensive. If read literally as Rushdie's attack on Islam, these metaphors put into question the very sanctity of the Koran (the *Qur'an*). According to this view, the novel, written in bad faith by a religious "deserter," is dangerous for the true believer. In 1989 Ayatollah Khomeini's notorious interpretation of the novel as a book that "has been compiled, printed, and published in opposition to Islam, the Prophet, and the Qur'an" brought a death sentence on the author for questioning and mocking the basic premises of Islam; in other words, for questioning a totalizing myth of the birth of the Koran and the sanctity of the Prophet Muhammad (qtd in Pipes 2004: 27). To this accusation, and the many that followed the publication of *The Satanic Verses*, Rushdie answers straightforwardly,

> To put it as simply as possible: *I am not a Muslim*. It feels
> bizarre, and wholly inappropriate, to be described as some
> sort of heretic after having lived my life as a secular, pluralist,
> eclectic man [...] I do not accept the charge of blasphemy,
> because, as somebody says in *The Satanic Verses*, 'where there is
> no belief, there is no blasphemy.' (1991: 405)

This early clarification and the numerous subsequent interviews and
apologies to Muslims—but not to the theocratic state of the "Actually
Existing Islam"—made Rushdie's intent in writing the novel clearer to
people who believe literature requires, and provides at the same time,
freedom of mind, a transcendence which is "that flight of the human
spirit outside the confines of its material, physical existence [...]"
(1991: 421).

On the other hand, *The Satanic Verses* offends many Westerners by
implicitly critiquing capitalism and the racism of Thatcher's British
society. From a post-colonial perspective, Rushdie rejects the claim of
the West to be a metropolitan center, a righteous illuminator of backward nations and savior of indigenous cultures. The political dema-
gogy of the West is a form of fundamentalism, one just as dangerous
as religious fundamentalism. That is why, as Rushdie points out,

> Writers and politicians are natural rivals. Both groups try to
> make the world in their own images; they fight for the same
> territory. And the novel is one way of denying the official,
> politicians' version of truth. (1991:14)

Thus, Rushdie makes it clear—not only in *The Satanic Verses*, but also in
the rest of his works—that postmodern and post-colonial questioning
of dominant social discourses inevitably clashes with the enshrined
doctrines of society, regardless of there being "Western" or "Eastern."
The Satanic Verses implodes such doctrines, addressing the anxiety of
living in a world that incessantly outgrows the wildest fictional reality.
As Finney points out, the novel "can be seen as a *bricolage* of conflicting
discourses framed by the controlling discourse of fiction."

In the opening scene of *The Satanic Verses*, two colorful and memorable characters, Gibreel Farishta and Saladin Chamcha, fall from the
jumbo jet *Bostan*. While the reader is completely aware of this leap of
imagination, the fall and the ensuing surrealistic events turn the novel into

a meditation on the spiritual and tangibly physical obstacles that divide people of different races, religions, and cultures. The clash between Good and Evil, in literature and real life, and, moreover, the difficulties in easily discriminating between the two, seem to be the underlying issues in this black comedy. To this effect Rushdie introduces an interesting twist in the choices he provides to his two main characters. As he explains,

> *The Satanic Verses* is the story of two painfully divided selves. In the case of one, Saladin Chamcha, the division is secular and societal: he is torn, to put it plainly, between Bombay and London, between East and West. For the other, Gibreel Farishta, the division is spiritual, a rift in the soul. He has lost his faith and is strung out between his immense need to believe and his new inability to do so. The novel is 'about' their quest for wholeness. (1991: 397)

Rushdie does not shy away from offering outrageously critical (as well as poetic) contemplations on the human condition and that elusive quest for "wholeness" in the pastiche reality of the postmodern world. Using the techniques of magic realism, Rushdie never seems to settle completely on a particular view point, but creates a mosaic of "truths" and observations. Thus, the insistence of the omniscient narrator in the novel, which sets the tone of the novel,

> Once upon a time—*it was and it was not so*, as the old stories used to say, *it happened and it never did*—maybe, then, or maybe not [...] (1998: 35)

A world of possibilities and multiple meanings is set into motion by this invocation, with its ambiguous "maybe's." Who speaks and what is said are relatively clearly delineated choices in *The Satanic Verses*; what is more interesting, though, remains in the silences between these choices. Thus the magic transformation in which Gibreel acquires a saintly halo, while a pair of hornlike protrusions grow on Saladin's head, does not settle the question of who is who, or what—or who—is Good and Evil. In an act of spiritual rebirth, each character has to define themselves against the backdrop of a world which favors easy—if incorrect—answers rather than accepting an ever-changing, pluralistic world devoid of certainty. The narrator asks:

How does newness come into the world? How is it born? Of what fusions, translations, conjoinings is it made?

How does it survive, extreme and dangerous as it is? What compromises, what deals, what betrayals of its secret nature must it make to stave off the wrecking crew, the exterminating angel, the guillotine? (8)

Thus "mongrelization" and its potential to change the perceived world, rather than the power of grand narratives to maintain certainty, recurs in several of Gibreel's dreams, in the stories of Gibreel's and Saladin's experiences in Britain, in the story of Muhammad, and so on.

Gibreel's dreams about Muhammad are the primary source of controversy that made Rushdie so unpopular with the Islamic clerics. The chapters "Mahound" and "Return to Jahilia" are particularly blasphemous: even Rushdie's choice of names—"Mahound" is the old derogatory name for the Prophet Muhammad, and "Jahilia" (meaning "ignorance" in Arabic) is the author's name for the holy city of Mecca—are enough to raise the ire of Moslem clerics.

As the central doctrine of Islam, the Koran is accepted as the transcription of the exact words of God, and Muhammad, via the dictation of the angel Gabriel, is the Prophet who brings God's message to people. Rushdie's title references the "satanic verses," an extra couplet that Muhammad supposedly pronounces (after being falsely misled by Satan) and then, under the guidance of Gabriel, he retracts these verses (cf Pipes 2004). In *The Satanic Verses*, Mahound is portrayed as advancing his own agenda by pronouncing the "satanic verses," and not prompted by Satan; therefore the author emphasizes the human aspect (mistake and self-interest) of writing the Koran, not on its sacred origin. Gibreel, the angel, not Gibreel the actor who is actually *dreaming* it all, is a mere disinterested observer,

[. . .] hovering-watching from his highest camera angle, knows one small detail, just one tiny thing that's a bit of a problem here, namely that *it was me both times, baba, me first and second also me.* From my mouth, both the statement and the repudiation, verses and converses, universes and reverses, the whole thing, and we all know how my mouth got worked. (123)

It is easy to see how Rushdie, undoubtedly taking fictional liberty, turns this story—a cornerstone of Islamic belief—upside down to vex authorities. Yet, the author is not questioning the belief itself, but the structure of dogma and its tendency to arrest the thinking of true believers, making them the pawns of pseudo-religious gurus. Rushdie writes of his "glaring dissent" in *The Satanic Verses*:

> What does the novel dissent from? Certainly not from the people's right to faith, though I have none. It dissents most clearly from imposed orthodoxies *of all types*, from the view that the world is quite clearly This and not That. It dissents from the end of debate, of dispute, of dissent. (1991: 396)

It is obvious, then, that Rushdie does not glorify atheism just for the sake of it, but targets the lack of critical understanding and the narrow-minded acceptance of dogmas on different levels and by different social groups. Thus, for example, the narrator in *The Satanic Verses* lashes freely at another modern guru, Maggie the Bitch (269), and the Thatcherite racist regime in the UK. The treatment of immigrants in the eighties is just as hypocritical as the treatment of believers: the discourse of "natural right" and "obligations," combined with a vocabulary harkening back to Enoch Powell's nationalistic speeches in the House of Commons in 1969 threatening the average Englishman with "rivers of blood," proves equally dogmatic even for a writer like Rushdie who is accepted—not assimilated—by the former imperial center. The author's critique of capitalism is also embodied in the character of Hal Valance, the advertising executive, an exploiter who knows an opportunity when he sees one, with no discrimination against geographical detail or cultural bias, because, after all, money is a universal language.

As succinctly put by the author himself, a thoughtful reading of *The Satanic Verses* makes any simplistic conclusion difficult, especially one that charges Rushdie with being *against* Islam and human belief:

> [...] the opposition of imagination to reality, which is also of course the opposition of art to politics—is of great importance, because it reminds us that we are not helpless; that to dream

is to have power. [...] Unreality is the only weapon with which reality can be smashed, so that it may subsequently be reconstructed. (191: 122)

That same "unreality" called "fiction," the dreams made into stories, is entwined in the texture of *The Satanic Verses* to challenge any open-minded reader—not Islamic clerics—to think about the world as a kaleidoscope of uncertainties, identities, and experiences, not as a "flattened world," as Mimi philosophically concludes in the book (261). In the novel, the dissent from monotheism, which imagination and creativity naturally foster in their liberating effect over the soul, vex Mahound to the extent to sentence Baal, the poet, to death for "bringing the worst out of people," through mocking the sacred dogma. Thus the poet challenges a clear response from the Prophet,

> 'Whores and writers, Mahound. We are the people you can't forgive.'
> Mahound replied, 'Writers and whores. I see no difference here.' (392)

As Pipes observes in his study of the controversies surrounding the book and its author, "Rushdie has undeniably great artistic talents, and *The Satanic Verses* is a crowded, elusive and sophisticated tale" (2004: 53). Dense as it is, the novel more than welcomes dissent in our own interpretations as long as the essential freedom to think and to dream is granted. Ultimately, what Rushdie achieves in his book is probably the answer to his own question,

> How is freedom gained? It is taken: never given. To be free, you must first assume your right to freedom. In writing *The Satanic Verses*, I wrote from the assumption that I was, and am, a free man. (1991: 396)

"A love-song to our mongrel selves," *The Satanic Verses* rejects totality in favor of the colorful mosaic of pieces (394). Writers, readers, critics, and prophets all try, with only some success, to put together these pieces.

WORKS CITED

Finney, B. "Demonizing Discourse in Salman Rushdie's *The Satanic Verses*." <http://www.csulb.edu/~bhfinney/SalmanRushdie.html> 20 April 2009.

Pipes, D. *The Rushdie Affair*. New Brunswick, NJ, and London: Transaction Publishers, 2004.

Rushdie, S. *Imaginary Homelands: Essays and Criticism 1981–1991*. London: Granta Books, 1991.

———. *The Satanic Verses*. London: Vintage Books, 1998.

THE POETRY OF ANNE SEXTON

❧

"The Poetic Heroism of Anne Sexton"
by Diana Hume George,
in *Literature and Psychology* (1987)

INTRODUCTION

In her essay "The Poetic Heroism of Anne Sexton," critic
Diana Hume George examines the taboo subject matter that
appears throughout Sexton's poetry and its resonance with
the Oedipus myth, as interpreted by Sigmund Freud and
Bruno Bettelheim. For George, Sexton's attempts to confront
her childhood neuroses recall Oedipus' search for truth.
Sexton "thought herself guilty of her mother's death, and of
marrying her father," and struggles to resolve her feelings
through poetic disclosure. By writing about her time spent in
mental institutions and her feelings of familial guilt, George
demonstrates how many of Sexton's poems play with this
most sacred taboo.

❧

What the story of the Sphinx seems to emphasize is that the
answer to the riddle of life is not just man, but each person

---

George, Diana Hume. "The Poetic Heroism of Anne Sexton." *Literature and
Psychology* 33.3–4 (1987): 76–88.

himself. . . . In contemplating Sophocles' *Oedipus* as Freud did, one realizes that the entire play is essentially Oedipus' struggle to get at the hidden truth. It is a battle for knowledge in which Oedipus has to overcome tremendous inner resistance against recognizing the truth about himself, because he fears so much what he might discover. . . . What forms the essence of our humanity—and of the play—is not our being victims of fate, but our struggle to discover the truth about ourselves.

—Bruno Bettelheim, *Freud and Man's Soul*[1]

Not that it was beautiful,
but that I found some order there.
There ought to be something special
for someone
in this kind of hope.
This is something I would never find
in a lovelier place, my dear,
although your fear is anyone's fear
like an invisible veil between us all . . .
and sometimes in private,
my kitchen, your kitchen,
my face, your face.
—Anne Sexton, "For John, Who Begs Me Not to
        Enquire Further" *To Bedlam and Part Way Back*[2]

Bettelheim's Oedipus

Oedipus, Sophocles, Freud: this is preeminently a man's story, told by men to and for men, about a tragically fated hero who unknowingly slays his father and marries his mother. Despite Freud's attribution of the Oedipus complex to women as well as to men, the story of Oedipus has also remained essentially masculine in the popular imagination. That imagination, sensing perhaps the culturally masculine tenor not only of the myth but of its symbolic meanings, has even tried (with a brief assist from psychoanalysis) to provide a womanly equivalent: The Elektra complex. But Freud stuck stubbornly to his assertion that the story of Oedipus was that of all humankind, and a number of revisionist theorists and practitioners have attempted to explain why. Among the most convincing retellings is Juliet Mitchell's in *Psychoanalysis and Feminism*, in which she urges us to construe the Oedipus complex as more than a term for normal childhood sexual conflicts revolving around intense attachments to the parents, by which measure the significance attributed to it by psychoanalysis may indeed seem inflated. According to Mitchell, the Oedipus complex designates a set of internal and external acts through which every person is initiated into the cultural order; it is not only "a metaphor for the psychic structure of the bourgeois nuclear family under Viennese capitalism," but "a law that describes the way in which all [Western] culture is acquired by each individual."[3]

Critics have been endlessly irritated by the recurring themes of infancy and the relationship to the mother and father in Anne Sexton's poetry. Beginning with her first teacher, John Holmes, Sexton has been accused of childishness and of infantile preoccupations. She insisted that these themes were at the heart of the matter—and not only her matter, but by implication, everyone's. "Grow up," said the decorous world of poetry to her throughout her career; "Stop playing in the crib and the sandbox—and especially stop sniveling about your childhood." Her poetic reply frightened the critics who disliked her work—most of them transparently opposed to psychoanalytic theory—for that reply asserted again and again that grown woman though she might be, successful professional though she might be, the process of working out her relationship to her parents and her childhood was a life's work. Nor did she permit the poetic community to suppose it was only *her* life's work. If we acknowledged it as hers, and as the legitimate domain of poetry, then we would have to come to terms with the possibility that it might be our own lifelong process as well. Blind as Teiresias, she revealed to all of us the truth about Laius' murder. As Bruno Bettelheim writes in *Freud and Man's Soul*, "we encounter in Teiresias the idea that having one's sight turned away from the external world and directed inward—toward the inner nature of things—gives true knowledge and permits understanding of what is hidden and needs to be known."[4]

But it is not Teiresias, finally, with whom I identify Anne Sexton. Rather, it is Oedipus, and specifically the Oedipus of *Freud and Man's Soul*. Bettelheim attempts yet another re-reading of Freud's Oedipus, and I find it the most moving and accessible that contemporary psychoanalysis has offered to an audience larger than its own members. Freud's Oedipus, through Bettelheim, takes on the luminosity of the prophet, and becomes not merely a tragic victim, but an embattled seer. According to Bettelheim, the suggestiveness and referential richness of the Oedipal story only *includes* the implication that little boys want to kill the man they *know* is their father and marry the woman they *know* is their mother. This "common and extreme simplification" ignores the fact that Oedipus did not know what he was doing when he killed Laius and married Jocasta, and that "his greatest desire was to make it *impossible* for himself to harm those he thought were his parents." This crucial detail expands the story's mythic power to include "the child's anxiety and guilt for having patricidal and incestuous wishes," and the consequences of acting on such wishes.[5]

As Bettelheim reads both the Sophocles play and Freud's adaptation of it, the central issues are Oedipus' guilt and his discovery of the truth. Oedipus' lack of initial awareness about what he has done is reflected in psychoanalysis's version of the story by the repression in adulthood of both the murderous feelings toward the parent of the same sex, and the incestuous feelings toward the parent of the opposite sex. Oedipus behaved as he did as a consequence of his real parents having rejected him in the most brutal and literal way possible; he loved the parents he thought were his. "It is only our love for our parents and our conscious wish to protect them that leads us to repress our negative and sexual feelings for them."[6]

Bettelheim also emphasizes another portion of the story often glossed over by theory and by practice: when he fled Corinth, Oedipus did not fully heed the temple inscription, "Know thyself," which implicitly warned against misunderstandings of the oracle's prophecies. He was not sufficiently self-aware in his flight, and later acted out his metaphorical blindness by literally blinding himself. So Oedipus, truth-seeker, sought the complex truths too late; or, translated into psychic parlance, self-knowledge requires an understanding of the "normally unconscious aspects of ourselves." It's Bettelheim's conviction and that of psychoanalysis—and here I part company with him and it regretfully—that knowledge really is power, that to know the unconscious is to be able to control it, and more or less completely. "This is a crucial part of the myth," writes Bettelheim: "as soon as the unknown is made known ... the pernicious consequences of the Oedipal deeds disappear."[7] That is indeed the most hopeful reading of the cease of pestilence in Thebes, but not the only one. No one, after all, can restore Oedipus' sight to him, and his wanderings toward ultimate peace in Colonus are still torturous and tragic. Not until he awaits death does he find his peace. Bettelheim sees the Oedipus in us all as able to be "free" from our own "destructive powers" and their ability to "harm us."[8] This is, of course, the expression of psychoanalysis's own profound wish that it might provide "cure," a wish that Freud himself became suspicious of near the end of his life. I prefer a more realistic phrasing of what the search for self-knowledge might hope to accomplish: a lessening of the destructive hold of unconscious material over people's lives, and a diminished likelihood that one might single-handedly cause a pestilence in the city.

This important reservation aside, I find Bettelheim's reading of Oedipus convincing and important, if not entirely new: Oedipus is a hero who is fated to feel guilty for something he has done but did not know he was doing and did not mean to do; and, more importantly, he is a quester after truth against tremendous inner and external odds, determined to recognize that truth when he finds it, no matter how painful it may be for him and for other people he loves. That truth is peculiarly his own—Bettelheim points out, through DeQuincey, that the Sphinx posed different problems for different people, so that the answer to the riddle is not merely man in general, but Oedipus in particular. But it is also universal. "The answer to the riddle of life is not just man, but each person himself."[9]

In the Oedipus story, it is the woman/mother/wife, Jocasta, who says that she does not want to know the truth and who cannot cope with it when it is revealed. She kills herself because she possesses unwanted knowledge—not, as Bettelheim points out, the knowledge that she has committed incest, but repressed knowledge that she helped to abandon her son to death years earlier. Perhaps it is ironic that I should see Anne Sexton as Oedipus and not as Jocasta. Anne Sexton killed herself. Yet despite that final irony, the essential characteristics of Anne Sexton's poetry identify her not with the overwhelmed and helpless victim/victimizer, Jocasta, but with the hero Oedipus, whose struggle for the truth was determined and tragic. As Alicia Ostriker says in a comparison of Plath and Sexton, Sexton "fought hard with love, greed, and laughter to save herself, and failed."[10] Her "failure" was heroic rather than pathetic, courageous rather than cowardly. Unlike Jocasta, who is immediately defeated by the revelation of the truth, Sexton grappled with her truth again and again, in a deadly hand to hand combat she might be said, on some terms, to have won.

ANNE'S OEDIPUS

That Anne Sexton identified herself with Oedipus is evident in only one modest place in her poetry, in the first collection, *To Bedlam and Part Way Back*. The epigraph for the collection is from a letter of Schopenhauer to Goethe in 1815:

> It is the courage to make a clean breast of it in face of every question that makes the philosopher. He must be like Sophocles' Oedipus, who, seeking enlightenment concerning his terrible fate, pursues his indefatigable enquiry, even when he divines that appalling horror awaits him in the answer. But most of us carry in our heart the Jocasta who begs Oedipus for God's sake not to inquire further . . .

Sexton's biographer, Diane Middlebrook, reveals the previously unavailable details of the story that led to Sexton's use of this epigraph, and to the poem that opens Part II of *Bedlam*, which contains the most intensely confessional material in the collection.[11] "For John, Who Begs Me Not to Enquire Further," was Sexton's ultimate poetic reply to John Holmes's fierce objections to Sexton's "sources and subject matter." She should not, he warned, write about her experiences in mental institutions or her private neuroses; these were not legitimate subjects for poetry, and were more dangerous than useful. Although Sexton could not have known it at the time, Holmes was to be only the first of a series of Jocastas whom Sexton would have to confront in the many years of productivity remaining to her. Her argument in this poem is that of the truth-seeking Oedipus:

> Not that it was beautiful,
> but that, in the end, there was
> a certain sense of order there;
> something worth learning
> in that narrow diary of my mind,
> in the commonplaces of the asylum . . .

Like Oedipus, Sexton does not pretend to be a seeker after beauty here, though she will seek beauty as well later in her poetic life; she seeks, rather, "a certain sense of order," if knowing the truth about oneself, however awful, can yield a pattern, a structure, that will teach one "something worth learning" about how one's mystery can be unwoven. The "narrow diary of my mind" elicits images of the private person confiding confidences to a small and secret book, and she is aware that in employing this image, she addresses the implicit reservations anyone might have about the divulgence of confidences. Yet it seems to me that straight as this image is, Sexton must have intended some slight irony, angry as she had been during the process that led up to this finally loving, forgiving, giving poem addressed to a father figure, teacher, and friend who was, as she later said, "in the long run, ashamed of me where you might be proud of me."[12] The "commonplaces of the asylum" include the "cracked mirror," in which the beholder must acknowledge the fragmented pieces of the self, held up to the scrutiny of whatever wholeness that perceiver can manage. It also prefigures the next and central image of the poem, which Diane Middlebrook finds central not only to this poem, but to Sexton's entire poetics:

> I tapped my own head;
> it was glass, an inverted bowl,
> It is a small thing
> to rage in your own bowl.
> At first it was private,
> Then it was more than myself;
> it was you, or your house
> or your kitchen.

Like that other star-crossed poet, Plath, Sexton is trapped in her bell jar, "an inverted bowl." But by the act of tapping it, she tentatively releases powers that reveal to her that her pain is more than private, that she shares with other isolated beings this "small thing" enlarged by sympathy and empathy.

The scene of this coming into connection with others trapped in their inverted bowls is, significantly, the "house," and more particularly the kitchen, locale of so many of Sexton's scenes of recognition, as it was of Plath's. It is not only, I think, that the kitchen is such a female place, but that here the ritual of preparing and eating food takes place: here all modern people are most literally nourished. This is the room in which her world, suburban America, finds itself most at home. The domesticity suggested by the kitchen implies that here, in this most ordinary and yet formally ritualized room, the most extraordinary human truths will emerge, in the midst of simple converse about the everyday matters of commonplace lives. In this respect, the kitchen and the asylum are perhaps closely related. Neither is Thebes or Corinth, but either may be the crossroads at which one kills one's father, or the ceremonial place in which one marries one's mother.

> And if you turn away
> because there is no lesson here
> I will hold my awkward bowl,
> with all its cracked stars shining
> like a complicated lie,
> and fasten a new skin around it
> as if I were dressing an orange
> or a strange sun.

It is on this passage that Middlebrook bases her contention that tapping the head "produces 'stars,' signs radiant with significance, uniting sufferer and beholder despite the 'glass bowl' that shuts them off from other forms of contact."[13] To that insight, I would add that the cracked stars resulting from tapping the bowl are yet another reflection of the cracked mirror in the asylum, that we all, in kitchens or madhouses, aim toward the same general human truths that shine differently in different lives. The speaker, under the critical scrutiny of the one who has "turned away," must hold her bowl awkwardly, partially disarmed by the withdrawal of an invited commonality. The cracked stars shine "like a complicated lie," Sexton's acknowledgement that we each create our own story, are trapped within our own private perspectives in which we style and shape a truth that has as much of the necessary lie as of authenticity; the lie is "complicated" by our complicity in the egotistical desire to make ourselves, perhaps, the heroes of our stories. There is also a suggestion here, muted from reprimand into plea, that the stars will more likely constitute that "complicated lie," that partial denial of the sought truth, if the invited other rejects the partnership by which a complicated *truth* might emerge: "And if you turn away . . ." When the fellow sufferer changes to the detached or disdainful observer, the speaker has no choice but to "fasten a new skin" around the bowl, an action which defensively separates her from him, and blocks any progress that they might together make toward an understanding; yet the stars still shine underneath, a luminous invitation toward truth.

> This is something I would never
> find in a lovelier place, my dear,
> although your fear is anyone's fear,
> like an invisible veil between us all . . .
> and sometimes in private
> my kitchen, your kitchen,
> my face, your face.

Whatever truth the speaker seeks, it will not be available in "lovelier places" than the private mind speaking its halting language to another private mind, trying to make contact. What separates them, she knows, is the hearer's fear, "anyone's fear," not only of the sick or mad or sordid; "your fear" is also the subject of the inquiry itself. Although the grammatical construction of the last lines is ambiguous, I read them to mean secondarily that the fear pulls down the veil between them in their kitchens and on their faces, and primarily that this "something," this "special sort of hope," takes place in the kitchen and is revealed, through the mutually cracked glass bowls, on their distorted, human, striving faces.

The two lengthy poems that follow this preface to Part II of *Bedlam* reveal the "source and subject" of the cracked stars that John/Jocasta does not want to hear. "The Double Image" and "The Division of Parts" show us this other "cracked mirror" of the mother, image of fragmentation and wholeness for the speaker.

> . . . my mocking mirror, my overthrown
> love, my first image. She eyes me from that face,
> that stony head of death
> I had outgrown.

Addressed to her daughter, "The Double Image" tells the story of a thirty-year-old mother who goes to live with her own mother after the speaker's suicide attempt. An "outgrown child," she inhabits her mother's house as an unwelcome guest who must submit to her mother's resentment for her suicide attempt, and who must sit for a portrait of herself to be hung on a wall opposite her mother's portrait, freezing in time her dependence on her mother, herself as reflection of that "mocking mirror," and her stubborn refusal to become that bitter woman. The mother contracts cancer (blaming her daughter), the daughter is institutionalized again, and the mother begins her slow dying. The speaker estranged from her own daughter by her inability to mother her tells herself one of those complicated lies, and then unravels it:

> . . . And you came each
> weekend. But I lie,
> You seldom came. I just pretended
> you . . .

The lesson she learns that she must pass on to her daughter—this complicated truth made up of so many self-serving lies that must be exploded—is "why I would rather / die than love." And this has much to do, she knows, with her relationship to that "overthrown love," and the speaker's need to turn away from her:

> The artist caught us at the turning;
> we smiled in our canvas home
> before we chose our foreknown separate ways.
> And this was the cave of the mirror,
> that double woman who stares
> at herself, as if she were petrified
> in time . . .

If she is to survive, she will have to acknowledge that she is unwillfully guilty of her own mother's sin, passed now to another generation:

> And this was my worst guilt; you could not cure
> nor soothe it, I made you to find me.

In telling her young daughter this truth, she is giving that child a chance to escape the prison of poisonous identifications handed from mother to daughter to mother to daughter. Mary Gray, Sexton's mother, could not admit or acknowledge this human truth inherent in the reproductive urge; it is Sexton's hope that in admitting her own complicity in this complicated lie, she will provide her child with a way to escape its implications; or if not to escape them entirely, then to know that the trap lies baited for her.

But I have called Anne Sexton Oedipus, and Oedipus wanted to marry his mother, not to harm her. Sexton's Oedipus/Anne knows that the mother is the "first overthrown love" for both sexes, and that the differentiation of desire in males and females occurs later. It is my contention that Oedipus/Anne does "slay" her mother and "marry" her father, just as Oedipus slew his father and married his mother. That Sexton thought herself guilty of her mother's death, and of marrying her father, is explicit throughout her canon. (In "All My Pretty Ones," she also acknowledges the possibility of an unconscious guilt connected with her father's death). Here I will concentrate on her self-perception of this deadly configuration in three poems ranging throughout her career: "The Double Image," (*Bedlam*); "Those Times . . ." (*Live or Die*); and "Divorce, Thy Name is Woman" (*45 Mercy Street*). In "Double Image," she is accused of her mother's death; in "Those Times" she acknowledges this unintentional sin; and in "Divorce, Thy Name is Woman," she speaks of her "marriage" throughout life to her father. This is what Oedipus must discover himself guilty of: the murder of the parent of the same sex, and forbidden incest with the parent of the opposite sex.

"The Double Image" includes one of the most startling and frightening of Sexton's stanzas, made more so by the clever facility and unexpectedness of the rhyme:

> They hung my portrait in the chill
> north light, matching
> me to keep me well,
> Only my mother grew ill.
> She turned from me, as if death were catching,
> as if death transferred,
> as if my dying had eaten inside of her.
> That August you were two, but I timed my days with doubt.
> On the first of September she looked at me
> and said I gave her cancer.
> They carved her sweet hills out
> and still I couldn't answer.

The speaker of this poem is the same woman who remembers putting "bees in my mouth" to keep from devouring her mother in the nursing process as an infant; who knows that "all my need took you down like a meal"; who, though she does not know it as a child, will utterly defeat her mother in "Those Times . . ."

> I did not know that my life, in the end,
> would run over my mother's like a truck
> and all that would remain
> from the year I was six
> was a small hole in my heart, a deaf spot,
> so that I might hear
> the unsaid more clearly.

The "hole in the heart," that "deaf spot," becomes the poet's source of the knowledge of absence; blocked by childhood indignities from hearing the ordinary music of daily life, she takes on the special sensual acuity of the handicapped: what she will hear is the unsaid, just as blind Oedipus will "see" with the sight of the blind visionary.

And like Oedipus, Sexton did not want to run over her mother's life like a truck, or to give her cancer, or to defeat her, or to slay her; she intended, rather, like Oedipus, the opposite; to protect that beloved if rejecting parent. Oedipus is utterly rejected by his biological parents, who wish to murder him that he might not murder his father; his other parents, unknowingly adoptive, are those he loves and flees Corinth to protect when he hears the Oracle. In so fleeing, he fulfills the prophecy. In the Oedipus myth, then, the parental figures are split; the actual and rejecting parents, and the adoptive and loving ones, who might after all be called the "real" parents. In the normative infant and childhood psyche, these roles of rejecting and loving parents are united, so that reality and imago emerge from the same identities and bodies; it is the real parents we love and wish to protect, their imagos we wish to murder and marry. Seeking this complex truth, Sexton knows that she must make reparation for the split inside her that duplicates the split in the psyches of her parents, who both rejected *and* loved her, just as she rejects *and* loves them.

Having "murdered" her mother in the psychic sense, she processed such guilt as if fated to do so. It matters little, I would say, whether or not Mary Gray actually told Anne Sexton that Sexton "gave her cancer," matters equally little whether the mother's trauma over her daughter's suicide attempt actually contributed to the development of her disease. Like Oedipus, she has sought and found her psychic truth: she slew her mother, who had literary aspirations that Sexton would fulfill, who was jealous of this beautiful daughter; *and* she dearly loved the mother that she slew. That is a hard truth. It is peculiarly Anne Sexton's; it is also mine, may be any woman's. Daughters both "love" and "slay" their mothers.

Oedipus/Anne acknowledges the other half of her sin in the countless father poems distributed throughout the canon. Having detailed this intense and lifelong romance elsewhere, I will here rely on the late poem, probably composed almost fifteen years after "The Double Image," in which she most explicitly acknowledges her marriage to the father. Part of the sequence in *45 Mercy Street* called "Eating the Leftovers," "Divorce, Thy Name is Woman" begins in the aftermath of that lifelong marriage:

> I am divorcing daddy—Dybbuk! Dybbuk
> I have been doing it daily all my life . . .

In this poem, Sexton constructs a kind of allegory for woman in western culture. The marriage of daughter to father is represented as literal.

> Later,
> When blood and eggs and breasts
> dropped onto me,
> Daddy and his whiskey breath
> made a long midnight visit
> in a dream that is not a dream
> and then called his lawyer quickly.
> Daddy divorcing me.

The "dream that is not a dream" is a psychic fact, a fact of mental life, something that "actually happens" in the netherland of unconscious primary process. The father seduces the daughter, then rejects her, disowning his own passion and hers. "I have been divorcing him ever since" in the interior world of psychic realities, where the Mother is her witness in the courtroom. The daughter keeps on divorcing him,

"adding up the crimes / Of how he came to me, / how he left me."
Sexton's speaker takes on the voice of any woman working out her
childhood love for her father, any woman still

> waiting, waiting for Daddy to come home
> and stuff me so full of our infected child
> that I turn invisible, but married,
> at last.

To be born a woman in a patriarchy is often to be compelled to live
out precisely this ritual. The maternal urge becomes a parody of its first
manifestation in the desire to present the father with a child. This, in
the tortured psychic world of the poem, is the only true marriage; all
others are only pale and inadequate reflections of this primal union. To
marry one's father is, indeed, to "turn invisible," for it means that the
daughter, becomes not herself, not her mother, but an inverted parody
of herself *and* her mother, of wife *and* daughter. Acknowledging the
incestuous foundations of romantic love on which not only the family,
but all western culture is based, Sexton exposes the underbelly of the
myth—that we are all "the infected child" of incest, that we all become
"invisible," effaced, in the need to "marry, at last." Marriage is the
sanctification of incest, the sacred profanity whose nature we expend
our sublimated energies denying. We are all possessed by the dybbuks
of our personal and cultural pasts. What Sexton speaks of here is as
narrow as the room of each womb we come from, and as broad as
our dedication to Classical culture. We are all implicated, fathers and
daughters alike, all dwelling in a shadow world in which the realities
we perceive are shadows of original forms—and of original desires.
We stay in the cave willingly, perceiving reflected forms, because we
cannot look upon those forms directly without becoming "invisible."
Yet we seek that original form, that original desire, never quite content
with its substitute.

While Sexton breaks this ultimate taboo, thereby acknowledging
her self-effacement, her speaker also wants to affirm the divorce. The
"solution" of the poem is a continual process of divorce, an unending
courtroom scene, but one which always returns from courtroom to
bedroom, where the woman is "opening and shutting the windows.
Making the bed and tearing it apart." Before and after the divorce
of man and wife is this continuous marriage to and divorce from the

father, a permanent oscillation between two conflicting desires: to divorce and be done with; and to "marry, at last."

* * * * *

Far from being done with the horrors he discovers in his pursuit of truth when he does indeed uncover it and blind himself, Oedipus does not find peace until he awaits death at Colonus, in the wake of years of blind wandering. The Jocastas in Anne Sexton's life begged her not to inquire further; when she did, psychoanalysis held out to her the hope of which Bettelheim speaks on behalf of psychoanalysis: that knowledge of the truth will set one free. Her truth, tougher by far than either the willed ignorance of Jocasta which cannot endure revelation, or the mandated "liberty" of analytic cure, is more like that of the original Oedipus: complex, tragic, visionary. Sexton did not, like Jocasta, find the sought truth and simply die of it; in the many years between her first exploration of truth in *Bedlam* and her death in 1974, she triumphed over her guilt and her ghosts again and again. The "strange goddess face" of the slain mother whom the infant ate— "all my need took / you down like a meal"—is redeemed in a dream of reparation and mutual forgiveness in "Dreaming the Breasts:"

> The breasts I knew at midnight
> beat like the sea in me now.
> Mother, I put bees in my mouth
> to keep from eating
> yet it did you no good.
> In the end they cut off your breasts
> and milk poured from them
> into the surgeon's hand
> and he embraced them.
> I took them from him
> and planted them.

The planting of the mother's severed breasts enables "those dear white ponies" to "go galloping, galloping, / wherever you are;" and the daughter, for the moment of this poem, is renewed into her own life, free of guilt and pain. In "All My Pretty Ones," the daughter discovering her father's flaws after his death in her mother's diary is able, by coming to terms with them and with their small duplications in her own life, to reach some kind of catharsis of pity and fear:

> Only in this hoarded span will love persevere.
> Whether you are pretty or not, I outlive you,
> bend down my strange face to yours and forgive you.

If this act of mutual forgiveness with mother and father must be repeated more than once, this is not a sign of weakness of resolve and will and heart, but of their strengths and determination. No resolution is ever quite so permanent as humans might wish. Anne Sexton could not be utterly and finally freed of her ghosts and her guilt in this life, and her poetry thus reveals these other "complicated lies:" of poetry as celebration only, of knowledge as ultimate freedom. "What forms the essence of our humanity—and of [*Oedipus Rex*]—is not our being victims of fate, but our struggle to discover the truth about ourselves."[14] What forms the essence of Anne Sexton's poetic achievement is not her status as victim, but her struggle to discover the truth about herself, to turn her blindness into insight. And unless we "turn away," like Jocasta, like John Holmes, there ought indeed to be "something special" in "this kind of hope," perhaps in private.

> my kitchen, your kitchen,
> my face, your face.

NOTES

1. Bruno Bettelheim, *Freud and Man's Soul* (New York: Alfred A. Knopf, 1983), pp. 27–31.
2. Anne Sexton, *The Complete Poems* (Boston: Houghton Mifflin Company, 1981), p. 34.
3. Juliet Mitchell, *Psychoanalysis and Feminism* (New York: Random House, 1974), p. xxi.
4. Bettelheim, pp. 23–24.
5. Bettelheim, p. 22.
6. Bettelheim, p. 23.
7. Bettelheim, p. 24.
8. Bettelheim, pp. 26–27.
9. Bettelheim, p. 27.

10. Alicia Ostriker, *Writing Like A Woman* (Ann Arbor: University of Michigan Press, 1983), p. 5.

11. Diane Middlebrook, "Housewife into Poet: The Apprenticeship of Anne Sexton," *New England Quarterly*, 56, No. 4 (December 1983), pp. 483–503.

12. Middlebrook, p. 496.

13. Middlebrook, p. 494.

14. Bettelheim, p. 30.

THE PROSE WORKS OF JONATHAN SWIFT

"Biographical Introduction"
by W.E.H. Lecky, in *Swift's* Tale of a Tub *and Other Early Works* (1897)

INTRODUCTION

In this passage from his biographical essay on the life and works of Jonathan Swift, W.E.H. Lecky attempts to illuminate the temperament that produced such "coarse and irreverent" works as *Tale of a Tub* and *Gulliver's Travels*. "Pouring a torrent of ridicule and hatred on all its opponents," Swift incorporated taboo material in his writings for moral purposes. For Lecky, though Swift "indulged more habitually in coarse, revolting, and indecent imagery" than any other author of the period, "his faults in this respect are rather those of taste than of morals." Lecky concludes that Swift's satirical use of the taboo was also precipitated by his melancholic worldview: "It was his deliberate opinion that man is hopelessly corrupt, that the evil preponderates over the good, and that life itself is a curse." According to Lecky, this perspective informs *Gulliver's Travels*: as Swift himself once wrote, he intended his most famous work "to vex the world rather than to divert it."

Lecky, W.E.H., M.P. "Biographical Introduction." *Swift's* Tale of a Tub *and Other Early Works*. Ed. Temple Scott. *The Prose Works of Jonathan Swift, D.D., Volume I.* London: George Bell and Sons, 1897.

It is remarkable that a writer who was destined to become the greatest of English humourists, and one of the greatest masters of English prose, should have wholly failed to discover his true talents before his twenty-ninth year. There is some reason to believe that the first sketch of "The Tale of a Tub" was written at Kilroot, but it was on his return to Moor Park in 1697 that this great work assumed its complete form, though it was not published till 1704. To the same period also belongs that exquisite piece of humour, "The Battle of the Books," the one lasting fruit of the silly controversy about the comparative merits of the ancient and modern writers which then greatly occupied writers both in France and England, and into which Temple, though totally destitute of classical scholarship, had foolishly flung himself. Of the merits of the controversy which such scholars as Bentley and Wotton waged with the Christ Church wits, the world has long since formed its opinion; but the fact that the burlesque was intended to ridicule the party who were incontestably in the right does not detract from its extraordinary literary merits. It appears to have been written to amuse or gratify Temple, and it was not published till 1704.

[...]

"Whoever has a true value for Church and State," Swift wrote at a later period, "should avoid the extremes of Whig for the sake of the former and the extremes of Tory on account of the latter." In these words we have the true key to his politics. He was at no period of his life a Jacobite. He fully and cordially accepted the Revolution, and either never held the Tory doctrine of the divine right of kings, or at least accepted the king *de facto* as the rightful sovereign. As long as the question was mainly a question of dynasty he was frankly Whig, and it was natural that a young man who was formed in the school of Temple should have taken this side. On the other hand, Swift was beyond all things a Churchman, and was accustomed to subordinate every other consideration to the furtherance of Church interests. In each period of his life this intense ecclesiastical sentiment appears. Coarse and irreverent as are many passages in the "Tale of a Tub," which was published in 1704, the main purport of the book was to defend the Church of England, by pouring a torrent of ridicule and hatred on all its opponents, whether they be Papists, or Nonconformists, or Freethinkers. In his "Project for the Reformation of Manners," in his "Sentiments of a Church of England Man," in his "Argument against the Abolition of Christianity," in his "Letter to a Member of Parliament concerning the

Sacramental Test," all of which were written when he was still ostensibly a Whig, the same decided Church feeling is more reverently expressed. It appeared not less clearly in his later Irish tracts, when it was his clear political interest to endeavour to unite all religions in Ireland in support of his Irish policy. The abolition of the Test Act, which excluded Nonconformists from office, was opposed by Swift at every period of his life. In the reign of Queen Anne, and especially in its later years, party politics grouped themselves mainly on ecclesiastical lines. It was on the cry of Church in danger that the Tory party rode into power in 1710, and the close alliance between the Whigs and the Nonconformists, and between the Tories and the Church, was the main fact governing the party divisions of the time. There could be no doubt to which side Swift would inevitably gravitate.

[...]

In that remarkable "Essay on Public Absurdities," which was published after his death, he deplored that persons without landed property could by means of the boroughs obtain an entrance into Parliament, and that the suffrage had been granted to any one who was not a member of the Established Church, and he condemned absolutely the system of standing armies which had recently grown up. On the other hand, on some questions of Parliamentary reform, he held very advanced views. Like most of his party he strenuously advocated annual Parliaments, believing them to be the only true foundation of liberty, and the only means of putting an end to corrupt traffic between ministers and members of Parliament. He blamed the custom of throwing the expense of an election upon a candidate; the custom of making forty-shilling freeholders in order to give votes to landlords, and the immunity of members and of their servants from civil suits. "It is likewise," he says, "absurd that boroughs decayed are not absolutely extinguished, because the returned members do in reality represent nobody at all; and that several large towns are not represented, though full of industrious townsmen."

The four years of the Harley administration form the most brilliant and probably the happiest period of his life. His genius had now reached its full maturity, and he found the sphere which beyond all others was most fitted for its exercise. In many of the qualities of effective political writing he has never been surpassed. Without the grace and delicacy of Addison, without the rich imaginative eloquence or the profound philosophic insight of Burke, he was a far greater master of that terse, homely, and nervous logic which appeals most powerfully to the English mind, and no writer has ever excelled him in the vivid force of his illustrations, in trenchant, original, and inventive wit, or in concentrated malignity of invective or satire. With all the intellectual and most of the moral qualities of the most terrible partisan he combined many of the gifts of a consummate statesman—a marvellous power of captivating those with whom he came in contact, great skill in reading characters and managing men, a rapid, decisive judgment in emergencies, an eminently practical mind, seizing with a happy tact the common-sense view of every question he treated, and almost absolutely free from the usual defects of mere literary politicians. But for his profession he might have risen to the highest posts of English statesmanship, and in spite of his profession, and without any of the advantages of rank or office, he was for some time one of the most influential men in England. He stemmed the tide of political literature, which had been flowing strongly against his party, and the admirable force of his popular reasoning, as well as the fierce virulence of his attacks, placed him at once in the first position in the fray. The Tory party, assailed by almost overwhelming combinations from without, and distracted by the most serious divisions within, found in him its most powerful defender.

[...]

Another source of annoyance to Swift was the difficulty with which he obtained Church preferment. He knew that his political position was exceedingly transient; he had no resources except his living. He appears to have taken no pains to make profit from his writings. "I never got a farthing," he wrote in 1735, "by anything I wrote, except once about eight years ago, and that was by Mr. Pope's prudent management for me." By his influence at least one bishopric and many other places had been given away, and yet he was unable to obtain for himself any preferment that would place him above the vicissitudes of politics. The antipathy of the queen was unabated; the Duchess of Somerset, whose influence at Court was very great, and whom Swift had bitterly and coarsely satirized, employed herself with untiring hatred in opposing his promotion, and all the remonstrances of the ministers and all the entreaties of Lady Masham were unable to overcome the determination of the queen.

The charge of scepticism was one which Swift bitterly resented, and there is no class whom he more savagely assailed than the Deists of his time. At the same time no one can be surprised that such a charge should be brought against a writer who wrote as Swift had done in the "Tale of a Tub" about the Roman Catholic doctrine concerning the Sacrament and the Calvinistic doctrine concerning inspiration. And although the "Tale of a Tub" is an extreme example, the same spirit pervades many of his other performances, especially those wonderful lines about the Judgment of the World by Jupiter, which Chesterfield sent to Voltaire.[1] His wit was perfectly unbridled. His unrivalled power of ludicrous combination seldom failed to get the better of his prudence, and he found it impossible to resist a jest. It must be added that no writer of the time indulged more habitually in coarse, revolting, and indecent imagery; that he delighted in a strain of ribald abuse peculiarly unbecoming in a clergyman; that he was the intimate friend of Bolingbroke and Pope, whose freethinking opinions were notorious, and that he frequently expressed a strong dislike for his profession. In one of his poems he describes himself as—

"A clergyman of special note
For shunning those of his own coat,
Which made his brethren of the gown
Take care betimes to run him down."

In another poem he says:

"A genius in a reverend gown
Will always keep its owner down;
'Tis an unnatural conjunction,
And spoils the credit of the function.

. . . .

"And as, of old, mathematicians
Were by the vulgar thought magicians,
So academic dull ale-drinkers
Pronounce all men of wit freethinkers."

At the same time, while it must be admitted that Swift was far from being a model clergyman, it is, I conceive, a misapprehension to regard him as a secret disbeliever in Christianity. He was admirably described by St. John as "a hypocrite reversed." He disguised as far as possible both his religion and his affections, and took a morbid pleasure in parading the harsher features of his nature. If we bear this in mind, the facts of his life seem entirely incompatible with the hypothesis of habitual concealed unbelief. I do not allude merely to the vehemence with which he at all times defended the interests of the Church, nor yet to the scrupulousness with which he discharged his functions as a clergyman, to his increasing his duties by reading prayers on Wednesdays and Fridays at Laracor, and daily at St. Patrick's, to his administering the Sacrament every week, and paying great attention to his choir, and to all other matters connected with his deanery. In these respects he appears to have been wholly beyond reproach, and Hawkesworth has described the solemnity of his manner in the pulpit and the reading-desk, and in the grace which he pronounced at meals. But much more significant than these things are the many instances of concealed religion that were discovered by his friends. Delany had been weeks in his house before he found out that he had family prayers every morning with his servants. In London he rose early to attend public worship at an hour when he might escape the notice of his friends. Though he was never a rich man, he systematically allotted a third of his income to the poor, and he continued his unostentatious charity when extreme misanthropy and growing avarice must have rendered it peculiarly trying. He was observed in his later years, when his mind had given way, and when it was found necessary to watch him, pursuing his private devotions with undeviating regularity, and some of his letters, written under circumstances of agonizing sorrow, contain religious expressions of the most touching character. Many things which he wrote could not have been written by a reverent or deeply pious man, but his "Proposal for the Advancement of Religion," his admirable letter to a young clergyman on the qualities that are requisite in his profession, the singularly beautiful prayers which he wrote for the use of Stella when she was dying, are all worthy of a high place in religious literature. His sermons, as he said himself, were too like pamphlets, but they are full of good sense and sound piety admirably and decorously expressed. Of the most political of them—that "On Doing Good"—Burke has said that it "contains perhaps the best motives to patriotism that were ever delivered within so small a compass."

It must be added that the coarseness for which Swift has been so often and so justly censured is not the coarseness of vice. He accumulates images of a kind that most men would have regarded as loathsome, but there is nothing sensual in his writings; he never awakens an impure curiosity, or invests guilt with a meretricious charm. Vice certainly never appears attractive in his pages, and it may be safely affirmed that no one has ever been allured to vicious courses by reading them. He is often very repulsive and very indecent, but his faults in this respect are rather those of taste than of morals.

[...]

That morbid melancholy to which he had ever been subject assumed a darker hue and a more unremitting sway as the shadows began to lengthen upon his path. It had appeared very vividly in "Gulliver's Travels," which was published in 1726. Like nearly all Swift's works this great book was published anonymously, and like nearly all of them it met with a great and immediate success. It is, indeed, one of the most original as well as one of the most enduring books of the eighteenth century. Few things might have seemed more impossible than to combine in a single work the charm of an eminently popular children's story, a savage satire on human nature, and a large amount of shrewd and practical political speculation. Yet all this will be found in "Gulliver." Of all Swift's works it probably exhibits most frequently his idiosyncrasies and his sentiments. We find his old hatred of mathematics displayed in the history of Laputa; his devotion to his disgraced friends in the attempt to cast ridicule on the evidence on which Atterbury was condemned; his antipathy to Sir Isaac Newton, whose habitual absence of mind is said to have suggested the flappers; as well allusions to Sir R. Walpole, to the doubtful policy of the Prince of Wales, and to the antipathy Queen Anne had conceived against him on account of the indecorous manner in which he had defended the Church. We find, above all, his profound disenchantment with human life and his deep-seated contempt for mankind in his picture of the Yahoos. Embittered by disappointment and ill-health, and separated by death or by his position from all he most deeply loved, he had learnt to look with contempt upon the contests in which so much of his life had been expended, and his naturally stern, gloomy, and foreboding nature darkened into an intense misanthropy. "I love only individuals," he once wrote. He "hated and detested that animal called man," and he declared that he wrote "Gulliver" "to vex the world rather than to divert it." It was his deliberate opinion that man is hopelessly corrupt, that the evil preponderates over the good, and that life itself is a curse. No one who really understands Swift will question the reality and the intensity of this misanthropy. It was one of his strange habits to celebrate his birthday by reading the third chapter of the Book of Job, in which the patriarch cursed bitterly the day of his birth. "I hate life," he once wrote on learning the early death of a dear friend, "when I think it is exposed to such accidents, and to see so many thousand wretches burdening the earth while such as her die makes me think God did never intend life for a blessing." "Life," he wrote to Pope, "is not a farce: it is a ridiculous tragedy, which is the worst kind of composition."

The melancholy of Swift was doubtless essentially constitutional, and mainly due to a physical malady which had long acted upon his brain. His nature was a profoundly unhappy one, but it is not true that his life was on the whole unprosperous. Very few penniless men of genius have had the advantages which he obtained at an early age by his connection with Sir William Temple. He tasted in ample measure all the sweets of literary success, and although his political career was chequered by grave disappointments he obtained both in England and in Ireland some brilliant triumphs. A deanery in an important provincial capital, where he was adored by the populace, and where he had warm friends among the gentry, may not have been all to which he aspired, but it was no very deplorable fate, and although the income attached to it was moderate and at one time greatly diminished, it was sufficient for his small wants and frugal habits. Above all, few men have received from those who knew them best a larger measure of affection and friendship. But happiness and misery come mainly from within, and to Swift life had lost all its charm.

Note

1. "With a whirl of thought oppress'd,
   I sunk from reverie to rest.
   A horrid vision seized my head,
   I saw the graves give up their dead!
   Jove, arm'd with terrors, burst the skies,
   And thunder roars and lightning flies!
   Amazed, confused, its fate unknown,
   The world stands trembling at his throne!
   While each pale sinner hung his head,
   Jove, nodding, shook the heavens, and said:

'Offending race of human kind.
By nature, reason, learning, blind;
You who, through frailty, stepp'd aside;
And you, who never fell—from pride:
You who in different sects were shamm'd,
And come to see each other damn'd;
(So some folk told you, but they knew
No more of Jove's designs than you;)
—The world's mad business now is o'er,
And I resent these pranks no more.
—I to such blockheads set my wit!
I damn such fools!—Go, go, you're bit.'"

TESS OF THE D'URBERVILLES
(THOMAS HARDY)

❧

"*Tess of the D'Urbervilles*: The 'Pure Woman'"
by Geoffrey Wagner, in *Five for Freedom:*
A Study of Feminist Fiction

INTRODUCTION

In his wide-ranging discussion of *Tess of the D'Urbervilles*, Geoffrey Wagner examines Thomas Hardy's portrayal of femininity and its relation to the views of D.H. Lawrence and Simone de Beauvoir, as well as biological and anthropological debates regarding gender difference. Writing "in a culture which constantly took offence at the reading of erotic betrayal as prototypical of religious betrayal, and/or vice versa," Hardy's novel explores how society "executes Tess, as it did Camus's Meursault, and for not entirely dissimilar reasons. In neither case is the murder the guilt; the revolt against convention is the real guilt." Thus, for Wagner, Hardy's novel criticizes the double standard of an unjust, male-dominated society where feminine sexuality is held to be taboo and "the female is the victim of the species."

❧

Wagner, Geoffrey. "*Tess of the D'Urbervilles*: The 'Pure Woman'." *Five for Freedom: A Study of Feminist Fiction*. 1972. Madison, NJ: Fairleigh Dickinson University Press, 1973. 183–93, 196–211.

'Woman is truly less free today than ever she has been since time began, in the womanly sense of freedom. Which means, she has less peace, less of that lovely womanly peace that flows like a river, less of the lovely, flower-like repose of a happy woman, less of the nameless joy in life, purely unconscious, which is the very breath of a woman's being.'

D. H. Lawrence

Hardy asks—What is love? In *Tess of the D'Urbervilles*, his thirteenth novel in order of composition and possibly his first in emotional commitment, we have the heroine as victim, 'a visionary essence of woman—a whole sex condensed into one typical form'.[1] She is perhaps the most firmly fleshed-out person in these pages, as also the most fully sexed. What is more, Hardy takes pains to present her as both a living, breathing, individual woman and one trying hard to defer to the models in her culture. In short, she exemplifies what one feminist has defined as modern woman's true tragedy—'the sad thing for women is that they have participated in the destruction of their own eroticism'.[2]

It is important to be clear about Hardy's intentions here from the start. For his own reticences, compounded with those of his time, sometimes obscure—certainly for the contemporary student steeped in libertine literature—what shimmers through the imagery, in a manner in which of course it does in life. Tess liked sex.

In the serial publication in the *Graphic*, for instance, Tess's account to her mother of her own seduction by Alec d'Urberville is wholly changed; in it Tess is deceived into a false marriage ceremony in a 'private room' with Alec. This sop to contemporary bias (the term morality can barely be used), apparently echoing the similar deception of Thomasina in *The Return of the Native*, was reinforced by the expunging of all references to Tess's child from the serial story, including the whole of Chapter XIV. The first episode involving the text-painter, whose fire-and-brimstone hortations Tess instinctively felt to be 'Crushing! killing!', was also omitted.[3]

While Hardy was no Flaubert in this respect—after all, he had had Harper's American offer for *Tess* in his pocket for over a year before British serialization—he nevertheless went about faithful thematic restoration for eventual book publication, letting Angel Clare carry the dairymaids in his arms over the flooded lane where his magazine editor had successfully suggested his transporting them by wheelbarrow ... and, above all, restoring the famous, eloquent subtitle 'A Pure Woman', which estimate, as he himself put it in his Preface to the Fifth and Later Editions, 'was disputed more than anything in the book'.[4]

So between Phase The First ('The Maiden') and Phase The Second ('Maiden No More,' explicitly enough) there is an interval or lacuna during which Tess must be conceived as having been carried away by her sexual side, to which she obviously yielded with a degree of pleasure. Alec's initiation into sex—bully though he is—was not, in short, wholly unpleasant. She was, in Hardy's words, 'stirred to confused surrender awhile ...', and, in her own to Alec, 'My eyes were dazed by you for a little, and that was all.' He, meanwhile, was the kind of man who makes James's Doctor Sloper exclaim in exasperation, 'You women are all the same! But the type to which your brother belongs was made to be the ruin of you, and you were made to be its hand-maids and victims.'

We must establish all this securely at the start since it influences so much later on. The structural response comes in the pivotal confession scene with Angel, whom Tess realizes she could at this point win over by the wiles of sex yet refrains from so doing, sensing that (in a shame-culture for women) seduction can be no solution—'she might have used it promisingly', we read here, 'it' being 'her exceptional physical nature'. Hence Tess hates herself for her initial weakness, really a little rape when we compare its similarity with that of the dying pheasants later on when she again sleeps outside. So at the very beginning of her destiny she turns with flashing eyes on Alec to cry, 'My God! I could knock you out of the gig! Did it never strike your mind that what every woman says some women may feel?'

We now know, or think we know, very much more about Thomas Hardy's private life and it may be that his liaison with Tryphena Sparks, who probably bore him the only child he ever had, urged further reticences on an already inordinately shy author. Sue Bridehead of *Jude the Obscure* and Tryphena are indeed astonishingly alike, and Hardy himself said that 'some of the circumstances' of this book were suggested by the death of a lady in 1890, the year in which Tryphena herself died. *Jude* was written not long after *Tess*. The model for Tess herself was apparently a dairymaid called Marian, four years older than himself and 'one of the few portraits from life in his works' (Florence Emily Hardy).

Appearing in 1895, *Jude* was the last novel Hardy ever wrote, so far as we know. 'A man must be a fool to deliberately stand up to be shot at', as he put it, splitting an infinitive, in a diary entry of 15 April 1892. He had already been astonished at, and soured by, the extraordinary reception of *Tess*, and *Jude*'s was worse, the *Pall Mall Gazette* heading their review 'Jude The Obscene', while the Bishop of Wakefield bragged that he had thrown the book into the fire. According to his second wife, Florency Emily Dugdale, Hardy hated even to be touched. Yet his reticences may have been a protective persona, or mask—we note Ezra Pound's high estimate in his *ABC of Reading*, while quite independently Virginia Woolf saw the public stance of the late Hardy as a kind of self-protective pose. He liked to touch his vast bevy of cats, at any rate.

Surely the man had to grow some self-protection in a culture which constantly took offence at the reading of erotic betrayal as prototypical of religious betrayal, and/or vice versa. In view of the reception of his novels, to which we will return below, then, Hardy can scarcely be called hypersensitive if he soon reverted to poetry, which he deemed his 'more instinctive kind of expression'. Indeed, the best of his novels are pure prose poems.

And actually, a lot of Hardy's reticences are what might be called semantic hang-ups of his time (see his article 'Candour in English Fiction', first published in *The New Review* for January, 1890). The marvellous metaphor in *Tess* of the mechanical reaper making a noise 'like the love-making call of the grasshopper'—marvellous in that the two arms of the image comprise so much of our time—is revised for first publication to 'the love call of the grasshopper'.[5]

As with *Jane Eyre*, an initial (anti-familial) breach with convention starts out others. In Tess's case, of course, for she is surely one of the most charming heroines in literature, this breach of convention is based on obeisance to another. For if it had not been for her father's egregious infatuation with aristocracy, Tess would never have been urged forward by her mother in the first place (pimped by her maternal parent would be the less polite, if more accurate, term). Flatteringly described as 'foolish', her mother blames her oldest daughter for not having got Alec to marry her, later chides her again for telling Angel the truth about the resulting bastard ('christened' Sorrow, in book form), and can still round on her at the end for not having practised general sexual deception as a life principle—'O, Tess, what's the use of your playing at marrying gentlemen, if it leaves us like this!'

Finally, the 'maternal' Joan Durbeyfield is responsible for pressuring Tess to marry Angel, and so sets in train the eventual tragedy. In fact, Hardy's ironies can become a shade heavy-handed in these contexts, at least for modern taste, as when he has Alec d'Urberville, who has watched Tess tortured by treadmill-like labour on the steam thresher all day long, tell her—the woman he himself had seduced—'You have been the cause of my backsliding.'

But a novel, as Hardy wrote in a Preface to this one, is 'an impression, not an argument'. As a young critic has put it, 'Nobody thinks of T. S. Eliot or D. H. Lawrence as model democrats, or of *The Waste Land* or *Women in Love* as being about good citizenship. But both *are* about the impact of modern civilization on the finest, keenest, most intelligent, most serious minds involved in it.'[6]

Hardy has here seen that a moment has come in our civilization when meekness and humility are no longer values in the true sense ... and all the less so since we pay such loud lip-service to them in church. We talk a lot about the virtues of humility but, in America at any rate, encourage our sons to be aggressive, 'tough', to 'flay' and 'whip' their opposition in sports, to make a 'killing' on the market. We give meekness few emotional rights any more. So the two strands of our culture are being unravelled in different directions, as it were (one of Tess's sisters is called Modesty). Flaubert anticipated this important feminist insight in his late story *Un Coeur simple*. Gogol also comes to mind.

Male sexual aggression, incarnate here in Alec d'Urberville, is thus virtually half of the Puritan conscience. James's Dr Sloper had said as much. 'The man submits', in the words of another writer, 'to the force of nature; the woman submits to the man. Sex is an act of aggression with which she complies only because she is physically the weaker.'[7] So Alec can cry out, 'You have been the cause of my backsliding'. Forever Eve! As a woman, it must seem, at times, that you cannot win. For, as Hardy brilliantly if indirectly demonstrates, to put woman on a pedestal is to take the defence of her honour out of her own control, to tie her hands behind her back. Man is then encouraged to attack purity *per se* ... as does Alec d'Urberville (or Dostoevsky's Svidrigailov). I am suggesting that in another culture Tess could take care of herself very well, thank you.

In so doing, however, one must also confess that Hardy considerably loads the dice by making Tess, an unlettered country girl, after all, 'quite a Malthusian towards her mother for thoughtlessly giving her so many little sisters and brothers' (a reflection from Hardy rather than Tess) and by having her, in her teens, think of her siblings as 'six helpless creatures, who had never been asked if they wished for life on any terms'. This unlikely consideration on the part of a teenage Wessex girl is almost immediately succeeded by a slighting reference to Wordsworth and his belief in 'Nature's holy plan' (from 'Lines Written in Early Spring'). Almost the most violent authorial outbreak in the whole of *Tess* replies to this in the penultimate Phase The Sixth ('The Convert'), where we read:

> 'for to Tess, as to not a few millions of others, there was ghastly satire in the poet's lines—
> Not in utter nakedness.
> But trailing clouds of glory do we come.
> To her and her like, birth itself was an ordeal of degrading personal compulsion, whose gratuitousness nothing in the result seemed to justify, and at best could only palliate.'

Hardy is here advancing another sexological insight, namely that woman has laboured too long—in all senses—under the ban of the concept that sexual pleasure is a concomitant of reproduction. As Ruth Herschberger well puts it:

> 'In a very basic sense, a child is the only admission of marital eroticism that wins the approbation of society . . . It is of the utmost importance to make clear that reproduction and the sex act are far more closely allied in the man's case than in the woman's for in the normal man the sex act is by Nature's design specifically a reproductive act as well.'[8]

Intercourse must always have reproductive significance for the male. It does not do so for the female: A woman ovulates, sheds an egg, usually but once a month, and during the long child-bearing period of her life is generally infertile; furthermore, ovulation is not with her a response to copulation (as with horses and sheep).

It is far from far-fetched to bring this into a discussion of *Tess* for the imagery surrounding the heroine is so succulently suggestive of what sexual union is for a woman—'The coordinated system of the male is merely the negative reflection of the positive features of the female. The male functions to produce sperm to give to the female' (Herschberger). As far as the sexual side of the book goes, this could have been Hardy's epigraph. It is another sense in which his heroine is a 'pure' woman.

Some of the sweetest pictures of Tess are tactful reinterpretations of this 'woman's view' of biology; here is Tess on that June evening when she wanders out 'conscious of neither time nor space' and hears Angel's harp:

> 'Tess had heard those notes in the attic above her head. Dim, flattened, constrained by their confinement, they had never appealed to her as now, when they wandered in the still air with a stark quality. like that of nudity. . . . The outskirt of the garden in which Tess found herself had been left uncultivated for some years, and was now damp and rank with juicy grass which sent up mists of pollen at a touch; and with tall blooming weeds emitting offensive smells—weeds whose red and yellow and purple hues formed a polychrome as dazzling as that of cultivated flowers. She went stealthily as a cat through this profusion of growth, gathering cuckoo-spittle on her skirts, cracking snails that were underfoot, staining her hands with thistle-milk and slug-slime, and rubbing off upon her naked arms sticky blights which, though snow-white on the apple-tree trunks, made madder stains on her skin; thus she drew quite near to Clare, still unobserved of him.'

This little still life of fecundity, reminding us in passing, perhaps, that of all our authors Hardy is the only considerable poet, is repeated again and again at this 'phase' in Tess's development. Living 'at a season when the rush of juices could be almost heard below the hiss of fertilization', she exhibits to Angel Clare 'a dignified largeness both of disposition and physique, an almost regnant power, possibly because he knew that at that preternatural time hardly any woman so well endowed in person as she was likely to be walking in the open air within the boundaries of his horizon'. Again when he comes across her shortly after this, 'The brim-fulness of her nature breathed from her. It was a moment when a woman's soul is more incarnate than at any other time; when the most spiritual beauty bespeaks itself flesh, and sex takes the outside place in the presentation.'

* * *

Tess, then, is ironically enough Nature's 'holy plan', though strictly speaking, if she could comment about novel-reading as cited, it is unlikely she would have been familiar with Wordsworth. 'She was not an existence, an experience, a passion, a structure of sensations, to anybody but herself. She simply existed.' It is a pity de Beauvoir did not study Hardy; and he, in turn, might have subscribed to much of what she wrote in *The Second Sex*, one passage of which could well be superscribed over much of *Tess*:

> 'Woman is the victim of no mysterious fatality; the peculiarities that identify her as specifically a woman get their importance from the significance placed upon them.'[9]

The existential sanguine is there again when Hardy—once more somewhat spuriously—attaches a little Sully Prudhomme to his heroine's reflections, and remarks that she could 'hear a penal sentence in the fiat, "You shall be born".' Then after Tess has been betrayed—that is, after she has 'fallen'—we are asked:

> 'In a desert island would she have been wretched at what had happened to her? Not greatly. If she could have been but just created, to discover herself as a spouseless mother, with no experience of life except as the parent of a nameless child, would the position have caused her to despair? No, she would have taken it calmly, and found pleasures therein.'

It is something of a pity Hardy felt he had to make Tess an aristocrat by birth, for the book is really unconcerned with class, except inasmuch as that through Alec a rural West Country girl is betrayed by common trade turned pseudo-squireen.[10] It is a pity if only since it led D. H. Lawrence into some maddeningly self-indulgent passages on the novel, in which, however, genuine insights lie buried.

Possibly not meant to be published, and only posthumously so (in the *Phoenix* collection edited by Edward D. McDonald), these pages are rendered almost unreadable by Lawrence's assumption that we will all share his love ethic, together with its attendant and highly arbitrary terminology. Tess is an aristocrat and, for him, 'has the aristocratic quality of respect for the other being'. What does this mean, if anything? We need a key. 'She could attend to the wants of the other person, but no other person, save another aristocrat—and there is scarcely such a thing as another aristocrat—could attend to her wants, her deepest wants.' This is infuriatingly suggestive and, indeed, Lawrence nearly always strikes through to the marrow of some truth—Tess does respect the rights of others, only to have her own infringed. The 'embodiment of desire' is destined to be betrayed in this fashion. Meekness marries aggression. We shall return to Lawrence's critique below. It is a valuable one, well worth the tedium of having to plough through Lawrentian rhetoric at its most intolerable, e.g. 'The murder is badly done, altogether the book is botched, owing to the way of thinking in the author, owing to the weak yet obstinate theory of being. Nevertheless, the murder is true, the whole book is true, in its conception.' Which is really to asseverate that Lawrence's sex ethic differed from Hardy's.

For Lawrence's interest was chiefly in what he was forever calling the male principle. Hardy's was not, as Virginia Woolf well saw:

> 'For the women he shows a more tender solicitude than for the men, and in them, perhaps, he takes a keener interest. Vain might their beauty be and terrible their fate, but while the glow of life is in them their step is free, their laughter sweet, and theirs is the power to sink into the breast of Nature and become part of her silence and solemnity, or to rise and put on them the movement of the clouds and the wildness of the flowering woodlands.'

One thinks of the charming frieze of the three milkmaids always hovering behind Tess at the Talbothays farm in a real picture of feminist solidarity:[11] never spiteful nor vicious toward Tess, as well they might have been, only, as mortally dependent beings, gently envious of her good luck ('Such supplanting was to be'), and two of them serving to warn Angel at the end. In the dairy dormitory they twist in their beds at night 'under the oppressiveness of an emotion thrust on them by cruel Nature's law. . . . The differences which distinguished them as individuals were abstracted by this passion, and each was but portion of one organism called sex.'

[. . .]

Tess Durbeyfield grows up to be a strong county girl, able to face a walk of twenty-five miles with equanimity and to write a long impassioned letter to her husband after stoically enduring a dawn-to-dusk thumping on the platform of a steam-thresher at Flintcomb-Ash (a Hardy name, if ever there was one). It is important to stress her physique since it is made much of, and is clearly meant to fit her character as a Gea-Tellus, Earth Mother. At the end she kills a strong man with evident ease with a table knife ('Fulfilment' is the title of this section, or Phase).

Now it is far from frivolous to suggest that a great deal of the present ranting about feminine inferiority in a pretentiously egalitarian world is a sort of tight-shoes syndrome . . . women are told, and therefore feel, they have inferior physiques. A firm way of classifying men, that is, appears to be by the fact that they are physically stronger. Our laws embed this distinction within them at points.

But is this a biological parentage or a social construct? It seems hard to discern. Professor Juliet Mitchell of the University of Reading asks, 'how can we tell whether there would be sexually determined differences in a society not dedicated to their production?' The arguments here can become circular, if not frankly self-contradictory. One school of anthropology would have it that the vulnerable female breasts are ersatz buttocks, a rump-presentation duplicated in the breastless chimpanzee and forced on the human primate when he stood erect: 'The protuberant, hemispherical breasts of the female must surely be copies of the fleshy buttocks, and the sharply defined red lips around the mouth must be copies of the red labia.'[13]

Surely . . . must be? As a layman I remain relatively unconvinced by the bizarre theory. Anyone who has studied chimps must concede that they are far more upright than researchers report them to be, and indeed do know frontal genital exposure (the cause of much of the bother here). And the theory relies on, and strongly supports, the idea that the female orgasm is originally 'borrowed' from the male, which we are now industriously disproving.

Yet even within a short span of time woman seems able to alter her physique to conform to social norms, unaided by corset, hobble-skirt and bustle. It has been said, for instance, that the sloping shoulders of the idealized Victorian heroine were more an attempt to copy patterns of elegance to be found in fiction, written largely by males, than a received reality. A section of my own study of popular iconography,

Parade of Pleasure, tried to show that the size of women's breasts in America of the early fifties followed fantasy rather then function (receiving ultimate reductio in the early pages of *Playboy*). Women have simply been assigned subordinate physique-roles for so long. Lady athletes in the last Olympics, one dating a steady boyfriend, were surprised and indignant to find themselves reclassified males (sometimes on the mere basis of testes concealed in the labia major). Such sex tests indeed provoked one British doctor to declare, in 1966, 'There is no definite line between male and female.'

Margaret Mead had told us this years ago, showing how certain societies institutionalize types and traits in both men and women:

> 'No culture has failed to seize upon the conspicuous facts of age and sex in some way, whether it be the convention of one Philippine tribe that no man can keep a secret, the Manus' assumption that only men enjoy playing with babies, the Toda prescription of almost all domestic work as too sacred for women, or the Arapesh insistence that women's heads are stronger than men's. In the division of labour, in dress, in manners, in social and religious functioning—sometimes in only a few of these respects, sometimes in all—men and women are socially differentiated and each sex, as a sex, forced to conform to the role assigned to it. In some societies, these socially defined roles are mainly expressed in dress or occupation with no insistence upon innate temperamental differences.'[14]

In her valuable *Adam's Rib* Ruth Herschberger starts off with a denunciatory dissection—indeed a 'ribbing'—of the famous findings made by Robert M. Yerkes with his Yale chimpanzees, on which so many 'norms' of male dominance have been based, norms already intentionally present in the all-too-male experimenters—desiderata. Female chimps of the same weight as male seem to be far more aggressive in almost every activity, including and especially mating:

> 'If a mother discovers her young son and daughter wrestling, she usually feels there is something vaguely indecent about it. Even though the little girl may on this occasion have established a half-nelson and be about to pin her brother to

the ground, the mother's injunction will be the same; "Junior! Don't hurt Joan! You know girls aren't as strong as you!" As the children get shamefully to their feet, obedient to their mother's note of horror (and it *was* pleasurable), Joan really believes she was about to be hurt in some uncalculated way, and Junior thinks he was about to forget his strength and wound a lady. Already pleasure begins to smack of the harmful.'[15]

This was not always so. Certainly not in the pre-agricultural period. 'We do not even know whether woman's musculature or her respiratory apparatus, under conditions different from those of today, were not as well developed as in man.'[16] Tacitus reports that notions of feminine inferiority are basically physical, since women have had leading roles as prophetesses and priestesses without disfavour. In France we have recently seen male writers promoting a veritable cult of the muscular woman, ranging from Henry de Montherlant's poems on thousand-meter women runners to Jacques de Lacretelle's *La Bonifas*, the portrait of a masculine woman haunted by fatality. And in contemporary America we can observe the distortions and difficulties being created for women by introduction of the muscle rhetoric into their lives. The desire for women to compete in men's sports is doubt- less laudable, and has worked in swimming, but it can be dangerous as well as ridiculous in other games.

It is natural that 'Masculine arrogance provokes feminine resis- tance', as de Beauvoir puts it. Male demands are met symmetrically. If we look at the dominant–subordinate polarity between the sexes as one partially originating in physique, we at least fight free of some of the silly squabbling that has lately been obscuring reality. And we can come to agree with Mrs Herschberger when she suggests that 'Some woman scientist ought to start passing it around that males must be unnatural because they don't have cyclical changes during the month.'[17]

In view of woman's superiority in sensitivity—of skin, breasts, nipples and of course the clitoris, capable of extraordinarily varied response—it must rank as a tragedy of our times that something called penis envy came to be regarded as even an idea. Who said that women suffer from penis envy? His Embarrassing Eminence from Vienna. It is experientially untrue and has vulgarized and degraded women. Who said that boys have secret envy of their father's sexual organs? Do they?

Did they? None that I ever knew. Nor do many women seem notably galvanized by the idea of penis envy on the part of their sex:

> 'Authorized to test her powers in work and sports, competing actively with the boys, she would not find the absence of the penis—compensated by the promise of a child—enough to give rise to an inferiority complex.'[18]

There is probably no such thing as penis envy at all, except in the eyes of adults like Freud. De Beauvoir elsewhere hints as much:

> 'Thus, far from the penis representing a direct advantage from which the boy could draw a feeling of superiority, its high valuation appears on the contrary as a compensation—invented by adults and ardently accepted by the child—for the hardships of the second weaning.'[19]

The conception of the boy child being in constant fear of castration at the same time as envious of his father's penis is, in other words, only a baffling absurdity until you recognize it as an adult rationalization for a repressive male society.

This of course is the hub of most of D. H. Lawrence's unfortunate verbal dervish-dancing about something called the phallus. We notice his prose—as in the *Fantasia of the Unconscious*—becoming unreadably rhetorical directly he touches on this subject. For if the universe can only be apprehended through the phallus, woman is deprived of all rights at the start of the game. Man is saying, Come and play tennis with me, but only I am allowed a racquet. Significantly, therefore, Lawrence keyed his love ethic to monogamous relationships in which woman discovers her derivation in man. Perversions of this plan generally proved disastrous.[20]

Now this is not surprising in a sensitive male. For at times the phallus does seem to act rather like some existential 'Other'. Maddeningly so. It erects itself whimsically, will refuse to perform at will, and then goes and ejaculates at night without permission. Surely it must be a god. What man of middle age, who has made love regularly all his adult life, would deny, on the threshold of paradise, that the clitoris is a far more reliable, and sensitive, organ? 'Feminine sexual excitement can reach an intensity unknown to man',[21] writes de Beauvoir; but it is not only intensity that is at issue here, it is *variety*. To admit as much, however, would be to topple Lawrence's entire love ethic, or mis-ethic.

It is ironic that America should discover the clitoral organism in the laboratories of the Masters-Johnson sex research team, aided by a US government grant, when every second page of the uncharted sea of Victorian pornography tells the same story, and far more organically. Laboratory lovers are the electroded robots of sex. And it will be more than ironic, it will be tragic if the public consciousness accepts the aggressive, self-seeking role placed on the clitoral orgasm by so many noisy, and sometimes noisome, feminists in our midst today. It will be to play directly into the hands of the dominant technology to objectify this experience, seal it off and code it as some sort of independent rival of the male ejaculation. Why make the mistakes of a masculine society all over again? As Susan Lydon puts it:

> 'female sexuality is subtle and delicate, conditioned as much by the emotions as by physiology and sociology. Masters and Johnson proved that the orgasm experienced during intercourse, the misnamed vaginal orgasm, did not differ *anatomically* from the clitoral orgasm. But this should not be seen as their most significant contribution to the sexual emancipation of women. . . . As they wrote, "With orgasmic physiology established, the human female now has an undeniable opportunity to develop realistically her own sexual response levels." Two years later this statement seems naive and entirely too optimistic. Certainly the sexual problems of our society will never be solved until there is a real and unfeigned equality between men and women. This idea is usually misconstrued: sexual liberation for women is wrongly understood to mean that women will adopt all the forms of masculine sexuality. As in the whole issue of women's liberation, that's really not the point.'[22]

Equality, in other words, doesn't mean sameness, and I for one think Hardy was trying to show this. Women's sexuality is immensely varied and delicate, and literature—even the subliterature of pornography—may be a better guide to it than the clinics. It is currently a sort of platform with American feminists to attack pornographies as 'encouraging rape and other forms of sexual sadism and exploitation. They are an insult and a crime against women'.[23]

Such writers have probably not read the pornography they are so bitterly attacking and which, in fact, contains more than a modicum of completely enfranchized and extremely dominant women, all thoroughly enjoying the sexual experience. America has been the first country to mass-produce pornography (in the last century it was, in England, a prerogative of the elite); I am not suggesting that *pornos* replace sex manuals, but they have certainly given lower-class people in America lately a new rhetoric of sex and one that does not show it as a response to a biological need alone. Clitoral orgasm is invariably enjoyable, in such pages, and sometimes even linked with affection, tenderness and awareness. Once more, Fem Lib contradicts itself. To lock up pornography is to work for just those forces of repression that have kept women down so long. Herbert Marcuse has a whole theory of sexual liberation in which Eros and Agape are conjoined:

> 'The regression involved in this spread of the libido would first manifest itself in the reactivation of all erotogenic zones and, consequently, in a resurgence of pregenital polymorphous sexuality and in a decline of genital supremacy. The body in its entirety would become an object of cathexis, a thing to be enjoyed—an instrument of pleasure.'

Certainly it was so for Tess.

For women are in a majority, and they have several superior faculties, including that of memory.[24] Monique Wittig, in her recent novel *Les Guérillères*, played amusingly on a reversal of our assumptions of male physical superiority. Undoubtedly these assumptions were spurred on by Puritan capitalism. In *Patriarchal Attitudes* Eva Figes makes this indictment: 'The rise of capitalism is the root cause of the modern social and economic discrimination against women, which came to a peak in the last century.' When Angel Clare, by this time married to Tess, makes his proposal to Izz Huett to come to be his mistress in Brazil, he footnotes the offer as follows: 'But I ought to remind you that it will be wrong-doing in the eyes of civiliza-tion—western civilization, that is to say.' The accent is on western, and it is the man he meets in South America who shrugs his shoulders at Angel's erotic problem.

Under Roman law, at the end of the Antonine jurisconsults at any rate, women were legally equal with men in most matters, a position of which the matrons seem not to have profited. As we know, the troubadour period later perfected a form of matrism which, while it undoubtedly turned men's minds to the Virgin Mary in another world, concomitantly civilized their behaviour to the Lauras and Beatrices of this. 'It may be questioned', Burckhardt wrote of the Holy Virgin, 'whether, in the north, a greater devotion was possible.' Under such matrism women certainly began to emerge more as fellow-beings than they had for some while before, thus making the Portias and Rosalinds of a later century possible. 'The period soon became one of enhanced status for women. They were given an education similar to that of men, and were regarded as their equals, even if it was held to be proper for them to work by influencing men rather than to engage directly in politics.'[25]

Such is stressed here since Hardy has been called, by Lord David Cecil, one of the last of the heroists. Two strains meet in Tess, the Gea-Tellus or all-powerful fecundator (*queen* in the original sense, one shared with *quim*) and, of course, the all-too-human equal and companion of man. For it is likely that Bachofen's famous study over-stressed the feminine quotient in the alleged early matriarchies of the Mediterranean basin. De Beauvoir shows herself uncomfortable with the Bachofen view:

> 'These facts have led to the supposition that in primitive times a veritable reign of women existed: the matriarchy. It was this hypothesis, proposed by Bachofen, that Engels adopted, regarding the passage from the matriarchate to the patriarchate as "the great historical defeat of the feminine sex". But in truth the Golden Age of Woman is only a myth. To say that woman was the *Other* is to say that there did not exist between the sexes a reciprocal relation: Earth, Mother, Goddess—she was no fellow creature in man's eyes; it was *beyond* the human realm that her power was affirmed, and she was therefore *outside of* that realm.'[26]

With Molly Bloom, Tess very much wanted to be within that realm; she earnestly longed to be a fellow creature in man's eyes here and now. By this route we can come logically back to Lawrence and his twin insights concerning her plight. For she is very strong physically and quite unafraid of Groby at the end: 'To have as a master this man of stone, who would have cuffed her if he had dared, was almost a relief after her former experiences.'

Tess's physicality has been thoroughly insisted on since she is the flower of her sex and race: so much so that it sometimes suggests her as older than she is. She is thoroughly natural, a 'pure' woman, and 'her exceptional physical nature' causes her to ask Angel to marry her sister after she has been hanged, as if she were some generous tree, giving off another branch of life. By this request, too, to which Angel evidently accedes, she urges him to join her on the other side of convention: of her own crime Hardy had at once commented, 'She had been made to break an accepted social law, but no law known to the environment in which she fancied herself such an anomaly.'

It must be clearly established, too, that Angel Clare was far more anti-conventional than a modern reader (certainly a modern American reader) might assume. Dairyman Crick tells us that he is 'one of the most rebellest rozums you ever knowed', he is described as 'un-Sabbatarian' and 'preferred sermons in stones to sermons in churches'. At one point the adverb 'communistically' is used of him, the word only having acquired English currency around 1850. But Angel fails at the brink and can only go the whole way 'Too late, too late!' (in Tess's terms before the murder).

The story is archetypally simple. A young country girl is seduced, has an illegitimate child which dies in infancy, marries another and tells her husband the truth before consummation of the wedding. The latter cannot tolerate the idea and abandons her to go to Brazil. Now at this turn in the narrative we may, in fact, tend to judge Angel too harshly. But his identity and whole relationship with the world depended on things being what they were. Tess tells him she has a child by another man. As James Baldwin puts it of another regional writer, William Faulkner, 'Any real change implies the breakup of the world as one has always known it, the loss of all that gave one an identity, the end of safety.'

Pestered by her first lover, Tess gives in to live with him since he will then support her family—the words 'He bought me' in the 1892 text were expunged by Hardy from the later Wessex edition. On her husband's return and subsequent discovery of her new menage, Tess kills her paramour, has a few days' elegaic happiness with her new-found husband and is apprehended for her crime lying, like a sacrificial victim, on an altar at Stonehenge, an episode of overcrude symbolism for many critics. She is hanged.

We see that Hardy carefully arranged for chance to interfere with Tess's first confession of her supposed fault and then for Angel, before

the marriage consummation, to see fit to make his own admission of
sexual 'backsliding'. Overjoyed, Tess then makes hers 'because 'tis just
the same'.

But of course it isn't, given the society. Convention intervenes
and though 'nothing had changed since the moments when he had
been kissing her', ignorant of her lapse, 'the essence of things had
changed'—the essence, not the existence. Tess slides to her knees and
begs for forgiveness, saying 'I will obey you like your wretched slave',
and asking, from the depths of her instincts, how he can suddenly stop
loving her on the mere receipt of information—'It is in your own mind
what you are angry at, Angel.' In truth, it is. Angel's position is put in
the following exchange:

> "'In the name of our love, forgive me!" she whispered with a dry
> mouth. "I have forgiven you for the same!"
> And as he did not answer, she said again—
> "Forgive me as you are forgiven! I forgive you, Angel."
> "You—yes, you do."
> "But you do not forgive me?"
> "O Tess, forgiveness does not apply to the case! You were
> one person; now you are another.'"

If we have been correct in tracing two themes working through
Tess so far, fecundating Earth Mother and social and political equal,
we can see that there is far more at stake here than a simple attack on
the double standard of male convention. As with Emma Bovary, the
characterization is saturated with civilization. And we can return to
Lawrence's analysis.

For Tess is longing to be *whole* and neither man in her life will
let her be so. Lawrence sensed the psychodynamics of this, writing of
Angel Clare:

> 'He had no idea that there was such a thing as positive
> Woman, as the Female, another great living Principle
> counterbalancing his own male principle. He conceived of the
> world as consisting of the One, the Male Principle.'

Spattered as it is with capital letters, this statement is an unneces-
sarily over-complicated way of saying that Angel was the classic

case of the Puritan. But Lawrence proceeds astutely to observe that you can't have the one without the other, the Puritan without the Cavalier; and his interpretation of the other social pole repressing sex by exploiting it, and also refusing full consciousness to woman, is extremely interesting.

For him Alec d'Urberville is the opposite of Angel Clare, he has 'killed the male in himself, as Clytemnestra symbolically for Orestes killed Agamemnon'. So his is really another way of hating the flesh (indeed Hardy writes, 'd'Urberville gave her the kiss of mastery'). 'It is a male quality to resolve a purpose to its fulfilment', Lawrence here claims, 'to receive some impulse into his semen, and to transmit it into expression'. Woman, that is, needs the mediation of the male, the reverse view, of course, of a feminist sexologist like Mrs Herschberger ('The male functions to produce sperm to give to the female'). Thus Alec 'seeks with all his power for the stimulus in woman. He takes the deep impulse from the female'.

Though Schopenhauer, of all people, could hardly be called pro-feminist, Hardy comes close to his thinking here, and indeed Helen Garwood's study of Hardy's work as an exposition of Schopenhauer's was published as early as 1911. What Lawrence is saying is structured to show the destruction of a woman's psyche: this happens in two ways—(a) Angel denies woman, (b) Alec identifies woman and destroys her by betrayal. The result is death since in neither case is the woman left whole. In short, 'The female is the victim of the species.'[27]

* * *

Thomas Hardy was one of the last great heroic writers—'Elizabethan' for Cecil—lodged in a time that was running down. His God, or anti-God, was Immanent Will, President of the Immortals, The Spinner of the Years, a purblind Doomster (the diffidence of specification, in Hardy's semantic here, is itself an 'ironic' acknowledgement of taboo). Once more, Lord David, in his admirable little book on *Hardy The Novelist*, comes to our rescue and can be brought to the feminist bar in evidence.

For, as he observes, when the black flag moves up the prison pole as Tess drops to her death, we are given to read, '"Justice" was done, and the President of the Immortals, in Aeschylean phrase, had ended his sport with Tess.' The 'Aeschylean phrase' may be a literal translation of two words in line 169 of *Prometheus Bound*, but in the given context it has a sneering, sarcastic ring that is curiously insecure . . . 'strange terms for an atheist', as Lord David well puts it.

Precisely. With one side of himself (the rational) Hardy tried to adumbrate a universe of sheer fatality, chance, 'hap'. As the fields are cut in *Tess* rabbits and rats, friend and foe alike, cluster together in panic and misery, then run for their lives. Like humans, it is a matter of luck which of them is killed, and which escapes. We are all, that is, in the words of one of Hardy's best poems ('Neutral Tones'), 'Alive enough to have strength to die.'

There is a whole philosophy in that line, which seems to be Hardy's inheritance from those urns of Zeus of which the weary Achilles talks to Priam at the end of the *Iliad*.[28] Angel once confesses to his father 'that it might have resulted far better for mankind if Greece had been the source of the religion of modern civilization'. And again, after the chance but most important meeting with the stranger in Brazil, a cosmopolite who thought Tess's slip 'of no importance beside what she would be', Angel reflects that he had himself 'persistently elevated Hellenic Paganism at the expense of Christianity, yet in that civilization an illegal surrender was not certain disesteem'.

This is all very well, but Hardy proceeds to people his fiction with omens, and his poetry with ghosts. Intuitions, hauntings, spectral voices usually have a habit, with Hardy, of coming true. Cecil pinpoints the difficulty:

> 'You simply do not get a dyed-in-the-wool rationalist writer employing omens to increase his effect in a serious work. As a matter of fact, Hardy was not altogether consistent. Though his intellect accepted rationalism and materialism, his imagination never did. . . . Intellectual inconsistency, however, is often aesthetic gain.'

Tess may be part of nature, but she *has to be* part of society. 'Thus Tess walks on, a figure which is part of the landscape. . . . ' This is the existentialist Hardy who could write, with some fervour in his prose:

> 'Tess was no insignificant creature to toy with and dismiss; but a woman living her precious life—a life which, to herself who endured or enjoyed it, possessed as great a dimension as

the life of the mightiest to himself. Upon her sensations the whole world depended to Tess; through her existence all her fellow-creatures existed, to her. The universe itself only came into being for Tess on the particular day in the particular year in which she was born.'

This could be straight Camus, and in fact it really is for, as Cecil suggests, Hardy's mnemonic side had to concede what the Greeks called a human nature. We can, after all, talk about persistence beyond death; rabbits and rats cannot. 'Despairing literature', as Camus once put it, 'is a contradiction in terms'.

So society executes Tess, as it did Camus's Meursault, and for not entirely dissimilar reasons. In neither case is the murder the guilt; the revolt against convention is the real guilt. Meursault is decapitated 'in the name of the French people'. Tess is hanged in the name of male society. And yet her touching, tentative revolt against inhuman laws affirms something irreducibly human, and makes us all her murderers, as well as her fellow-condemned.

Of course, the great difference, aesthetically, between Hardy's brand of existentialism and Camus's is that the latter writer could already locate his in a social situation where the values of solitude, alienation, revolt (during German occupation) were normatively heroic. As a matter of fact, there may even have been an artistic penalty for this; however sympathetic Camus's fiction was, he was again giving testimony, acknowledging public truths, rather than (or just as much as) writing out of private discovery, apart. We feel he is as honest as Hardy all the way, but does he maintain the same creative energy over long stretches (his best work is short)? As Irving Howe once put it, 'Camus has not yet given himself irrevocably to the powers of art, he has not yet taken the final step that would bring him from the realm of reflection to the realm of imagination.'[29] Yet Camus's tragic optimism replies to, rounds out, Hardy's ironic pessimism. Surely he would have agreed with Camus that 'a human nature does exist, as the Greeks believed. Why rebel if there is nothing permanent in oneself worth preserving?'[30]

So Tess, this 'mere child of the soil', is also a child of our time, a truly delicate organization of appetencies. No wonder Tolstoy approved her (at least in serial shape). She is 'Alive enough to have strength to die', all right, and cannot imagine no further life for the true lovers of this world. She speaks closely to women since she lives 'under an arbitrary law of society which had no foundation in Nature'. For although we may all be pawns in the hands of the purblind Doomster, there is a sense of joy in the very copiousness of nature: as we read in *Tess*:

> 'The "appetite for joy" which pervades all creation, that tremendous force which sways humanity to its purpose, as the tide sways the helpless weed, was not to be controlled by vague lucubrations over the social rubric.'

Nature itself is guiltless, and Tess a sample of its innocence. For, if not the first, Hardy is certainly one of the best of our writers to use landscape as psychic state, and sometimes one of the most daring (in *Tess* there is a lengthy description of the Vale of the Var as a vaginal cleft). So Hardy makes his 'pun.' woman cry out for all women when, exhausted by field labour, she lashes at Alec with her glove, then sinks on the straw, on which his blood is dropping, to cry out in agony, 'Now, punish me. . . . Whip me, crush me; you need not mind those people under the rick! I shall not cry out. Once victim, always victim—that's the law!'

NOTES

1. The text used here is the Wessex edition of 1912.
2. Susan Lydon, 'Liberating Woman's Orgasm', *The New Eroticism*, edited by Philip Nobile, New York: Random House, 1970, pp. 225–6 (reprinted from *Ramparts* magazine).
3. The composition of *Tess* and the concessions Hardy had to make for an illustrated weekly newspaper have been thoroughly covered by two works: Richard Purdy, *Thomas Hardy: A Bibliographical Study*, Oxford University Press, 1954, and Ian Gregor and Brian Nicholas, *The Moral and the Story*, London: Faber and Faber, 1962. *Tess* appeared in the *Graphic* in twenty-four illustrated weekly installments from 4 July to 26 December 1891. Both books show what happened to odds and ends of the original conception.
4. Hardy complained at the omission, in the first American edition, of 'the second title, which is absolutely necessary to show its meaning'.

5. For a brief but enlightening review of Hardy's revisions of *Tess* in manuscript (now in the British Museum), see the relevant chapter in Wallace Hildick, *Word for Word: A Study of Authors' Alterations*, London: Faber and Faber, 1965, pp. 109–25.
6. Martin Green, *Science and the Shabby Curate of Poetry*, New York: Norton, 1965, p. 82; London: Longman, 1964.
7. Herschberger, p. 27.
8. Herschberger, pp. 42, 76, with accompanying footnotes provenancing Amram Scheinfeld's *Women and Men*.
9. De Beauvoir, p. 685.
10. I would maintain this despite the minor theme of the snobbery of the senior Clares—'she *is* a lady, nevertheless—in feeling and nature', Angel objects to his mother of Tess, and again, 'Distinction does not consist in the facile use of a contemptible set of conventions, but in being numbered among those who are true, and honest . . .', etc. Others have preceded Hardy here.
11. Cp. 'WSPers [members of Women Strike for Peace], wearing Vietnamese "coolie" hats made of newspaper, bearing black flowers and signs and tolling small bells, marched down Broadway reminding passers-by that "We're all POWs".' *WSP Peaceletter*, vol. II, no. 9, October, 1971.
13. Desmond Morris, *The Naked Ape*, New York: Dell, 1969, p. 63; London: Corgi, 1969.
14. Margaret Mead, *Sex and Temperament in Three Primitive Societies*, London: Routledge, 1935, pp, xix–xx.
15. Herschberger, p. 139.
16. De Beauvoir, p. 56.
17. Herschberger, p. 9.
18. De Beauvoir, p. 683.
19. *Ibid.*, p. 253.
20. The classic pro-Lawrentian view on these matters, one which takes all the posturing at face value and reduces it to exposition, must be read to be believed: Mark Spilka, *The Love Ethic of D. H. Lawrence*, Indiana University Press, 1955. It is studied in university courses.
21. De Beauvoir, p. 367.
22. Lydon, pp. 226–7.
23. 'BOYCOTT ALL Newsstands Selling Pornography', *Woman's World*, 15 April, 1971, p. 1.

24. Viola Klein, *The Feminine Character: History of an Ideology*, with a foreword by Karl Manheim, New York: International Universities Press, 1949, p. 99; this book was first published in 1946, reviews various writings on women, and here resumes the theories of Helen B. Thompson. American women are 106 millions strong in 1972.

25. Rattray Taylor, p. 131: Maurice Valency's *In Praise of Love* (New York: Macmillan, 1958) beautifully complements this text from the literary side.

26. De Beauvoir, pp. 64–5.

27. De Beauvoir, p. 18.

28. 'There are two urns that stand on the door-sill of Zeus. They are unlike for the gifts they bestow: an urn of evils, an urn of blessings. If Zeus who delights in thunder mingles these and bestows them on man, he shifts, and moves now in evil, again in good fortune.' Homer, *Iliad*, Book Twenty-Four, ll. 527–30 (translated by Richard Lattimore).

29. Irving Howe, 'Between Fact and Fable', *New Republic*, 31 March, 1958, p. 17.

30. Albert Camus, *The Rebel: An Essay on Man in Revolt*, with a foreword by Sir Herbert Read, translated by Anthony Bower, New York: Vintage Books, 1959, p. 16; Harmondsworth: Penguin, 1969.

Ulysses
(James Joyce)

ᴼᵏ ᴷᴼ

"Fetishizing the Bread of Everyday Life: The Taboo Gaze in 'Nausicaa'"
by Blake Hobby and Dustin Ryan, University of North Carolina at Asheville

---

Don't you think there is a certain resemblance between the mystery of the Mass and what I am trying to do? . . . To give people some kind of intellectual pleasure or spiritual enjoyment by converting the bread of everyday life into something that has a permanent artistic life of its own.

—Joyce, in conversation with his brother, Stanislaus

When we think of James Joyce's *Ulysses*, it is easy to think of taboos, those things that we normally do not talk about in literature: fornication, excrement, urine, adultery, sadomasochism, racial epithets and slurs, foul language, and "mutton kidneys that leave a faintly scented urine taste on the tongue" (see the first line of the book's fourth chapter). But, for the purposes of understanding what made and often still makes Joyce's *Ulysses* seem taboo, it might be profitable to focus on one chapter where Joyce conflates religion and sex, turning both into a voyeuristic spectacle, the thirteenth chapter we refer to as "Nausicaa." During this chapter, Leopold ("Poldy" as his wife calls him) Bloom masturbates in the beach scrubs while a disabled woman flashes her knickers on the Sandymount Strand beach. At the same time, a congregation at a Roman Catholic church called *Mary, Star of the Sea* adores the Most Blessed Sacrament, the consecrated body of Jesus. In both cases, a ritual is played out in which the taboo is fetishized.

A fetish is any object believed to have magical powers; fetishes are often surrounded by taboos. According to *The Encyclopedia of Taboos*, the term "fetish"

> has been used by anthropologists to describe anthropomorphic, animal or abstract figures that are carved from wood, bone or ivory, or molded in clay or termite secretions as well as natural objects such as the gnarled roots and branches of trees, dried leaves, animal claws, nails, fur and horns, tortoise shells, sacred rocks and minerals. More recently, the word has been applied to objects of religious devotion such as the Christian crucifix, religious relics and icons, while it is also used to define something that is irrationally reverenced such as goods in a capitalist economy or substitutes for the sexual object. (86)

There are two kinds of fetishized experiences working in "Nausicaa," both revolving around an adoring gaze. Within sight of each other, a man peers at a young woman on the beach while a congregation at a temperance retreat worships the Most Blessed Sacrament. As Bloom fetishizes Gerty and endows her with the "pure" and "angelic" qualities of the Virgin Mary, the *Mary, Star of the Sea* worshippers fetishize the consecrated Body of Christ. The adoring gaze unites sexual and religious scenes as the narrative voice shifts between the two fetishes. Thus, the objects of the "Nausicaa" are not only deified, but are also sexualized.

Drawing attention to the farcical nature of Ireland's self image as a bastion of moral purity and religious fervor, Joyce juxtaposes the two scenes. As Joyce's fiction often deals with the disparity between the real and the ideal, in "Nausicaa," Joyce attacks a number of ideal-ized perceptions of experience by comparing them to realities that are profane or immoral. He also exposes the futility of attempting to create a moral society, critiquing a State where the Church censors immoral thoughts and deeds. The most obvious juxtaposition of the real and the ideal lies in Gerty's character, which is presented with an array of Marian symbols. Joyce associates her with the Virgin Mary, whose color blue is present throughout this chapter and whose "blue banners" grace the Marian church (13:447–48). The blue-eyed Gerty wears a blue blouse, a hat with a blue ribbon under the brim, blue garters, blue stockings, and blue underwear, which she wears "for luck" (13:179). Blessed with the Virgin Mary's disposition, Gerty is sensitive and pure: "from everything in the least indelicate her finebred nature instinctively recoiled" (13:660–61). With a childlike innocence, she daydreams about fairytale romances. She also thinks with disdain about prostitutes and promiscuous women: "she loathed that sort of person" (13: 61). While Bloom watches her, she fantasizes about being his wife in an asexual marriage, a platonic romance in which she and Bloom would be best friends rather than lovers. In her reverie, Gerty thinks Bloom is probably a nice man and they could be "good friends like a brother and sister without all that other" (13:665–66). This childish romance plays out in her mind while Bloom lusts after her, "eying her as a snake eyes its prey" (13:517). Here, Joyce compares romantic, childish fantasies with a more realistic portrayal of human sexuality, one where the desire for physical gratification is natural.

Rather than an ideal of social purity and sexual naiveté, Gerty is a mockery of that ideal and is described as being "womanly wise" (13:223). She believes she knows what men want from a woman, and she knows how to attract the male gaze. This knowledge has been gained from women's magazines and from gossiping with her friends. Yet she is not merely a social construct or an object to be consumed by men. From one perspective, the narrative frames Gerty as a tantalizing seductress who reveals her body to Bloom. Gerty, in turn, derives erotic pleasure of her own from the realization that she is arousing Bloom's libido. On one level, she is the erotic voyeur, one who, like a man, gazes at pornography.

More than a seductress, however, Joyce presents her as a compassionate Mary figure. Gerty is not angry or insulted by the fact that Bloom is masturbating while he stares at her. Instead, she demonstrates compassion for him as she notices that he is dressed in mourning and wonders for whom he mourns (Bloom has attended a burial service for his friend Paddy Dignam earlier in the day). Like Mary, Gerty is a "comfortress of the afflicted" and a "refuge of sinners" (13:442). She wants to understand Bloom and comfort him and distract him from his mourning, yet she does so in a much more profane sense. Gerty is a seductive Virgin Mary, one who comforts her followers, easing them in times of sexual distress. In terms of her compassion and symbolic connections to Mary, Joyce establishes Gerty as a goddess-like character. However, he does not allow the reader to accept this image at face value. There are a number of decisively human aspects to Gerty as well. Her concern with fashion and attractiveness is worldly. Further, Gerty is menstruating during this scene, another very human element. Bringing Gerty down to earth from the status of a goddess, Joyce reminds the reader that she is experiencing an explicitly human, natural process. Yet Gerty in many ways remains an elusive character, one who, like Flaubert's Emma Bovary, Milton's Eve, or Homer's Penelope, is complex and capable of being seen from diverse perspectives. Thus, it is possible to see her as goddess and seductress, as angel and whore, while also recognizing her as a representation of the sentimentalized nineteenth-century woman.

Critics have contended that popular, sentimental fiction and "Nausicaa" alike sexualize women. Kimberly Devlin interprets Gerty's character in relation to the sentimental literature of the day, focusing on *The Lamplighter*, a sentimental romance novel contemporary to Joyce that is referenced in the episode. Gerty has read this book, and it is prominent in her consciousness throughout her presence in the scene. In a sense Gerty is a representation of what young female readers of books like *The Lamplighter* are not supposed to be and what they are supposed to be protected from by reading didactic, moral literature. Yet this very same literature, filled with advertisements and purple prose, appeals to the feminine imagination.

Gerty's self-awareness and her overdone romantic fantasies combine to parody the ideal woman as presented in *The Lamplighter*. Gerty dreams about the chaste *Lamplighter* heroine and desires to be like her. Unlike Molly Bloom, who reads smutty novels by Paul de Kock, Gerty seeks moral guidance in literature. Thus, it is ironic that she ends up becoming aroused when thinking about the very moral literature she seeks guidance from. Here Joyce takes a jab at those who had and continued to try to censor him. While Gerty's character is seen as being a social or cultural construct, she is more of a parody of her culture than its reflection. In this way, Joyce mocks Victorian ideals of womanhood and sexual chastity through Gerty MacDowell, a young woman trying to live up to feminine ideals while falling prey to the "corrupting" influence of consumer culture.

The perception of Gerty as an impossibly romanticized ideal of purity is compounded by the unmistakably mock-romantic tone with which the episode begins:

The summer evening had begun to fold the world in its mysterious embrace. Far away in the west the sun was setting and the last glow of all too fleeting day lingered lovingly on sea and strand, on the proud promontory of dear old Howth guarding as ever the waters of the bay, on the weedgrown rocks along Sandymount shore and, last but not least, on the quiet church whence there streamed forth at times upon the stillness the voice of prayer to her who is in her pure radiance a beacon ever to the stormtossed heart of man, Mary, star of the sea. (13: 1–8)

In this passage, whose style is reminiscent of cheap romance novels, the evening is personified as a man, one who holds a woman in a sensual embrace. Simultaneously, however, amidst all the overly romanticized, sensual prose, this paragraph establishes Mary's presence, and more importantly, the theme of purity underlying "Nausicaa." Furthermore, Gerty is described as "as fair a specimen of winsome Irish girlhood as one could wish to see" (13:80–81). Here, she is depicted in an almost mythical tone, as the romanticized ideal of what an Irish girl should be: a symbol of perfection and purity.

In a number of ways, Joyce challenges this seemingly flawless image, offering an all-too-human Gerty, a disabled woman who walks with a noticeable limp. Bloom is taken aback when he sees her walk: "She walked with a certain quiet dignity characteristic of her but with care and very slowly because—because Gerty MacDowell was ... Tight boots? No. She's lame! O!" (13: 769–71). The reader, like Bloom, does not discover she is lame until after the episode on the beach has reached its climax, as Gerty carefully hobbles away, worrying about tripping and falling on the rocks. Despite Gerty's fantasies about a happy marriage and home life, her own experience has been much different. Her father is an alcoholic who abuses her mother seemingly on a regular basis, something we come to learn in the same paragraph with the temperance retreat activities:

She had even witnessed in the home circle deeds of violence and intemperance and had seen her own father, a prey to the fumes of intoxication, forget himself completely for if there was one thing of all things that Gerty knew it was that the man who lifts his hand to a woman save in the way of kindness, deserves to be branded as the lowest of the low. (13:297–302)

The idea that Irish society could be characterized by temperance or moral superiority is also brought to task in "Nausicaa." This is another instance of Joyce comparing an idealized perception, in this case dealing with the supposed morality of Irish society in general and family life in particular.

Such a realistic, if not nightmarish, picture of marriage and Irish domesticity counters Gerty's fantasy of a marriage of quaint happiness and mutual respect, a vision of an Irish utopia where lofty moral codes are respected and upheld. As all of Joyce's works convey, Ireland is as ridden with flaws and moral depravity as any other human society. Just as the censors and the Church construct an idealized image of Ireland, so too does Gerty fashion a dream-like vision of marriage. All rely upon idealizations rather than actual experience. We can see this dichotomy in the chapter; it appears most poignantly in the radically different picture of Gerty's own domestic experience Joyce paints. Although she knows that marriage can be far from perfect, she still believes in the myths propagated by women's magazines and sentimental literature, believing that marriage "would be like heaven" (13:214). Gerty's idealized notions of reality benefit the publishers of sentimental literature. Their job is to encourage young women like Gerty to embrace this ideal and to pursue it. Ultimately, they cultivate desire, most especially the desire to hold the male gaze.

Joyce actually takes a mocking tone regarding Gerty's romantic fantasies about Bloom, emphasizing her childishness:

> Every morning they would both have brekky, simple but perfectly served, for their own two selves and before he went out to business he would give his dear little wifey a good hearty hug and gaze for a moment deep down into her eyes. (13:239–42)

"Brekky" and "dear little wifey" are pejorative terms that mock Gerty's romantic, childlike imagination. The narrative itself, rendering Gerty's perspective, demeans the very object of Bloom's desire. Gerty's fantasy of an idealized marriage, from the perspective of the overall narrative (which includes objective reporting, Gerty's stream-of-consciousness thoughts, and Bloom's stream-of-consciousness thoughts) is ludicrous. Bloom objectifies her, glad he did not know she was disabled, which might have ruined his fantasy and interrupted his masturbation. Of course, as we later learn in the novel, Bloom does indeed engage in debased sadomasochistic fantasies, delighting in a woman of the night who treats him as an insolent pig, riding him and putting out a cigarette in his ear. These fantasies, a Joycean parody of Freud's ideas about repression and sexuality, are also the focus of Joyce's *A Portrait of the Artist as a Young Man*, where Joyce indicts Irish religion and culture.

Repression is a fitting topic for Joyce to discuss and especially to think about in terms of "Nausicaa's" taboo subject matter. For, while the chapter presents repressions and repressive mechanisms in a comic light, "Nausicaa," originally published in *The Little Review* (July-August 1920 issue), was seized by the U.S. Postal Service, one of the many times Joyce's works fell victim to a censor who deemed them immoral. While the U.S. Postal Service had a definite sense of moral turpitude in mind, such grandiose moralizing is just the sort of thing that Joyce satirizes in the chapter. "Nausicaa" is both a representation of our humanity and also a jarring text, one where the religious and sexual collide—both presenting fetishized taboos. While such a collision gives us a humanistic chapter, this weaving of the sacred and the illicit was, and still is, too jarring for many. Joyce will not allow the reader to accept a comforting view of the world. Rather, Joyce presents the ideals we believe in and juxtaposes them with flaws that mar our utopian ideals, making our moralizing polemical hypocrisy at best. In doing so he reminds us that imagining the world to be one way does not change what it actually is. Rather than a debased portrait of what is illicit, Joyce presents our desires and our fantasies, the stuff of the taboo, as sacramental. In that sense, Joyce ruins the sacred truths, leaving us with a portrait of our humanity with all of our foibles intact, presenting our taboos for the fetishes we make them to be.

WORKS CITED AND CONSULTED

Devlin, Kimberly. "The Romance Heroine Exposed: 'Nausicaa' and *The Lamplighter*." *James Joyce Quarterly* Vol. 22, No. 4 (Summer 1985): 383–96.

Foucault, Michel. "The History of Sexuality, Volume One." *The Norton Anthology of Theory and Criticism*. Ed. Vincent B Leitch. New York: W.W. Norton & Company, 2001. 1648–59.

Gibbons, Luke. "'Have You No Homes To Go To': Joyce and the Politics of Paralysis." Ed. Derek Attridge and Marjorie Howes. Cambridge: Cambridge University Press, 2000. 150–71.

Gunn, Daniel P. "Beware of Imitations: Advertisement as Reflexive Commentary in *Ulysses*." *Twentieth Century Literature* Vol. 42, No. 4 (Winter 1996): 481–93.

Hug, Chrystel. *The Politics of Sexual Morality in Ireland.* New York: St. Martin's Press, 1999.

Jackson, Tony E. "'Cyclops,' 'Nausicaa,' and Joyce's Imaginary Irish Couple." *James Joyce Quarterly* Vol. 29, No. 1 (Fall 1991): 63–81.

Joyce, James. *Ulysses.* New York: Random House, Inc., 1986.

Law, Jules David. "Pity They Can't See Themselves: Assessing the Subject of Pornography in 'Nausicaa'." *James Joyce Quarterly* Vol. 27, No. 2 (1990): 219–38.

Leckie, Barbara. "Reading Bodies, Reading Nerves: 'Nausicaa' and the Discourse of Censorship." *James Joyce Quarterly* Vol. 34, No. 2 (Winter 1997): 65–81.

Leonard, Garry. *Advertising and Commodity Culture in Joyce.* Miami: University Press of Florida, 1998.

Mullin, Katherine. *James Joyce, Sexuality and Social Purity.* Cambridge: Cambridge University Press, 2003.

Nietzsche, Friedrich. "On Truth and Lie in an Extra-Moral Sense." *The Portable Nietzsche.* Ed. Walter Kaufmann. New York: Penguin Books, 1976. 42–46.

Ochoa, Peggy. "Joyce's 'Nausicaa:' The Paradox of Advertising Narcissism." *James Joyce Quarterly* Vol. 30–31, No. 1–4 (Summer & Fall 1993): 783–91.

Parkes, Adam. "Literature and Instruments for Abortion: 'Nausicaa' and the *Little Review* Trial." *James Joyce Quarterly* Vol. 34, No. 3 (Spring 1997): 283–99.

Richards, Thomas Karr. "Gerty MacDowell and the Irish Common Reader." *ELH* Vol. 52, No. 3 (Autumn 1985): 755–76.

Sicker, Philip. "Alone in the Hiding Twilight: Bloom's Cinematic Gaze in 'Nausicaa'." *James Joyce Quarterly* Vol. 36, No. 4 (Summer 1999): 825–47.

◈ *Acknowledgments* ◈

Baudelaire, Charles. "Les Paradis Artificiels." 1860. *Les Fleurs du mal, Petits poèmes en prose, Les Paradis artificiels.* trans. Arthur Symons. London: Casanova Society, 1925. 243–88.

George, Diana Hume. "The Poetic Heroism of Anne Sexton." *Literature and Psychology* 33.3–4 (1987): 76–88. © 1987 by *Literature and Psychology*. Reprinted by permission.

Kermode, Frank. "1925–1930." *D.H. Lawrence.* New York: Viking Press, 1973. © 1973 by Frank Kermode. Reprinted by permission.

Lecky, W.E.H., M.P. "Biographical Introduction." *Swift's* Tale of a Tub *and Other Early Works.* Ed. Temple Scott. *The Prose Works of Jonathan Swift, D.D., Volume I.* London: George Bell and Sons, 1897.

Marshall, Cynthia. "Totem, Taboo, and *Julius Caesar." Literature and Psychology.* 37.1–2 (1991): 11–33. Reprinted by permission.

Martin, Wendy. "'God's Lioness'—Sylvia Plath, Her Prose and Poetry." *Women's Studies* 1.2 (1973): 191–98. © 1973 by Gordon and Breach Science Publishers Ltd. Reprinted by permission.

Nietzsche, Friedrich. "Chapter Nine." *The Complete Works of Friedrich Nietzsche, Vol. 1: The Birth of Tragedy, or, Hellenism and Pessimism.* 1872. Ed. Oscar Levy. Trans. William August Hausmann. London: George Allen & Unwin, 1923. 72–75.

Rosenfield, Claire. "Men of a Smaller Growth: A Psychological Analysis of William Golding's *Lord of the Flies." Literature and Psychology* 11.4 (Autumn 1961): 93–101. Reprinted by permission.

Roth, Phyllis A. "Suddenly Sexual Women in Bram Stoker's *Dracula." Literature and Psychology* 27.3 (1977): 113–21. Reprinted by permission.

Stone, Edward. "Usher, Poquelin, and Miss Emily: the Progress of Southern Gothic." *Georgia Review* 14.4 (Winter 1960): 433–43. © The University of Georgia in 1960. Reprinted by permission.

Wagner, Geoffrey. "*Tess of the D'Urbervilles*: The 'Pure Woman'." *Five for Freedom: A Study of Feminist Fiction*. 1972. Madison, NJ: Fairleigh Dickinson University Press, 1973. 183–211. © 1972 by George Allen & Unwin Ltd. Reprinted by permission.

Index

Characters in literary works are indexed by first name (if any), followed by the name of the work in parentheses

45 Mercy Street (Sexton), 209, 211

A

ABC of Reading (Pound), 230
"Abortion, The" (Sexton), 130–131
"Abortion Attempt by My Mother, An" (Beatty), 131
abortion taboo
   in "the mother," 123–132
Adam's Rib (Herschberger), 237–238
"All My Pretty Ones" (Sexton)
   guilt in, 209, 213–214
Alvarez, A., 163
American
   culture and society, 38, 41, 45, 47–48, 185, 205
   feminism, 238, 240–241, 243
   history, 47, 167–168, 175
   literature, 91, 159, 163, 170, 173, 175, 177
   racial tension in, 39
   segregation in, 39
American Dream, An (Mailer), 161
Apollinaire, Guillaume, 40
"Applicant, The" (Plath)
   anger and bitterness in, 161

"Argument against the Abolition of Christianity" (Swift), 218
Ariel (Plath)
   poems, 159
Artaud, Antonin, 40
Artemis, Rossitsa
   on *The Satanic Verses*, 189–197
Atterbury Francis, 223
Awakening, The (Chopin), 159
Ayatollah Khomeini, 189, 191

B

Baldwin, James, 243
"Battle of the Books, The" (Swift), 218
Baudelaire, Charles, 40
   on *Confessions of an English Opium Eater*, 1–21
   death, 1
   drug use, 1
   Flowers of Evil, 1
   "Les Paradis Artificiels," 1–21
"Beast, The" (Plath)
   anger and bitterness in, 161
Beatty, Jan
   "An Abortion Attempt by My Mother," 131

Beauvoir, Simone de, 227
The Second Sex, 234, 238–239, 242
Bell Jar, The (Plath), 158
  alienation in, 159
  Buddy in, 160–161
  despair in, 157
  Doreen in, 160
  Esther Greenwood in, 157, 159–161
  Lenny in, 160
  sexuality in, 157, 159
  suicide in, 160
Beloved (Morrison), 126
Bentley, C.F., 218
  on *Dracula*, 32
Bettelheim, Bruno
  Freud and Man's Soul, 199–203
Birkerts, Sven, 47
Blake, William, 40–41
Blau, Herbert, 37
Bloom, Harold
  introduction, xv–xvi
Bolingbroke, Henry St John, 221
Bonifas, La (Lacretelle), 238
Brando, Marlon, 42
Brontë, Charlotte
  Jane Eyre, 88, 230
Brooks, Cleanth, 45
  Understanding Fiction, 165
Brooks, Gwendolyn
  "crowding darkness," 127
  "kitchenette building," 127–128
  "the mother," 123–132
  "the old-marrieds," 127
  "southeast corner," 127
  A Street in Bronzeville, 123, 125
Brooks, Van Wyck, 175
Burke, Kenneth, 219
Burroughs, Joan, 41
Burroughs, William, 41
  Junkie, 38

C

Cable, George Washington
  "Jean-ah Poquelin," 166–174
Campbell, Joseph
  The Hero with a Thousand Faces, 147–148
Camus, Albert
  The Stranger, 227, 247
Cannastra, William, 41
Cantos (Pound), 40
Carr, Lucien, 41
Carter, Jimmy, 124
Carter, Rosalynn, 124
"Cask of Amontillado, A" (Poe), 172
Cassady, Neal, 42–43
Céline, Louis-Ferdinand, 40
Chambers, Jessie, 87
Chase, Cynthia, 70
Chaucer, Geoffrey
  "The Miller's Tale," 113–122
Chopin, Kate
  The Awakening, 159
Civilization and Its Discontents (Freud)
  Eternal city in, 52, 63–65
Clark, Barrett H., 134
Clark, Walter Van Tilburg, 37
Colossus, The (Plath), 159, 161
Communism, 38
Company She Keeps, The (McCarthy), 159
Comstock laws, 131
Confessions of an English Opium Eater (De Quincey)
  dreams in, 6, 13, 17
  drug use in, 1–21
  escape in, 5, 9
  haschisch in, 3–7, 9–20
  immorality in, 7, 11–12, 18
  magic in, 21
  opium in, 5, 9–11, 20
  taboo in, 1–21

Crossing the Water (Plath), 159
"crowding darkness" (Brooks), 127
Cultural Cold War: The CIA and the World of Arts and Letters, The (Saunders), 39

D

"Daddy" (Plath)
  anger and bitterness in, 161
Dante
  Inferno, 40
"Death, Mourning, and Besse's Ghost" (Mellard), 184
Decay of Lying, The (Wilde), 152
De Quincey, Thomas, 203
  Confessions of an English Opium Eater, 1–21
Despair (Nabokov), 95
Devlin, Kimberly, 254
Dickinson, Emily, 158
"Division of Parts, The" (Sexton)
  cracked mirror in, 207
"Divorce, Thy Name is Woman" (Sexton)
  daughter-father relationship in, 209, 211–213
Dostoevsky, Fyodor, 231
Doty, Mark, 45–46
"Double Image, The" (Sexton), 211
  cracked mirror in, 207–208
  mother-daughter relationship in, 207–210
  suicide in, 207
Dracula (Stoker)
  Abraham Van Helsing in, 24–25, 27–28, 31, 34
  Arthur Holmwood in, 25–28, 31
  Count Dracula in, 25–34
  female sexuality in, 23–27, 29–30, 32–33

  Holmwood in, 28
  horror in, 23
  Jonathan Harker in, 25, 28–30, 32–34
  Joseph Bierman in, 26
  Lord Godalming in, 25, 29
  Lucy Westenra in, 25–26, 28–31, 33–34
  Mina Harker in, 24, 26–34
  Oedipal desire in, 23–24, 27–28, 31–34
  Quincey Morris in, 27
  Seward in, 27–31
  taboo in, 23–36
"Dreaming the Breasts" (Sexton), 213
drug use taboos
  in *Confessions of an English Opium Eater*, 1–21
Dylan, Bob
  "Mister Jones," 42

E

East, West (Rushdie), 189
"Eating the Leftovers" (Sexton), 211
Electra Complex, 200
  in *Mourning Becomes Electra*, 133
Eliot, T.S., 87, 97
  "The Love Song of J. Alfred Prufock," 125, 130
  The Waste Land, 47, 125, 231
"Elm" (Plath), 162
Enchantress of Florence, The (Rushdie), 190
Encyclopedia of Taboos, The, 252
Erlich, Jake, 38
"Essay on Public Absurdities" (Swift), 219
Essential Gwendolyn Brooks, The (Merrill), 125
Euripides
  The Orestes, 134–136, 139, 142

Evans, Robert C.
  on "The Miller's Tale," 113–122
Experience of Literature, The (Trilling),
  47

F

Fall of America, The (Ginsberg), 41
"Fall of the House of Usher, The"
  (Poe)
    compared to "A Rose for Emily,"
    165–166, 171–173, 175–176
Falvey, Kate
  on "the mother," 123–132
Falwell, Jerry, 47
Fantasia of the Unconscious
  (Lawrence), 239
Faulkner, William, 243
  "A Rose for Emily," 165–176
fear of death
  in *Sabbath's Theater*, 178–179, 181,
  183–185
Ferlinghetti, Lawrence, 37
"Fictional Convention and Sex in
  Dracula" (Fry), 24
Figes, Eva
  Patriarchal Attitudes, 241
Finney, Brian, 192
Fitzgerald, F. Scott
  This Side of Paradise, 159
Flaubert, Gustave, 15, 228, 254
  Un Coeur simple, 231
Flowers of Evil (Baudelaire), 1
"For John, Who Begs Me Not to
  Enquire Further" (Sexton)
    cracked mirror in, 205, 207
    Oedipus desire in, 200, 204–207
Forster, E.M.
  Maurice, 82
Frazer, James, 147–148
Freud, Sigmund, 25, 134

childhood, 56–61, 65
Civilization and Its Discontents, 52,
  63–65
The Interpretation of Dreams, 52,
  54–60, 68
Moses and Monotheism, xvi, 63
and Oedipal desire, 199–203
"Screen Memories," 58
theory in *The Lord of the Flies*,
  99–101, 106, 108
Totem and Taboo, xvi, 29, 51–52,
  58, 60, 63–67, 69–70, 108–110
Freud and Man's Soul (Bettelheim)
  Freud and the Oedipus complex
  in, 199–203
Fry, Carrol
  "Fictional Convention and Sex in
  Dracula," 24
Fury (Rushdie), 189

G

Garber, Marjorie
  on *Julius Caesar*, 52
Garwood, Helen, 245
Gay, Peter, 63
Gelb, Arthur, 136–37
Gelb, Barbara, 136–137
Genet, Jean, 40
George, Diana Hume
  on Anne Sexton, 199–215
  "The Poetic Heroism of Anne
  Sexton," 199–215
Gery, John, 126
Ginsberg, Allen
  death, 37, 45
  The Fall of America, 41
  Howl, 37–48
  humor and self-parody, 38
  "Kaddish," 38
  "Many Loves," 42–43

"Please Master," 43
"Supermarket in California," 47
"To Aunt Rose," 47
Ginsberg, Naomi
  and schizophrenia, 40–41
Goethe, Johann Wolfgang von, 70, 107, 204
Gogol, Nikolai, 231
Golden Notebook, The (Lessing), 159
Golding, William
  Lord of the Flies, 99–112
Goodbye, Columbus (Roth), 185
Gray, Jeffery
  on Howl, 37–48
Gray, Mary, 208, 210
Greenberg, Robert M., 185
Griffith, Melanie, 92
Ground Beneath Her Feet, The (Rushdie), 189
Guérillères, Les (Wittig), 241
"Gulliver's Travels" (Swift), 217, 223

H

Hall, Donald, 45
Hamlet (Shakespeare), 94, 173
  Oedipus complex in, 53–54, 61
  fratricide in, 134
  patricide in, xv
Hammett, Dashiell
  The Maltese Falcon, 38
  The Thin Man, 38
Hardwick, Elizabeth, 158
Hardy, Florence Emily, 229–230
Hardy, Thomas
  Jude the Obscure, 229–230
  The Return of the Native, 228
  Tess of the D'Urbervilles, 227–250
Hawthorne, Nathaniel, 173–174
Helms, Jesse, 47
Hemingway, Ernest

In Our Time, 159
Henry IV (Shakespeare)
  Oedipus complex in, 54
Hero with a Thousand Faces, The (Campbell), 147–148
Herschberger, Ruth
  Adam's Rib, 237–238
  on feminine sexuality, 232–233, 238, 245
Herzog, Arhur, Jr., 129
Hobby, Blake
  on Ulysses, 251–258
Holiday, Billie
  "God Bless the Child," 129
Holmes, John, 201, 204, 214
Homer, 254
Homo Ludens (Huizinga), 103, 110
Horn, Clayton, 37
Horoun and the Sea of Stories (Rushdie), 189
horror and gothic
  in "A Rose for Emily," 165–166, 170–172, 174, 176
Howe, Irving, 158
Howl (Ginsberg)
  anti-establishment climax of, 40
  banning of, 37–38, 42, 45–46, 48
  drug use and, 41
  "Footnote to Howl," 39, 46
  four-letter words in, 38–39
  madness in, 39–42
  Moloch in, 40–41
  N.C. in, 43
  outsiders in, 41
  saintly motorcyclists in, 42
  sexuality in, 37–39, 42–46
  taboo in, 37–48
Howl and Other Poems (Ginsberg), 37, 44
Hugh, Vincent, 40
Hughes, Te, 158–159

Huizinga, Johan
 Homo Ludens, 103, 110
Huncke, Herbert, 41
Huysmans, Joris-Karl
 A Rebours, 152

I

"Ignato" (Marlow), 38
Imaginary Homelands (Rushdie), 190
incest, xv
 in *Dracula*, 33
 in *Mourning Becomes Electra*, 133
 in *Oedipus Tyrannus*, 143–146
 in *Sabbath's Theater*, 177
Inferno (Dante), 40
"In Good Faith" (Rushdie), 190
In Our Time (Hemingway), 159
Interpretation of Dreams, The (Freud)
 dreams in, 55–62, 68
 Freud's childhood in, 56–61
 Julius Caesar in, 52, 54–59, 62
Irons, Jeremy, 92

J

Jaguar Smile, The (Rushdie), 190
James, Henry
 Washington Square, 229, 231
Jane Eyre (Brontë, C.), 88, 230
"Jean-ah Poquelin" (Cable)
 compared to "A Rose for Emily,"
  166–174
 Governor in, 168, 170
 Jacques Poquelin in, 167, 171–172
 Jean Marie Poquelin in, 166–172,
  174
Joyce, James
 censorship, 42
 *A Portrait of the Artist as a Young
  Man*, 257
 Ulysses, 38, 40, 251–258

Joynson-Hicks, William, 86, 88
Judaism, xvi
Jude the Obscure (Hardy)
 Sue Bridehead in, 229–230
Julius Caesar (Shakespeare)
 Antony in, 59, 66
 Brutus in, 51–58, 61–62, 65–66,
  68–70
 Caesar in, 52–54, 56–60, 62,
  65–66, 69–70
 Caesar's ghost in, 60, 62, 66–68, 70
 Calpurnia in, 59
 Cassius in, 53, 55, 66
 Oedipus complex in, 52–54, 58,
  62, 65
 patricide in, xv, 53, 56, 60, 67
 taboo in, xv, 51–75
Junkie (Burroughs), 38

K

"Kaddish" (Ginsberg)
 taboo in, 38
Kammerer, David, 41
Kermode, Frank
 on *Lady Chatterley's Lover*, 77–90
Kerouac, Jack
 censorship of, 38
 On the Road, 41–42
King Lear (Shakespeare), 182
"kitchenette building" (Brooks),
 127–128
Klimek, Julia F.
 on *Sabbath's Theater*, 177–187
Kubrick, Stanley, 92

L

Lacretelle, Jacques de
 La Bonifas, 238
Lady Chatterley's Lover (Lawrence)
 banning of, 38, 77, 84–85, 88

Clifford Chatterley in, 80–85
Constance Chatterley in, 80–85
critique of society, 77–79
Michaelis in, 81–82
Oliver Mellors in, 81–85
Puritanism in, 80, 86, 89
rebirth of phallus in, 79, 82, 84–86
sex in, 77–89
vulgar language in, 77, 79, 82
"Lady Lazarus" (Plath)
anger and bitterness in, 161–162
Langella, Frank, 92
Lawrence, D.H., 227–228
censorship, 42
Fantasia of the Unconscious, 239
Lady Chatterley's Lover, 38, 77–90
The Lost Girl, 89
on love ethic, 234–235, 240, 244–245
The Plumed Serpent, 80
Propos of Lady Chatterley's Lover, Pornography and Obscenity, 85–89
The Virgin and the Gypsy, 82
"When I Went to the Film," 89
The White Peacock, 80–81
Women in Love, 83–84, 231
Leaves of Grass (Whitman)
banning of, 37
Lecky, W.E.H.
on Jonathan Swift, 217–225
Les Fleurs de mal. See Flowers of Evil
"Les Paradis Artificiels" (Baudelaire)
drug use in, 1–21
narrative, 2
Lessing, Doris
The Golden Notebook, 159
"Letter to a Member of Parliament concerning the Sacramental Test" (Swift), 218–219
"Lines Written in Early Spring" (Wordsworth), 232
Live or Die (Sexton), 163, 209

Lolita (Nabokov)
Charlotte Haze in, 91–92, 95–96
Clare Quilty in, 91–92
Dolores Haze in, 91–97
Humbert Humbert in, 91–97
movie versions, 92
murder in, 91–92
narrative, 92, 94–95
pedophile affair in, 91–98
solipsism in, 95–97
Long Day's Journey Into Night (O'Neill), 137
Lord of the Flies (Golding)
amorality of childhood in, 100–104
Bill in, 105
Freudian theory in, 99–101, 106, 108–109
good vs. evil in, 100–101, 105, 107, 110
Jack in, 100–102, 104–107, 109–110
the kill in, 104–110
Maurice in, 105
narrative, 100, 108
Piggy in, 101–103, 106–111
Ralph in, 100–102, 104–107, 109–110
Simon in, 107–109, 111
Lost Girl, The (Lawrence), 89
"Love Song of J. Alfred Prufock, The" (Eliot), 125, 130
Lowell, Robert, 38–39, 158
Lydon, Susan, 240
Lyne, Adrian, 92
Lyon, Sue, 92
Lyotard, Jean-Francois, 190

M

MacGillwray, Royce
on *Dracula*, 24, 27
madness taboo
in *Howl*, 39–42

in "A Rose for Emily," 174
  in *Sabbath's Theater*, 181–182
"Maenad" (Plath), 162
"Magi" (Plath)
  anger and bitterness in, 161
magical realism
  in *The Satanic Verses*, 190, 192–193
Mailer, Norman
  An American Dream, 161
Maltese Falcon, The (Hammett), 38
"Many Loves" (Ginsberg), 42–43
Marcuse, Herbert, 241
Marett, R.R., 63
Marlow, Christopher
  "Ignato," 38
Marshall, Cynthia
  on *Julius Caesar*, 51–75
Martin, Wendy
  on Sylvia Plath, 157–164
Marx, Karl, 40
Mason, James, 92
matricide
  in *Dracula*, 33
  in *Mourning Becomes Electra*, 133
  in *The Oresteia*, 135
Maurice (Forster), 82
McCarthy, Joe, 38
McCarthy, Mary
  The Company She Keeps, 159
McDonald, Edward D., 234
Mead, Margaret, 237
Melhem, D.H., 124–125
Mellard, James M.
  "Death, Mourning, and Besse's
    Ghost," 184
Melville, Herman
  Moby Dick, 173–174
Merrill, James
  The Essential Gwendolyn Brooks,
    125
Middlebrook, Diane, 204–206
Midnight's Children (Rushdie), 189

Midsummer-Night's Dream, A
  (Shakespeare), 95
Miller, Arthur, 38
Miller, Henry
  censorship, 42
  The Tropic of Cancer, 38
"Miller's Tale, The" (Chaucer)
  Absolon in, 119–122
  Alison in, 116–121
  Christian teachings in, 114–122
  the Clerk in, 121
  flood imagery in, 120
  the Host in, 115–116
  John the carpenter in, 116–122
  the Knight in, 116, 121
  the Miller in, 114–116, 121–122
  the Monk in, 115–116
  narrative, 114
  Nicholas in, 116–122
  the Reeve in, 121
  religious taboos in, 114–122
  sex in, 116–119
  taboo behavior and speech in,
    113–116
Milton, John, 85, 254
  Paradise Lost, 93
"Mister Jones" (Dylan), 42
Mitchell, Juliet, 236
  Psychoanalysis and Feminism, 201
Montherlant, Henry de, 238
Moby Dick (Melville), 173–174
Moor's Last Sigh, The (Rushdie), 189
Moorton, Richard F. Jr., 137
Morrison, Toni
  Beloved, 126
Moses and Monotheism (Freud)
  patricide in, xvi, 63
"mother, the" (Brooks)
  abortion taboo in, 123–132
  imagery in, 126
  imagined lives of children in, 123,
    125, 127–130

self-absorbed narrator in, 123–126, 128–129

sexuality in, 124, 127

Mourning Becomes Electra (O'Neill)

Abe Mannon in, 134–135, 138–139

Adam, 133, 139

Adam Brantome in, 133, 137–141

Christine in, 133, 135, 137–140

David Mannon in, 134–135, 139–140

Electra Complex in, 133, 136

Ezra in, 133, 137–139

incest in, 133

internalized guilt in, 135

Lavinia in, 133, 136–141

Marie Brantome in, 133, 135, 137–138

murder in, 133, 138

Oedipus Complex in, 133

Orin in, 133, 136–141

Peter in, 140–141

sexuality in, 134, 138–139, 141–142

suicide in, 133, 136–141

N

Nabokov, Dmitri, 94

Nabokov, Vladimir

Despair, 95

Lolita, 91–98

necrophilia

in "A Rose for Emily," 165, 170–171, 173

Newton, Isaac, 223

Nietzsche, Friedrich, 87

on *Oedipus Tyrannus*, 143–146

Nobel prize, 189

O

"Ocean 1212-W" (Plath), 162

Oedipal desire

in Anne Sexton's poetry, 199–215

in *Dracula*, 23–24, 27–28, 31–34

and Freud, 199–203

in *Hamlet*, 53–54

in *Henry IV*, 54

in *Julius Caesar*, 52–70

in *Mourning Becomes Electra*, 133

in *Oedipus Tyrannus*, 143–146

Oedipus Rex (Sophocles), 134, 200, 202, 214

Oedipus Tyrannus (Sophocles), 65

incest in, 143–146

patricide in, 143–146

"old-marrieds, the" (Brooks), 127

"On Doing Good" (Swift), 222

O'Neill, Eugene

Long Day's Journey Into Night, 137

Mourning Becomes Electra, 133–142

O'Neill, James, 136–137

On the Road (Kerouc)

outsiders in, 41–42

sexuality in, 43

Orestes, The (Euripides), 139

Agamemnon in, 134, 136

Atreus in, 134–135

cannibalism in, 135

Clytemnestra in, 134, 136

Electra in, 134, 136

Eumenides in, 135, 142

matricide in, 135

Orestes in, 134–136

Thyestes in, 134–135

Orlovsky, Peter, 41

Ostriker, Alicia, 203

Othello (Shakespeare), 97

P

Paradise Lost (Milton), 93

Patriarchal Attitudes (Figes), 241

patricide
   and Freud, xvi, 63, 65, 67–69
   in *Oedipus Tyrannus*, 143–146
   in Shakespeare's tragedies, xv, 53,
     56, 60–61, 65
Perloff, Marjorie, 45
Picture of Dorian Gray, The (Wilde)
   Basil Hallward in, 147–150,
     152–153
   Dorian Gray in, 147–153
   Hedonism in, 147–148, 150
   Henry Wotton in, 147–153
   homosexuality in, 152
   moral corruption in, 149, 153
   murder in, 153
   narcissism in, 150, 153
   suicide in, 151–152
   Sybil Vane in, 148, 151–152
   youth and beauty in, 147–150, 153
Pipes, Daniel, 196
Plath, Otto, 158
Plath, Sylvia
   "The Applicant," 161
   Ariel poems, 159
   "The Beast," 161
   The Bell Jar, 157–161
   biography, 158–159
   The Colossus, 159
   Crossing the Water, 159
   "Daddy," 161
   "Elm," 162
   "Lady Lazarus," 161–162
   "Maenad," 162
   "Magi," 161
   "Ocean 1212-W," 162
   politics, 158
   Sexton compared to, 203, 205
   suicide, 157–159, 162–163
   "Three Women: A Poem for Three
     Voices," 163
   "Who," 162
   Winter Trees, 159, 163

"Witch Burning," 162
"Zookeeper's Wife," 161–162
"Please Master" (Ginsberg), 43
Plumed Serpent, The (Lawrence), 80
Poe, Edgar Allan, 9, 97
   "A Cask of Amontillado," 172
   "The Fall of the House of Usher,"
     165–166, 171–173, 175–176
   "A Tale of the Ragged Mountains,"
     10
"Poetic Heroism of Anne Sexton,
   The" (George)
   on the taboo in Sexton's poetry,
     199–215
political taboos
   in *The Satanic Verses*, 189–197
Pollock, Jackson, 39
Pope, Alexander, 218, 221, 224
Portnoy's Complaint (Roth), 177,
   184–185
*Portrait of the Artist as a Young Man,
   A* (Joyce), 257
Pound, Ezra, 45
   ABC of Reading, 230
   Cantos, 40
Powell, Enoch, 195
"Project for the Reformation of
   Manners" (Swift), 218
"Proposal for the Advancement of
   Religion" (Swift), 222
*Propos of Lady Chatterley's Lover,
   Pornography and Obscenity*
   (Lawrence), 85–89
Proust, Marcel, 40
Psychoanalysis and Feminism
   (Mitchell), 201

R

Rabkin, Norman
   on *Julius Caesar*, 53–54
Rank, Otto, 34

Ransom, John Crowe, 45
Raskin, Jonah, 38, 40
Rebours, A (Huysmans), 152
religious taboos
    in "The Miller's Tale," 114–122
    in *The Satanic Verses*, 189–197
    in *Ulysses*, 251–253, 255–257
Return of the Native, The (Hardy)
    Thomasina in, 228
Rexroth, Kenneth, 37
Richardson, Maurice
    on *Dracula*, 24–25, 27
Rimbaud, Arthur, 40
Robinson, Lillian S., 130
Roe v. Wade decision, 127
"Rose for Emily, A" (Faulkner)
    compared to "A Cask of
        Amontillado," 172
    compared to "The Fall of the
        House of Usher," 165–166, 170–
        171, 173, 175–176
    compared to "Jean-ah Poquelin,"
        166–174
    concealment theme in, 173
    Emily Grierson in, 165, 167–175
    erotic gratification in, 165–176
    father's death in, 168–169, 172–173
    Homer Barron in, 168–169, 171–
        172, 175
    horror and gothic in, 165–166,
        170–172, 174–175
    madness in, 174
    necrophilia in, 165, 170–171, 173
    time and place in, 166–167
Rosenfield, Claire
    on *Lord of the Flies*, 99–112
Roth, Philip
    Goodbye, Columbus, 185
    Portnoy's Complaint, 177, 184–185
    Sabbath's Theater, 177–187
Roth, Phyllis A.
    on *Dracula*, 23–36

Roussea, Jean-Jacques, 17
Rushdie, Salman
    censors, 189
    East, West, 189
    The Enchantress of Florence, 190
    Fury, 189
    The Ground Beneath Her Feet, 189
    Horoun and the Sea of Stories, 189
    Imaginary Homelands, 190
    "In Good Faith," 190
    The Jaguar Smile, 190
    Midnight's Children, 189
    The Moor's Last Sigh, 189
    Nobel prize-winner, 189
    politics, 189–191
    The Satanic Verses, 189–197
    Shalimar the Clown, 189
    Shame, 189
    Step Across This Line, 190
Ryan, Dustin
    on *Ulysses*, 251–258

S

Sabbath's Theater (Roth)
    awards for, 177
    Debby Cowan in, 180, 183, 185
    Drenka Balich in, 178–181,
        184–186
    fear of death in, 177–179, 181,
        183–185
    Fish in, 179, 185
    Helen Trumbull in, 179–180, 186
    incest in, 177
    Kathy Goolsbee in, 179–180, 186
    Lincoln Gelman in, 179, 182–183
    madness in, 181–182
    Michelle Cowan in, 179, 183
    Mickey Sabbath in, 177–186
    Morty Sabbath in, 177, 184–185
    narrator of, 178, 185
    Nikki Sabbath in, 178–179, 181–185

Norman Cowan in, 179–180, 182–183, 185
Roseanna Sabbath in, 178–179, 181, 183, 186
sexual taboos in, 177–187
suicide in, 177, 182–183, 185
Sanyal, Arundhati
 The Picture of Dorian Gray, 147–156
Satanic Verses, The (Rushdie)
attack on Islam in, 190–192, 194–196
divided selves in, 193
dreams in, 194, 196
Gibreel Farishta in, 192–194
Hal Valance in, 195
magical realism in, 190, 192–193
"Mahound" in, 194, 196
Margaret Thatcher's racism in, 190, 192, 195
mongrelization in, 191, 194
narrator, 191, 193, 195
political taboos in, 189–197
religious taboos in, 189–197
"Return to Jahilia" in, 194
Saladin Chamcha in, 192–194
Saunders, Frances Stonor
 The Cultural Cold War: The CIA and the World of Arts and Letters, 39
Schanzer, Ernest
 on *Julius Caesar*, 54
Schiller, Friedrich
 depiction of Caesar, 55–58, 69
Schopenhauer, Arthur, 204, 245
Schorer, Mark, 37
Schuman, Samuel
 on *Lolita*, 91–98
Second Sex, The (Beauvoir), 234, 238–239, 242
Sellers, Peter, 92
"Sentiments of a Church of England Man" (Swift), 218

Sexton, Ann, 158
 45 Mercy Street, 209, 211
 "The Abortion," 130–131
 "All My Pretty Ones," 209, 213–214
 compared to Plath, 203, 205
 death, 213
 "The Division of Parts," 207
 "Divorce, Thy Name is Woman," 209, 211–213
 "The Doubled Image," 207–211
 "Dreaming the Breasts," 213
 "Eating the Leftovers," 211
 "For John, Who Begs Me Not to Enquire Further," 200, 204–207
 Live or Die, 163, 209
 poetry of, 199–215
 "Those Times...," 209–211
 To Bedlam and Part Way Back, 200, 204, 207, 209, 213
sexual taboos, 1
 in *The Bell Jar*, 157
 female sexuality in *Dracula*, 23–27, 29–30, 32–33
 in *Howl*, 37–39, 42
 in *Lady Chatterley's Lover*, 77–89
 in *Lolita*, 91–98
 in "The Miller's Tale," 116–119
 in "the mother," 124, 127
 in *Mourning Becomes Electra*, 134, 138–139, 141–142
 in *On the Road*, 43
 in *The Picture of Dorian Gray*, 152
 in "A Rose for Emily," 165, 173
 in *Sabbath's Theater*, 177–183, 186
 in "Song of Myself," 37–38, 43–45
 in *Tess of the D'Urbervilles*, 227–250
 in *Ulysses*, 251–257
Shakespeare, William, 87
 Hamlet, xv, 53–54, 61, 94, 134, 173
 Henry IV, 54

Julius Caesar, xv, 51–75
  King Lear, 182
  A Midsummer-Night's Dream, 95
  Othello, 97
Shalimar the Clown (Rushdie), 189
Shame (Rushdie), 189
Shechner, Mark
  on *Sabbath's Theater*, 177, 181, 186
Shelley, Percy Bysshe
  on incest, xv
Shostak, Debra, 181
Siemon, James
  on *Julius Caesar*, 53
Simpson, Louis, 45
Slonin, Vera, 94
Smart, Christopher, 40
Snell, George, 175
Solomon, Carl, 41
"Song of Myself" (Whitman)
  banning of, 37–38
  sexuality in, 37–38, 46
Sophocles
  Oedipus Tyrannus, 143–146, 200, 202
  Oedipus Rex, 134
"southeast corner" (Brooks), 127
Sparks, Tryphena, 229
Spatz, Lois, 130
Spender, Stephen, 39
"Spontaneous Me" (Whitman), 45
Starbuck, George, 158
Step Across This Line (Rushdie), 190
Stoker, Bram
  Dracula, 23–36
Stone, Edward
  on "A Rose for Emily," 165–176
Stranger, The (Camus)
  Meursault in, 227, 247
Street in Bronzeville, A (Brooks)
  stories in, 123, 125, 127–131
Striker, Alicia, 203
suicide
  in *The Bell Jar*, 160

  in "The Double Image," 207
  in *Mourning Becomes Electra*, 133, 136–141
  in *The Picture of Dorian Gray*, 151–152
  in *Sabbath's Theater*, 177, 182–183, 185
"Supermarket in California" (Ginsberg), 47
Swain, Dominique, 92
Swift, Jonathan
  "Argument against the Abolition of Christianity," 218
  "The Battle of the Books," 218
  death, 219
  "Essay on Public Absurdities," 219
  "Gulliver's Travels," 217, 223
  "Letter to a Member of Parliament concerning the Sacramental Test," 218–219
  "On Doing Good," 222
  politics of, 217–225
  "Project for the Reformation of Manners," 218
  "Proposal for the Advancement of Religion," 222
  "Sentiments of a Church of England Man," 218
  "The Tale of a Tub," 217–218, 221

T

"Tale of the Ragged Mountains, A" (Poe)
  Augustus Bedloe in, 10
"Tale of a Tub, The" (Swift)
  coarseness of, 217–218, 221
Temple, William, 224
Terkel, Studs, 125, 131
Tess of the D'Urbervilles (Hardy)
  Alec d'Urberville in, 228–231, 233–236, 245

Angel Clare in, 228–231, 233, 235, 241, 243–246
feminine sexuality in, 227–250
ironies in, 231
Izz Huett in, 241
Joan Durbeyfield in, 231
Tess d'Urberville in, 227–232, 241–248
Thatcher, Margaret, 190, 192, 195
Thin Man, The (Hammett), 38
This Side of Paradise (Fitzgerald), 159
Thomas, Dylan, 38
"Those Times…" (Sexton), 209
murder of mother in, 210–211
"Three Women: A Poem for Three Voices" (Plath), 163
"To Aunt Rose" (Ginsberg), 47
To Bedlam and Part Way Back (Sexton)
poems in, 200, 204, 207, 209, 213
Tolstoy, Leo, 247
Totem and Taboo (Freud), 108
Julius Caesar in, 51–52, 63, 65–67, 69–70
neuroses in, 64
Oedipal conclusion of, 52, 58
patricide in, xvi, 29, 60
To the Lighthouse (Woolf), 162
Trilling, Lionel
The Experience of Literature, 47
Tristan und Isolde (Wagner), 88
Tropic of Cancer, The (Miller)
banning of, 38

U

Ulysses (Joyce)
banning of, 38, 40
Gerty MacDowell in, 252–256
Leopold Bloom in, 251–253, 255–257
Molly Bloom in, 251, 254

narrative, 252–253, 256
"Nausicaa" in, 251–252, 255–257
religious taboos in, 251–253, 255–257
sexual taboos in, 251–258
Un Coeur simple (Flaubert), 231
Understanding Fiction (Brooks and Warren), 165

V

Virgin and the Gypsy, The (Lawrence), 82
Voltaire, Francois-Marie Arouet, 221
vulgar language
in *Lady Chatterley's Lover*, 77, 79, 82

W

Wagner, Geoffrey
on *Tess of the D'Urbervilles*, 227–250
Wagner, Richard
Tristan und Isolde, 88
Walploe, R., 223
Walters, Scott
Mourning Becomes Electra, 133–142
Warren, Robert Penn, 45
Understanding Fiction, 165
Washington Square (James)
Dr. Sloper in, 229, 231
Wasson, Richard
on *Dracula*, 28–29
Waste Land, The (Eliot), 47, 125, 231
West, Ray B. Jr., 175
"When I Went to the Film," (Lawrence), 89
White Peacock (Lawrence), 80–81
White, Phil, 41
Whitman, Walt, 40–41
Leaves of Grass, 37

"Song of Myself," 37–38, 43–46
"Spontaneous Me," 45
"Who" (Plath), 162
Wilde, Oscar
   The Decay of Lying, 152
   The Picture of Dorian Gray, 147–156
"Wild One, The" (film), 42
Willbern, David, 65
Winters, Shelley, 92
Winter Trees (Plath), 159, 163
"Witch Burning" (Plath), 162
Wittig, Monique
   Les Guérillères, 241
Women in Love (Lawrence), 83–84, 231

Woolf, Virginia, 40, 163, 230, 235
   To the Lighthouse, 162
Wordsworth, William, 234
   "Lines Written in Early Spring," 232
Wotton, William, 218
Wright, Richard, 123–124, 131

Y

Yerkes, Robert M., 237

Z

"Zookeeper's Wife" (Plath)
   anger and bitterness in, 161–162